THE HEAT AND D[...]
The Broke Couple's Guide to Bharat

Devapriya Roy is the author of two novels, *The Vague Woman's Handbook* (2011) and *The Weight Loss Club* (2013). She has degrees in literature and performance studies from Presidency College, Calcutta, and Jawaharlal Nehru University, New Delhi, where she spent many years in pursuit of a PhD on the *Natyashastra*. Once upon a time, she was the Keo Karpin girl.

Saurav Jha was trained in economics at Presidency College, Calcutta, and Jawaharlal Nehru University, New Delhi. He is a commentator on energy and security issues and contributes regularly to varied national and international media. He also runs a popular blog, 'Geek at Large', on Indian defence issues. His first book, *The Upside Down Book of Nuclear Power*, was published in March 2010, and his next work on the sustainability of economic growth, *The Nexus*, is scheduled for end 2015.

THE HEAT AND DUST PROJECT

The Broke Couple's Guide to Bharat

Devapriya Roy and Saurav Jha

HarperCollins *Publishers* India

First published in India in 2015 by
HarperCollins *Publishers* India

Copyright © Devapriya Roy and Saurav Jha 2015

P-ISBN: 978-93-5136-749-9
E-ISBN: 978-93-5136-750-5

2 4 6 8 10 9 7 5 3 1

Devapriya Roy and Saurav Jha assert the moral right
to be identified as the author of this work.

The views and opinions expressed in this book are the authors' own and the facts are as
reported by them, and the publishers are not in any way liable for the same.

The names of many people and hotels have been changed.

Though every effort has been made to obtain permission for quoted matter, this has
not been possible in every case. Any omission brought to our notice will be acknowledged
in future editions.

HarperCollins *Publishers*
A-75, Sector 57, Noida, Uttar Pradesh 201301, India
1 London Bridge Street, London, SE1 9GF, United Kingdom
Hazelton Lanes, 55 Avenue Road, Suite 2900, Toronto, Ontario M5R 3L2
and 1995 Markham Road, Scarborough, Ontario M1B 5M8, Canada
25 Ryde Road, Pymble, Sydney, NSW 2073, Australia
195 Broadway, New York, NY 10007, USA

Typeset in 10.5/13.5 Warnock Pro, Cronos Pro
By Saanvi Graphics Noida

Printed and bound at
Thomson Press (India) Ltd.

For
Meenakshi, who was born two weeks before the journey and
was the fair star monitoring its mad course; Saksham,
who offered to write a part of the book (as long as
we helped with the spellings); and Priyanka, who heard all our
stories first and is reading our books now.

Contents

Authors' Note

In many parts of the world, there is something called a gap year. Not so in India. While young people elsewhere contemplate a gap year (amply aided by exchange rates), eighteen-year-old Indians of certain classes swot madly for entrance exams. It might not be off the mark to say that middle-class Indians truly peak in focus and ambition between the ages of sixteen and eighteen. It is great hormone management too in a way.

One hears of parents in the Western hemisphere who are mortally afraid that their children's jobs are going to be Bangalored, outsourced to some briskly busy Indian IT professional who thinks nothing of working fifteen hours a day, every day. If he were to go back in time though, and see his seventeen-year-old version, and the sheer amount of effort he put into cracking the exams – the ones that would morph him to the said IT professional – well, he'd have to confess he was taking it really easy at his fifteen-hour workday. *Their* kids, with all the cheerleading and prom and sex and protection talk, are *no* match whatsoever.

But, to cut a long story short, we did not come from a tradition of gap years, and now, past our mid-twenties, we'd missed that age group by nearly a decade. We lived yuppie lives in the heart of Delhi. We had decent, soulless jobs. We even had a garret apartment in a lovely neighbourhood that would be filled, on certain mornings, so generously with the sun and the sound of children playing outside that it was easy to decide in favour of householding and consumption.

We were the usual: nine-to-sixers, investment-makers, mall-goers, office-trippers and city-slickers. We were life-going-to-seeders.

Then we came up with an insane idea.

Everyone thought we were mad to put all our eggs in one basket: the idea of a transformational journey through India. On a very, very tight budget. We went ahead anyway.

This book is the story of what happened then.

Devapriya and Saurav

Atha
(Here, Now)

The bus is late. When we reach Jaipur, the touristy blue sky has begun to deepen incorrigibly. We hail an auto. By the time we get to the fork in the road – it is the hotel district close to Mirza Ismail Road, fairly central – dusk has leapt forward to night. Or perhaps, it is just the cold.

We know the first hotel at the mouth of the street: daintily designed and set back inside a little garden. It is quite expensive. (We'd stayed there once in the past – and we couldn't afford the prices then either.) We walk straight past it and pop into the next reception. Prices at the second hotel, a functional-looking structure, start from a shocking Rs 1,200 plus taxes.

Outside, the lane is streaked with dim shafts of light leaking from hotel rooms on either side. We stop religiously at every hotel; ask the rates, the facilities. True to the project, we step out and sigh, suffering a curious mix of outrage and nerves at room rents. But it is day one – it will not do to cave in already. It will not do to end up taking one of the better rooms with the promise of hot water.

Eventually, on to the last few 'deluxe 2-stars' in that series. The character of the neighbourhood has changed perceptibly. We are now deep within the recesses of that rough mohalla, down a typical Indian lane – which has seen several relayerings of asphalt over the years, but never once evenly – and ugly rooms are freely available for 400 rupees. They are painted an unvarying dull off-brown, if there were such a shade. Their Indian-style bathrooms are streaked with old red

1

stains, which, I can only hope, is paan. The straps of my backpack have begun to cut my shoulders.

At long last, the final hotel. A narrow building, terraced, with a name so elaborate that it sits off-kilter, almost wayward, on peeling walls: *Hotel Veer Rajput Palace*. We pause a moment to regroup.

'It'll have to be this one, I guess,' S says, almost relieved. 'Shall we try to settle at 300? I don't think they'll go lower than that.'

I am exhausted. I cannot think of returning to any of the hotels we've just left behind. In front, where the block ends, there is simply a claque of dogs guarding the entryway into a dark by-lane of small unpainted houses. No hotels.

I nod and follow him up the three steps. The door is ajar.

One

How (Not) to Grow Roots in Three Days

Dear God, this parachute is a knapsack.

– Chandler Bing, *Friends*

1

January 2010: It is a foggy winter day in Delhi when it begins.

Dilliwalas will, of course, say that *all* winter days in Delhi are foggy. But on some days, like this one, the fog that is barely endured in the morning stretches well into afternoon – making the city irritable and chilly, edgy with remorse.

Buses for Jaipur leave at regular intervals from Bikaner House.

It is about one-thirty now, midday, and we find ourselves rushing that way in an auto, unaccountably though, as there is no reason to rush. Not any more. We are – or so we would like to believe – free individuals. We have no bosses to report to, no landlords to be paid at the end of the month, not even a sad plant gathering dust at the office desk to chide us. We can, if fancy strikes, take a detour to Himachal Bhavan which is close by, take one of *their* buses and dash off to, say, Manali. I smile as I think this aloud, stretching my arms in an arch of delicious freedom.

'We can't,' S replies shortly. 'We have to stick to the plan. As it is, we are behind schedule. It takes a minimum of four-and-a-half hours

3

to get to Jaipur, by when it'll be evening. And then we will have to scout for a really cheap hotel. Don't imagine for a second that *that's* going to be easy. It's winter, high season in Rajasthan. Plus,' he adds, as if this were a clincher, 'we don't have enough warm clothes for Manali.'

It's not that I don't have appropriate answers to each of the above claims – because I do (I always do) – but, for now, I let it go. I busy myself checking if we've stashed our luggage alright. In addition to my cavernous canvas handbag, there are two backpacks – one red, one black – which we'd bought in Calcutta last month for about 700 rupees apiece from a luggage store in New Market. There had, naturally, been posher brands in the shop. A remarkable rust-coloured Samsonite, for instance, with a thousand loops and discreet zips and dinky pockets. It was for 5,000 rupees. Hung in a special alcove in the shop, a thing of beauty. S didn't even allow me to go within sniffing distance of it. Spending one-tenth of the entire (proposed) budget on gear? Not on his watch, apparently.

While we're on the subject, you might as well know there was a mighty row last night over the said backpacks.

To be honest, this is my first backpacking trip across India. Across anywhere, actually. So I did not want to take any chances with equipment. Given that we were to be gone for months, I came up with a pretty comprehensive list.

1. 3 jeans (one could get wet while the other is dirty, in which case I would thank my stars that I'd packed a third).
2. 9 8 7 6 t-shirts (they are ordinary cotton t-shirts – v.v. light).
3. A couple of salwar-kurtas (we may be travelling through rather conservative places where it might be considered too firang to prance about in jeans; for fieldwork, for people to talk to us freely, we need to be discreet and fit in).
4. One dressy top and one dressy salwar-kameez in case something comes up. (In my head it read as dinner with a princess or such like; after all, we *were* going to Rajasthan.)
5. An iron to ensure all the above were well-tended (one of the lightest irons possible; I had scoured the market).

6. A big bottle of Eezee for all the laundry. On a budget trip, that's the first place where one saves money – one hand-washes one's clothes.

7. Big box of tissues and one pack of wet wipes.

8. Hand sanitizer.

9. Two tiffin boxes – one each (in case we need to carry food). Preferably one red, one black, to match the bags.

10. Biscuits and protein bars in case we find ourselves locked up somewhere without food.

11. A medicine kit plus different kinds of vitamins.

12. A couple of notebooks.

13. Thermals.

14. Light sandwich toaster (?) ... bread could be bought anywhere.

15. A pot of Nutella (?).

I had only got this far and was wondering which books to take – you can't go on a transformative journey without a few soul-stirring books; Vivekananda had carried a copy each of the Gita and the *Imitation of Christ* on his wanderings through India – when S insisted on checking out the list. Not that he offered *his* list to me, which was a scrunched-up napkin with the words 'lots of underwear, one cheque book, charger' scrawled in a corner. He then went on to throw a mighty fit. Apparently, only the hand sanitizer in my entire list could be allowed. 'Who made *you* boss of the trip?' I bellowed. 'This project is *my* idea!'

And then he told me the following: Was I aware that over-preparation could have *dangerous* consequences? Did I even know of the strange case of Salomon Andrée?

I gulped. S warmed up to his theme. Salomon Andrée had, in 1897, dreamt of reaching the North Pole in a hydrogen balloon. Not just any old hydrogen balloon but one equipped so exhaustively and with such imagination that it would seem they had planned for every conceivable eventuality. They had the world's first primus stove, enough cutlery for fine dining, a Hasselblad camera, an on-board darkroom, even a cooker that could be lit remotely. Except, all this did not make any meaningful difference. Three days later the balloon sank, barely 200 miles from the starting point. Their bear-chewed bodies were discovered thirty-three years later.

'It doesn't prove anything,' I grumbled, sitting on the floor amid a bunch of clothes, in a sunless hotel room in Paharganj, secretly mulling over the possibility of our bear-chewed bodies coming home in gunny sacks.

2

There is a Silverline bus to Jaipur at half past two.

We rush to find the ticket counter. It is tucked away in a corner of the sprawling premises, the centrepiece of which is a pale pink faux-palace. S glances at me offhand, and remarks casually how my face is looking blue from all the weight I'm lugging. Am I up to it? he asks, offering to switch. It annoys me further.

Fact is, last night, in spite of the cautionary tale, my pride still couldn't come to terms with the fact that I might have to eat dinner with royalty in grotty jeans. So I sort of stuck to my original list.

I concentrate on the map of Rajasthan stuck on the wall in front. The names of places are delicious, rolling syllables that remind me of geography and history lessons half heard in school: 'Bijolia, Bundi, Kota,' I read aloud, and then squint to spot the smaller places dotting the far corners of the craggy state, 'Ganganagar, Nagaur, Chittor.' It is a moment of intense possibility, of such freedom. We can go almost anywhere, visit any of these places, even live there for a while. For a second, the heart swells.

Meanwhile, S has found the right queue. He is now standing behind a balding man in a shaggy black galabandh and corduroy trousers. The man is having a long chat with the guy at the counter. I find a chair nearby and lump the bag on it.

'Actually,' the man, elbows on the counter, says with deliberate emphasis, 'the boy is *physically handicapped*. So he always travels free.'

The guy at the counter scratches his ear. He is wearing a pair of thick black spectacles and a chocolate-brown monkey cap that covers his ears under woolly flaps. He replies excruciatingly slowly, 'That *is* the rule. Correct. Even the attendant can travel free. But you need a "physically handicapped" certificate for that. From an authorized government hospital. Do you have it?'

'No,' the man replies sadly. 'I should get this certificate made now, I think. Every time I am about to get it, something comes up.'

'Oh yes, of course. If you produce that, you don't have to pay for the ticket at all. Even the attendant can go free. If you come between eleven a.m. and one p.m. on weekdays ... the list of authorized government hospitals is available for five rupees at the next counter.'

'Can you at least give the handicapped kid and his attendant one of the seats in front?'

'Umm, no. The seats in front are *always* reserved for VIPs.'

S has been bursting to say something all this while and finally intervenes. 'Why don't you give his child the seat? In any case, which VIP will travel by a Silverline bus?'

The sad-looking man in the galabandh adds, 'Exactly. They take Volvos at least, the VIPs. Most of them take AC Qualises and all.'

'No, no, not true, not true.' The counter guy is most vehement. 'Many small VIPs take this bus. How many tickets do you want?' It is final.

The man replies.

The guy begins taking down names carefully. 'But that's only four names?' he asks, taking off his glasses and blinking rapidly. 'Didn't you want five tickets?'

'Yes, yes...' The sad-looking man has now lost interest and is busy SMSing. 'Plus the handicapped kid.'

'What's his name?' For all his unhelpfulness, the ticket guy is thorough.

'Mmm-hmm...' The man scratches his head distractedly as though trying to remember. 'Put it down as Pepsi.'

We are next.

In about ten minutes we are in the Silverline bus, its seats upholstered in bubble-gum-pink rexine, hungrily munching veg patties. After finishing, S vigorously dusts off crumbs and fishes out a small red notebook from his pocket. He throws me a stern look and notes neatly: Rs 240 (bus), Rs 40 (veg patties, 2). Then he tells me, 'Don't imagine for a *second* that Silverline buses and patties set the tone for this trip. We're on a budget and we have to stick to it, come hell or high water.' I nod with my mouth full. The soft flaky crust of the patty, dry, if flavourful, sticks slightly in my throat. I gulp down some water. 'Rs 15 (a bottle of water),' S notes, reminded.

The driver jumps onto his seat and bangs his door shut. Everybody scrambles in. The conductor jabbers something to the driver who appears not to hear. And then, suddenly, without any preamble, we are off.

3

Through the imprint of dust on the glass, the day outside seems more miserable than it probably is.

Having made its way out of the maze of Delhi, the bus lumbers through Gurgaon with its sandy earth, polythene litter, a few dull-grey hardy-looking trees and towering structures in steel and glass – offices and gleaming malls and gated residential communities with bombastic names. The new India. The chatter of co-passengers thins. There is only the grumble of traffic. The cold stills everyone into a stupor.

Beyond Gurgaon, fields of mustard begin in bright yellow waves, often interrupted by 'development', as though it were a pompous character from an ancient play that has wandered into current Indian vocabulary, and remained. 'The NCR is on fire these days,' one is told again and again, here and there. 'Development has come to stay.'

'You know what fire means, right?' S told me a week ago. 'Finance, Insurance, Real Estate. After that flash of fire, it could all be a downward trajectory.' He had much more to say on the subject, but at that time I'd been busy doing something else. I had shushed him. I think for a second if I should prod him on the subject now but decide against it. In any case, he's dozing.

'Become an airline pilot in 6 months,' a spectacular blue billboard announces. The words are spelled out brightly below a neat line of skyward-bound planes that seem to have just taken off from the large smooth forehead of a handsome pilot in white. The model who is the pilot has eerily even teeth.

I take notes.

Mounds of rubble – tyres, car parts, bricks; piles of hay; pockets of green that would look lush if it were a sunny day; huge hoardings for real-estate companies; garbage dumps; golden fields of mustard; industrial sheds; clumps of thorny bushes; one-room shops with lone unlit bulbs hanging in front; houses inside walled compounds which have tiny mud pens with thatched roofs in corners where goats are tied; brick kilns and one-off houses with walls that are entirely advertisements – Vodafone, Konark Cement, Dr X – godly healer of Gupt Rog; jungles of high-tension wires. These appear in different permutations, randomly, casually, in a landscape that is quintessentially modern-day Indian: where rural motifs unchanged for years easily coexist with noisy interventions from city life, neither category watertight and neither striking the Indian eye as incongruous.

Just after the bus crosses Starex International School, a gaudy mansion in the middle of nowhere – a sizeable plot of land although no children are sighted – I finally spot a milestone. Jaipur: 202 kilometres.

Over the last many months we have been reorienting our lives for this grand moment: this is it. The beginning. Yet somehow, I find, in some discomfort, that I am unable to feel the passion that *ought* to be coursing through me as the moment unfolds. There is only the present. We are in the bus; it is cold; the afternoon and the moment stretch out in front, unspooling like a quiet wintry track running parallel to the dusty grey road. That is all.

The bus winds its way along the road. S sleeps with his mouth open. Clots of truck drivers and khalasis are sitting around wood fires, their rides parked by the highway. I carefully drape my woollen shawl around my head. The young girl in the seat behind us was dropped off at Bikaner House by her parents, along with a hundred instructions in rapid Punjabi on *who* to talk to, *what* to eat at the midway stop, *how often* to call them and *how to* get to the hostel from the bus stop. She has just begun to open up to the young man sitting next to her. They speak softly. She's from north Delhi, studies in an engineering college outside Jaipur; he is Rajput, he informs her, from Ganganagar, far away, yes, but no, it's not a village, no, no, it's quite a sizeable town really, coming up in a big way, he works in Jaipur, comes to Delhi on tour regularly.

I eavesdrop for a while, wondering if they will exchange numbers.

Then evening comes in a flourish of electric rouge and casts a glow upon the mustard fields; the dry spare quality of the land and its vegetation suddenly softens in the colours of excess, of sunset. There is an aloof loneliness in the landscape at twilight that comes as a sudden stab. A calm cascade of beauty. I poke S awake.

A couple of hours later, we enter Jaipur. Soon, the walls of the old city are visible in the distance, through the rush of heavy traffic moving slowly, the buses and cars and hundreds of two-wheelers. The walls are saffron-orange in the distance, with patterns etched in white.

4

The lobby of Hotel Veer Rajput Palace, deluxe, is dimly lit and manned by two guys in identical green check sweaters, one reedy with a silver ear stud, one portly and balding, also with silver ear stud. The counter stretches like a redoubt around them. On one end is a small television set; it seems as though a righteous-cop film is playing.

By the door is a filthy couch covered in brown velvet. We dump our backpacks on it.

These guys know the rules of bargaining well. They size us up carefully and switch the TV off but say nothing.

'Do you have rooms available?' S asks. 'We want a double room.'

The lighting, the gaze and the cold night whistling outside combine to make this an extremely sexual sentence. For a bit, everyone is quiet.

'We have good double rooms, attached bathroom, hot water by buckets, room service,' the portly one recites. 'We can get you beer too.'

'Do you want to see one of the rooms upstairs?' the other asks.

We know this'll have to do; there is no real choice unless we want to return to the previous hotel with the paan-stained/bloodstained toilets, but it is good form to pretend we want to see the room before negotiating rates. So we nod. He adds helpfully, 'Don't worry. You can leave your bags here.'

We leave the bags there, not without misgivings. The portly chap, Rajinder, jangles a bunch of keys, small-talks politely, and leads the way into a dim corridor, then to a narrow mosaic stairway with an iron railing on one side. I realize that though the facade is narrow, the building is quite deep inside.

Rooms on the first floor open directly into the foyer. With the doors and windows open, one can see small dismal squares lit under 50-watt CFLs. The occupants of these rooms have spilled onto the landing. They look up as we pass. It is a large party of young men in colourful shirts and white trousers, hair slicked back, chunky watches on wrists. They are milling about the corridor, sitting on the bed, chewing chicken legs, humming loudly in the next room and talking on cell-phones; they seem to multiply before my eyes. There is a girl in a crimson salwar-kameez, tinkling jewellery, golden butterfly clips in her hair, standing outside the first room and talking to one of the white trousers earnestly. Another girl emerges from one of the other rooms, her hair tied in a topknot, her baby-pink salwar-kameez dotted with hundreds of glittery silver sequins. She interrupts the couple urgently, her high-heels clip-clopping. I am transfixed. S returns, and hustles me upstairs.

'We want a quiet room,' he tells Rajinder gruffly.

Rajinder reflects for a moment or two on our demand. He says, 'There *is* a quiet room in the corner, nice room, Western-style toilet, but it has only just been vacated. You can have it. But it will have to be cleaned first. Why don't you take a look?'

The room just vacated has seen better days. It is tucked away at the end of a long thin corridor and smells musty. A maroon carpet covers the entire floor, a patina of dust on it. The walls are a tube-lit green.

While S peeks into the bathroom with its cobwebbed but tiled corners and grimy sink, I gingerly push the polyester curtains open.

The window is surprisingly beautiful. It is latticed in the traditional style – leading to a dirty slab in front. But still, it is something. One sign of beauty. A good omen.

'Let's take this one,' I tell S, while Rajinder tries to discreetly remove empty bottles of Haywards from under the bed.

'How much?' he asks Rajinder.

'The reception will tell you that, sir,' Rajinder replies. 'I'll get the room cleaned.'

'Please change the sheets,' I beg. 'And the blankets.'

On the way to the reception, we see the white-trousered party who are still milling around, talking on cell-phones, humming loudly and indulging in intrigue with the girls. S smirks. 'Whose idea was this journey again?'

Down in the reception, there is fierce bargaining.

'How can you even ask for 375?' I demand. 'The room is so dusty. There is no view at all. The bathroom is a nightmare.'

'Jaipur is dusty city, madam,' the reedy fellow replies in English. 'We have power back-up. Other hotels here don't. Any food you want – Chinese, Indian, Italian, Thai – we serve in your room.' He waves a dog-eared menu in my face.

'Last offer 300.' I make to go.

The guys look glum but do not attempt to stop us.

'Three hundred fifty? That's final?' S settles.

I glower at him. He has given in *way* too easily.

The reedy guy opens the register. He asks, 'You have ID proof?' S nods and hands him his driving licence. I offer my PAN card. 'After David Headley was caught in a hotel in Pushkar, we are now *very* strict. Government instructions: no ID, no room. That's the new policy.' He carefully notes down the numbers.

'What relation are you to each other?' he now asks. 'Friends?'

I look away. S replies, 'She is my wife.'

The guy is disappointed. 'Full pay in advance. Twenty-four hours check-out.'

As S pays, Rajinder returns and hands me the keys.

Half an hour later, divested of our luggage, we step out, ravenous, into the streets of Jaipur. The night is deserted. Tipsy touts compare notes outside a hotel. The smell of old dust that has clung to the brain dissipates a little as we walk briskly in search of a restaurant. Rupees 500 − (350 + 40). That leaves about 110 rupees for dinner. And minus fifteen for the water bottle, S remembers. Only 95 for dinner. 'I think we'll have to keep the water bill separate,' I negotiate.

The air is nippy; a hint of wetness runs through as though it is raining somewhere close by. We walk on, quicker now to keep warm, pulling our coats closer, dreaming of hot chapatis with slightly blackened patches, shiny with butter.

Saurav

I wake up to the feel of rain in my bones. I cough and stir. There is dust in my throat. The chinks of light filtering in through the window remind me where I am: Veer Rajput Palace. At that I come round fully. I have not slept well. But that is nothing new. I stretch my arms and reach for my jacket. Distinctly odd, but it seems the dust on the carpet has somehow managed to rise upwards in the night, leaving dots on the sheets. I look around for a bottle of water.

Walking to the window, I push it open. A wet breeze drifts in. It is drizzling outside.

Our room is at the back of the building. It overlooks a block of modest houses with flat roofs. A short way across, through one or two trees glistening in the rain, one can see evidence of construction work. Several houses sport brown sackcloth hung from scaffoldings and a general collection of oddments: bricks, bamboos, cans of cement. New floors are being added, perhaps to rent out more rooms by the hour.

Very close by, though I cannot see it, stretch the saffron-pink walls of the old city, capital of Dhundhar.

⌐

The British insisted on referring to the principalities of Rajputana by the names of their respective capitals rather than the names of the historical regions under their sway. Thus Marwar was designated Jodhpur; Mewar was always Udaipur; hardly anybody knew that Bundi or Kota were used indiscriminately to refer to the region that is Haravati. So what was essentially Dhundhar was always called Amber (or Aamer) and later, after Sawai Jai Singh II established his glamorous new capital, simply Jaipur.

Historically, Dhundhar was the seat of the Kachhwaha Rajputs, a clan that claims descent from Kush, the younger son of Rama of Ayodhya. Their posh lineage notwithstanding, the story of how the Kachhwahas acquired the lands of Amber is one of betrayal.

It is believed by some that the descendants of Kush migrated from Rama's kingdom, Koshala, to what is now Rohtas in modern-day Bihar, and established a kingdom by the river Son. (The descendants of Lav apparently founded Lahore.) After a lapse of several generations, the legendary Raja Nal – hero of Kalidasa's eponymous play and lover of Damayanti, the princess of Vidarbha – migrated westward and established the kingdom of Narwar around AD 295. The thirty-third scion after Raja Nal was one Sora Singh whose son Dhola Rae – also called Dulhe Raja – established Dhundhar.

According to legend, when this Sora Singh died, his brother usurped the kingdom, divesting the infant Dhola Rae of his rightful inheritance. Dhola Rae's mother managed to escape, dressed as a commoner, her son hidden in a basket. She walked a long way, and finally, just outside the town of Khoganw, the capital of the Meenas, decided to take rest. She kept her precious basket on the ground and began to forage for berries. When she returned after a while, she found a serpent poised over the basket, its hood flashing in the sun.

Her shrieks for help attracted a travelling pandit who allayed her fears with great eloquence, insisting that she ought to celebrate, for this was a sign indicative of greatness to come. (The motif of a serpent identifying the heir is of course a recurrent one. Centuries later, Sangram Singh or Rana Sanga, then in exile, was similarly revealed by a cobra. But that is a different story.)

Dhola Rae's mother was not in a celebratory mood. She complained to the pandit that in her current state of hunger and thirst, not to mention homelessness, she could hardly harbour any fantasy of future glory for her infant. Chastened, the pandit gave her some useful advice. He urged her to go to the town of Khoganw, ruled by the Meenas, where, he was confident, her needs would be met.

The Meenas, incidentally, were an ancient race who claimed descent from the Matsya avatar of Vishnu; according to legends, they were fisherfolk who later became kings and founded the kingdom that has been identified through ancient history as Matsya. The capital of Matsya was Viratnagar (corresponding to Bairat in modern Rajasthan), and its most famous king was Virata, ally of the Pandavas and father-in-law to Abhimanyu, Arjun's favourite son.

In Khoganw, the former queen sought menial employment at the home of the Meena chieftain. One afternoon, a few days or weeks or months later, she was asked to prepare dinner by the Meena Rani. When the Meena Raja tasted the delicious dishes she'd cooked, a repast he deemed far superior to the usual fare, he invited her to an audience. The queen took this opportunity to reveal her antecedents.

After hearing the queen's tragic narrative, the Meena Raja immediately adopted her as his sister and the boy as his nephew. Thus, Dhola Rae was brought up an equal among the Meenas, and when he came of age, at fourteen, he was sent to Delhi as a representative of the Meena chief, carrying Khoganw's tribute.

In his five years in Delhi, however, egged on by his Rajput friends and cousins, Dhola Rae was seized with the idea of usurping the kingdom of the Meena Raja. Aided in the conspiracy by the Meena bard, Dhola Rae returned to Khoganw. On the occasion of Diwali, when it was customary for all the men to take a dip in the tank together and offer obeisance to ancestors, Dhola, along with his Rajput cohorts from Delhi, attacked his foster-brothers and swiftly filled the tank with dead bodies.

The first thing he did when he took possession of Khoganw was to put the treacherous bard to death. Since he'd been disloyal to the Meena Raja, why should Dhola believe he would be loyal to him?

The Meenas, though, were a doughty lot. The Meena Raja of Nain, for example, had been eulogized with the verse '*Bawan kot chhappan darwaja, Meena mard, Nain ka Raja*'. They nourished the enmity and continued guerrilla attacks against the Rajputs over the following centuries, hoping to win back their lands someday. The British, in a bid to cement their alliance with the Rajputs, eventually labelled the Meenas a criminal tribe. This appellation was only removed after Independence.

Many generations later, Dhola Rae's descendant, Sawai Jai Singh II, laid the foundation of Jaipur on 18 November 1727, under the guidance of auspicious stars and his architecture consultant from Bengal, Vidyadhar Bhattacharya.

⌐

This is not the first time I've come to Jaipur – D and I'd been here once before, our first holiday together, many years ago. It was not the happiest of trips. We were impecunious and still in the university. Intense bursts of anxiety about the future had quickly devoured our brief spells of bliss on that occasion and we'd distracted ourselves with brief bursts of sightseeing. D had taken many photos in Jantar Mantar with her five-hundred-rupee camera bought for the occasion. The Hawa Mahal, Nahargarh, the spectacular fort at Jaigarh. My young wife, I'd thought, every time I looked at her. And it was unsettling. But we always meant to come back. And here we are, thanks to a chain of bizarre decisions, in Jaipur, as poor as we were then, though older and fancy-free, beginning the journey that we like to imagine will refashion us. Refashion, renew, revolt. Funny how hopeful words begin the same way. D has always been a romantic. And it appears now that beneath the clipped jargon of energy economics and geopolitics – the things I analyse for a living – I have been as much of a romantic too.

Or insane. And like all insane ventures, this one too was born in a moment of false lucidity, infused with tremendous hope and bolstered by theory. The larger picture would put our minor moments in perspective. It is *exactly* what we need.

Over the last few months, we've taken turns reassuring each other. This is the right thing to do.

D is sleeping on her stomach peacefully, unaffected by dust or grime, curled into a ball in the cold. But it is important we begin our day – sally forth into Jaipur early on. In the late afternoon, we can board a bus to Pushkar which is around 130 kilometres away. I am not too enthused at the prospect of another night in Veer Rajput Palace. In any case, we'd decided to keep moving forward continuously, at rumbling speed.

The rain has now become insistent and drums on the dirty slab in front of our window. It is then that I think of D's elaborate list. It had, unfortunately, not included an umbrella.

5

Jaipur is shiny after the rain. Clouds with promising black bellies are still swirling in the sky but the drizzle has tapered off. As we walk, skirting puddles, we are still arguing about S's unilateral decision to travel onward. The decision has been taken though; I have even made a couple of calls to budget hotels in Pushkar. But I am not happy.

'The entire point of this journey is to keep moving,' S says, as I canter to keep up with him, '*keep* travelling, at a *hurtling* pace. How else do you propose to travel across thousands of kilometres in a hundred days?'

Yes, that indeed was the vague proposition we had agreed on at the outset. Around India in a hundred days. That sort of thing. Not much else. *That*, and the budget of course. We'd stick to 500 rupees a day for bed and board. (Water was put on the watch list. No decision had been taken on it.)

'We are yet to see what *the entire point of the journey is*,' I counter, 'but surely it is about getting a true feel of the place. How do you propose to do that in a few hours?'

'Oh, but you can *easily* do it in a few days. Hahaha.'

'Definitely. You can most definitely get a better flavour of a place in a few days as compared to a few hours.'

'Accept it,' S says smugly, 'you're sprouting roots. Even Veer Rajput Palace seems a passable proposition to you, compared to the uncertainty of another new place tonight.'

'What are you talking about?' I say, annoyed. How can he even suggest that I am less enthusiastic about uncertainty? *I'd married him.*

'This is exactly why Buddhist monks were cautioned against sleeping under the same tree for more than three nights in a row. Because people sprout roots. And you are sprouting roots in one night.'

I scowl and step back and contemplate a fitting reply.

It is around eight-fifteen now. We have been walking around the lanes and by-lanes near our hotel, and now emerge from one of them onto MI Road. We are to have some breakfast, acquire an umbrella, understand Jaipur. And then, apparently, by four in the afternoon or so, we ought to be off.

MI Road is one of the central arteries of Jaipur – broad and well laid out. Well maintained too, after a fashion. Traffic has begun to thicken as office-goers rush to work, the sudden shower notwithstanding. We stop for a while and watch them through the bluish haze that moisture in the air creates in dusty places, the road shining, the sky dipping low, grey and overcast. The signal changes. All traffic comes to a halt on the other side of the road – the motorbikes, the SUVs, the buses, the bicycles. And suddenly, a camel lurches forward, dragging behind her a cart. Her ride tries to stop her, and then, after a half-hearted flailing of arms, the man gives up and begins to laugh. Her head held high, she moves forward – to mix metaphors horribly – a ship with its mast tall and banners flying, sailing in style.

That surreal moment, suggesting perhaps the main point of the journey, marks our truce for now.

6

There are large batches of samosas being fried. The owner of the small eatery, dexterously lifting all fifteen or twenty at a time with his giant metal karchhi, waves us inside. It is a small room with a low ceiling and sooty walls. The effect is cosy. It begins to drizzle afresh. There are four mismatched tables, with a mix of chairs and benches surrounding them; all of these are occupied. We ask the lone member of the nearest table if we can join him. He is finishing a bowl of dal-bati-choorma; he smiles and wordlessly invites us to join him. For a while we sit quietly, all of us. S orders samosas. The man orders tea. The ice is broken.

'Are you from hereabouts?' I ask him, somewhat shyly and rather unoriginally. But it is, of course, the safest opener. Most people in India are not exactly from where you meet them; and even if they are, most Indians have a hometown beyond their hometown, a story of travel somewhere in the past which they are happy to narrate. (For instance, though I am from Calcutta and my dad is from Ranchi, my grandfather's family was originally from Deoghar, a pilgrim town in Jharkhand which I have never visited. Several generations ago, though, they were in Pabna, which is now in Bangladesh.)

'From near Ajmer,' the man replies. 'Though my mother was from the far west, from near the Pakistan border. But now I have been in Jaipur for sixteen years. I've got used to this place,' he half-complains. 'Can't seem to think of returning. What about you? Where are you coming from?'

'We are from Calcutta,' S answers, 'though now we've come from Delhi. We are rather fond of Jaipur – we've been here once in the past.'

The tea and samosas arrive at the same time. We dig in ravenously, dipping our samosas in the wildly hot chutney on the side. The man drapes his glass with the end of his shawl, and sips from it.

'I am a rickshaw driver,' he informs us, pointing to a smart rickshaw upholstered in electric blue, parked outside. It isn't his though; it's on rent. His own rickshaw was stolen a few months ago. As we rearrange our features into an appropriate expression, he shrugs, resigned. Early last winter he was at an eatery having lunch when it was stolen. It's apparently a big racket in Jaipur. He tells us that rickshaws are routinely picked up in Jaipur; in a matter of hours the colour schemes of the seats are changed, the wheels are replaced, and bam – nobody can prove anything! He's had enough of this. Now he rents a rickshaw for twenty-five rupees a day from a man who has 5,000 rickshaws. It's alright, he assures us. On a good day in the season he can make about 500 rupees. The twenty-five doesn't hurt so much then. There are even some benefits in this arrangement. The man with 5,000 rickshaws has mechanics who work directly for him, so repairs and things are all taken care of.

'Maybe the guy with the 5,000 rickshaws is the one who runs the racket, stealing rickshaws on the side. His army of mechanics can change their look in a jiffy,' S mutters at me darkly, while our friend looks philosophical.

I am curious if he would like to buy another rickshaw.

'I am tired of this trade now,' he replies. 'I would like to start a business of my own. You see, I had been apprenticed in the bakery business. We had a shop. We used to make breads and cakes and sell them. My father had a cycle rickshaw with a box for the baked goods.'

At the mention of the bread box on the bicycle we all feel a fleeting touch of wistfulness; it belongs to a time past, along with *Chitrahar* and the 'Sunday-ho-ya-Monday-roz-khao-andey' ad on Doordarshan. (This ad of course belongs in the innocent days before cholesterol was discovered.)

He continues, 'The shop was doing quite well. But it all came unstuck when my elder brother got married and became a complete joru ka ghulam. He cut us out of the business. By then my father was dead – there was no one to intercede on our behalf, me and my other brother. I want to get back into the bakery business. But my children are still young, so sometimes I think I should not take a risk and start something new. I know the rickshaw trade well; it's safe.'

We understand, we murmur. We've also changed trades recently, S tells him. It can't be easy if one has children.

His sisters, though, he is happy to report, have married better. One is in Gandhidham in Gujarat; one in Delhi. The Delhi sister's son is in Hong Kong, a house owner; the Gandhidham sister's son-in-law is in Dubai (also a house owner).

He motions for another chai while S calls out for another samosa.

'You must have been around these parts on work?' S asks, changing the subject. 'Rajasthan, Gujarat...'

'I have, actually,' he tells us. 'Before joining the rickshaw business, I travelled quite a bit. To Mundhra, Gandhidham, Surat – many other places, looking for work. Not been to Bombay though. Not *that* adventurous. I've been to Delhi several times; but nowadays I don't like going to my sister's place. They have become too posh for me.'

He has four children. The younger three clamour to be taken to Delhi to their aunt's house but he studiously avoids that set.

'Do many people from Rajasthan go to Gujarat for work?'

'Oh yes. Plenty! There are dalals who round up people and get them jobs in Gujarat every season. Mostly on contract though. All these jobseekers then travel together. Some become lifelong friends. But I'm too old for all that now. My eldest boy is in Gandhidham. He is sixteen.

After he dropped out of school, we sent him off – some other boys from our neighbourhood were going to Gujarat to look for work. He stays with my second sister. Our Dubai relative has promised to take him to Dubai after he turns eighteen. Let's see if he keeps his word. I did much for them once upon a time.'

The tables around us empty and then fill up again; we chat, the rain tapers off, there are regular splashes as buses trundle by.

The owner looks at us curiously. Perhaps if it weren't rush hour he'd have joined us at our table.

⌒

Later that morning we find ourselves wandering around old Jaipur, the pink city as it is called. An umbrella is acquired from Tripolia Bazaar.

But my memories of this jaunt and those on previous occasions, all the walks around the bazaars of the old city, coalesce. It should have been more hope than anxiety really that first time but for our predilection towards neuroses. I had wondered then why it was called *pink* city. When, in fact, the buildings are all the hue of sandstone. A reddish-saffron shade. The city had been bestowed this uniform look by Maharaja Ram Singh, in 1876, to welcome the Prince of Wales – and ever since, the residents are bound by law to follow the colour scheme. But then I'd seen the sunset: the extravagant gild the departing sun lends to the old city at cow-dust hour, a magic glow that turns the buildings into what is not quite golden pink but can only be called so.

The gloom of the present weather amplifies the romance of old Jaipur. But as usual, every medieval Indian moment gets interrupted by the aggressive signposting of MNCs – Coke and Lux – a study in postmodernity. Through the scattered raindrops, the bustle and the bargaining are a little muffled. But the rows of shops in long straight lines are doing brisk business. The bazaars with their silversmiths and gold johris, meenakars and cotton traders are full of tourists – local as well as foreign. From the Siredeori Bazaar I look up at the Hawa Mahal, Palace of Winds, the exquisite five-storey honeycombed structure built by Maharaja Pratap Singh in 1799 so that the women could witness the life of the city from its unique windows without anybody spotting them from outside. Once again, my memories meld, and I rapidly recede into my early twenties; S and I are standing at the edge of the bazaar, our skins raw, bumping into each other in the crowd like new lovers, enveloped by worlds of noise.

But that is late summer. The light is something else.

Two

How (Not) to Get Mixed Up in Other People's Pilgrimages

Tirtha belongs to a whole family of Indo-European cognates that are the great words of passage and pilgrimage in the West as well… 'thoroughfare', 'transition', 'transformation', 'transport', and 'transcend'.

– Diana L. Eck, *India: A Sacred Geography*

7

A year or so before the rainy day in Jaipur. We were still reasonably respectable yuppies living in Delhi. We had our jobs; I even had a tenuous link to the university, a higher degree that I was supposedly working on. S was away for a few days from office and while I stayed with friends in Chittaranjan Park, instead of my regular route to Vasant Vihar, cutting through Chanakyapuri, I took to returning home via Nizamuddin. Every evening I'd see a long line of buses parked there. Not the usual Delhi state transport buses or even the long-distance buses that plied from Delhi to neighbouring states. These were ancient weather-beaten vehicles with gaping windows and battered bodies, much the worse for wear.

Every evening, I'd observe the pavements as the signal changed and traffic around me stalled and heaved. Dusk would deepen; the remaining daylight would be sucked out from the sky, quart by quart as it were. The pavements would be filled with men cheerfully going about their business of life right there, cooking on portable stoves and washing vegetables and sitting in circles, talking, never mind the passers-by walking through their ranks swiftly, sometimes raising clouds of dust in their faces. But they did not look like squatters; they had instead the look and bearing of travellers, people passing through – and not merely passing through. The patience in their eyes indicated a confidence in what was awaited. One or two young men would sit away from the group at the edge of the footpath, their feet casually stretched on the road, fiddling with their mobile phones. Who were these people? I wondered. Why were they here?

On the fifth or sixth evening, I asked the autowallah what was going on. He was a man in his fifties. It seemed he knew what was what. He had also indicated a tendency to chat.

'Who are these people, bhaisahab?'

He took a quick look outside. 'Oh, them? They are going for Hajj, madam,' he replied. 'They're on their way to Mecca. You see these buses? That's what they've come by – and will take onward.'

I didn't quite understand. My geography was a bit dodgy but I was certain that Mecca was not just a bus-ride away.

The autowallah went on, 'These people have come from different parts of India. Each bus brings one party. It sometimes takes weeks for them to reach Delhi. Nizamuddin is the meeting ground. These people will *only* go on Hajj after paying their respects at the dargah. Only after all the buses reach and everybody has sought the blessings of the pir will the buses start.'

Enchanted as I was by this compelling account, I was still iffy about the route.

'But *how* will they go? Through Pakistan?'

'No, no, madam-ji,' he said, laughing, 'they'll go by jahaaz. From Bombay I think. Or maybe Gujarat, not sure. The buses will wait for them there and when they return, each party will be taken to their villages in the same bus that had brought them.'

I was seized with the sudden swirl of images this presented: the sea and piety, hope and grime, and long long days in buses through changing landscapes. The thin brown pilgrims, now baking rotis on a pavement as night beckoned.

The autowallah continued, 'Very difficult journey on the bus, madam. Long journey in ship. One person from my basti had gone a few years ago. A tailor. After he returned, he changed the name of his shop to Hajji Tailors from Pinky Tailors. It is doing much better these days. But then that is the thing about teerath: the more hardship you bear on the journey, the sweeter the results. But haan, it is not so easy to go on a teerath, after all. You can only go when Bhagwanji wills. In their case, they can only go after Allah permits, after all their duties are done. You know what happened to me one time? Many years ago, my wife had made a mannat when my youngest son developed meningitis and was critical, that if by God's grace he was cured, we would go to Haridwar and offer puja there. Feed at least a hundred people. He did become alright and every year, around his birth anniversary, my wife would start badgering me about this. But something or the other would intervene. Sister's wedding, children's education – never did I have enough money to take everybody to Haridwar. Seven years went by. One evening in August – I remember it was August because my youngest son was born in the rains and every time during monsoon my wife used to start the Haridwar gaana – I returned home and found a friend waiting. He told me that the next morning he was setting out for Haridwar to run some errands for his employer. He worked for a Delhi business family that hailed from Haridwar. He was driving an old Tata Sumo there and would come back after four or five days, along with a few boxes from the employer's ancestral house. Would we come? He would be glad of the company.'

The wind streamed in from both sides as the auto sped along. I was straining my ears, trying to collect his words in the right order as they ricocheted around my seat.

Luckily, we soon came to a signal.

'What can I say, madam?' The man now took his eyes off the road and turned to look at me. He had a square face with a high nose on which were perched gold-coloured spectacles. 'The offer was very kind. If we went in his jeep both ways, I wouldn't be spending anything at all. The employer was paying for petrol. The children would love a road trip. My mother would be thrilled. But what can I say? It was the end of the month. My hands were empty. I had just had my engine

changed to CNG. That had been expensive. On top of that, the auto
had been out of commission for a few days. Hardly any money for
groceries – how would we go on a teerath? Feed a hundred people?
My wife and I sat dispiritedly all evening. Where would I get eight to
ten thousand rupees at such short notice?'

The signal changed and we began to move again. Darkness had
fallen and the lights of the city glimmered around us.

Eyes on the road, the man continued.

'But, madam, you know the strange thing that happened that night?
You won't believe me if I tell you. At nine-thirty my brother-in-law
came. My brother-in-law, my sister's husband. He works as a house
painter and is often called away on projects here and there. He was
in a rush, going to Karnal that night. He gave me a bundle and said,
"Bhai-ji, there's ten thousand rupees here. All my savings from this
quarter. I am going to Karnal on a two-month project. Please keep it
safe." After he left, I rushed to my friend's house and my wife started
packing. The kids were jumping around. Two months later, when
my brother-in-law returned, I gave him his money and told him the
whole story. I told him he was a shareholder of the punya, since it was
his money that had enabled the daan. Five hundred people, we'd fed.'

We were outside the second market at C.R. Park. The air reeked of
fish. I scrabbled in my bag for money. 'Teerath is like *that*, madam-ji,'
he said, returning the change. 'When you are supposed to go, you will.'

I thanked him for the stories and began walking towards the house.
Like every evening, moths fluttered around the lamp posts. Large cars
were parked in double lines.

I remember that evening clearly. It was a listless night. Little chips
of grey stone crunched as I walked, leaving the smug bright lights of
the shops and the thrum of traffic behind, down a street dimly lit by
yellow pools of fluorescence. I have since convinced myself that it was
this evening when I found myself willing to admit, for the first time,
how unhappy we were.

It was not enough: the busy hours over unimportant tasks, the
shopping, the eating out, the investments we were learning to make.
Not enough to plug the hole through which everything black and scary
seemed to flood in diurnally.

Just why the fact of our unhappiness came to me thus, unbidden and mixed up with other people's pilgrimages, I cannot say, but that was how it was; I can see the lacklustre buses and the sprightly pilgrims and the moths around the lamp posts and the double lines of large cars. I can recognize the fish smell in the air.

I remember that I was at once afraid and free. I found myself stupidly crying on the road. It was a relief that nobody knew me in that neighbourhood. So I sat in the park and old men walked past. Leaves crushed under their feet and a smell of sap rose from the earth. I cried bitterly, in the grip of an exhaustion that was inexplicable.

Later that night I sent an email to S from my friend Gee's computer: 'I am willing to consider the alternative.'

Saurav

We have been assigned seats to the right, second row from the front. D scribbles in her notebook. I buy moongphali. Outside, the bus station buzzes with activity. Already our ears seem attuned to the familiar mixed noises: travellers, conductors, salesmen, eccentrics. Among the smells that stream in, the most prominent is a stench of urine. Over the months we will recognize this as the unifying trait of bus stands across the country. There are a few squabbles over the allocation of seats. A balding man in his late forties comes and claims the seat next to me. He waves his ticket at the conductor. He distributes his luggage hurriedly, a canvas bag and a small sturdy suitcase, here and there, and continues to look about his person cagily. As though somebody else might edge him out of his seat. When the bus leaves the depot, he relaxes, wipes his brow with the white gamchha on his shoulder and starts to chat.

A prosperous farmer, Kailash Chandra Jain grows moong when it rains, and jeera, bajra and makki round the year. On the side he runs a business. He is a supplier of white stone powder. There are many more marble centres in Rajasthan than before, now that groundwater is being exploited in many parts of the state. He has four children: three daughters followed by a son, a formula common enough across India. It is invariably accompanied by the joke that if the parents are fortunate, the son will bring back in dowry whatever was spent on the weddings of the (two, three, four or sometimes even five) daughters that came before. But his eldest daughter, Kailash Chandra adds, as though reading my thoughts, is extremely hoshiyaar. She has just finished school. As a matter of fact, he had come to Jaipur to admit her into a year-long coaching programme that would prepare her for engineering and medical entrances, the PMT. He emphasizes the PMT again and again, a mnemonic for his family's future plans. This year-long specialized college is an expensive proposition. But things are changing, even in this conservative state. Wouldn't it be better to spend this money now and let her stand on her own feet than spend it later on dowry, probably over a foolish boy who is not a professional but only depends on the lands of his forefathers and maybe a business or two? This was his wife's argument. He agreed. How many times can you sell the same land? he asks. But a degree? That's different.

When he hears that we are travelling in Rajasthan with no particular map, Kailash Chandra urges us to visit the Nisya Temple at Chand Khedi, one of the oldest pilgrimage sites of Jains, located around 80 kilometres from Kota, where, he claims excitedly, we are sure to witness a real miracle: water trickling out of a magic tumbler round the year. The phenomenon, he says, has intrigued rationalists for many years. He now stands up, swaying as the bus turns sharply, and begins to gather his belongings.

In a moment, the bus enters Kishangarh, his stop – the old town once famous for the painting style and now booming because of marble trade – and he repeats urgently, this time looking past me to D, who has copied down the words 'Chand Khedi' in her yellow notebook: 'Do note down, madam, there are many miracles connected to this temple. You must tell the public these legends through your writings. Even Aurangzeb tried to destroy the temple in Chand Khedi but failed. It is said, when his troops attacked, an axe damaged the toe of Lord Rishabha's statue. Immediately, a huge torrent of milk flowed out and the troops were washed away.' Rishabha or Adinatha is the Godhead of the Jain cult Kailash Chandra belongs to.

A large number of people disembark at Kishangarh. A bustling swirl of lights and sounds and corncob sellers, after the many miles of darkness. One of the hundreds of towns in India. Some other time this might be our destination. Today, though, Ajmer is 18 kilometres away.

'We must go to Chand Khedi,' D tells me seriously, stabbing the yellow notebook with her pen, her eyes shining behind the black spectacles. 'There must be something to that water-dripping-out-of-a-tumbler story.'
But we don't; it gets added to the List of Regrets.

8

We disembark at the wrong stop near Pushkar and, in our hurry, step right into a muddy patch. It is dark and cold and after the bus leaves, we find ourselves wavering by the highway. The quiet is occasionally broken by the rumble of buses or trucks that go past. Over the weeks, the melancholy of arrivals will become a familiar sensation – the slight stumbling over unfamiliar terrain, eyes trying to adjust to strange faces, the overwhelming feeling of suspicion that will mostly dissipate in the next hour or so, the weight on our shoulders – but now, it's still a reasonably new uneasiness. Like the melancholy of new love.

S shines his mobile on the map, trying to make sense of the tiny print in the *Lonely Planet* guide. (We have exchanged our bags, so at least I am able to breathe.)

But a few steps ahead there is a tea stall, and when we ask around, locals take us under their wing – the rucksacks, we understand later, are an important marker in hippie-friendly places – and a few men offer to lead the way. Through several dark galis and short cuts, during which I must confess I taste the acrid waves of doubt in my throat many many times though the men are unfailingly polite, we suddenly enter the main street of Pushkar, Sadar Bazaar Road. They are not touts and, in any case, we tell them our room has been booked already. Lights glimmer in houses and store-windows.

As we inhale the air and look around, there is a sudden spring in our step and our bags have become light. We grin at each other happily, linking fingers. The charm of Pushkar is immediate and affective. The whitewashed latticed houses. Homey restaurants promising Continental and Jewish cuisine, and entertaining spelling.

Quirky curio shops displaying wooden jewellery boxes, handmade paper notebooks and silk harem pants. Fat cows rambling past. We wander around in a sort of delirium, admiring everything. We even check out a few other hotels. Just like that.

Then we find a rickshaw and it quickly takes us to Mayur Guest House where I'd called in the morning. A family-run establishment, it turns out to be a delightful old house, designed and limewashed in the traditional style, nestled in a decent neighbourhood. One part of the main house is sectioned off for guests.

The considerable charms of Pushkar, however, will always be subservient in my mind to our room. For 250 rupees, we have been given a large clean room with skylights. Attached bath. The walls have a bluish tinge. There are clean white sheets on the bed and two clean white pillows smelling of starch. There is a Jaipuri rajai folded neatly and kept under the pillows. A slim mirror. Bare shelves on the wall. There is a large window with green fluted shutters. The room opens onto a tiny open courtyard with a few rattan chairs. While I knock off my shoes and socks and roll on the bed in hysterical happiness, S returns from signing the register and reports there is both hot water in our attached bath *and* a small collection of books to borrow.

Later, however, a photograph will tell me that the memory of the green fluted shutters is a false one, for the room seems to have had, at one end, a regular frosted-glass window, large and curtained. But when I shut my eyes and am in Pushkar again, in the room that spells out the formula for joy (clean sheets, hot water, books to borrow and the promise of blue hills in the distance), I see the window with its green shutters, casting the room in that happy gloom that only shuttered windows can.

I remember how the night in Pushkar gets cold. After the first flush of sleep, I lay awake, huddling for warmth next to S under that single quilt, imagining the darkness without. There is the occasional lowing of a cow; a random argument in French as footsteps pass by the window; and once, the escalated speeding of a scooter with a faulty silencer. It is like a noisy pebble in a lake, and it takes several minutes for the effect to wear off, even after stillness has descended again.

It is the middle of the night and I sit up and look critically at the soles of my feet. I can feel the roots sprouting.

Saurav

Pushkar. Afternoon. Brown hill against brilliant blue skies. (I do not know what this peculiar blue is called: renaissance blue is apparently the exact shade but it sounds idiotic in this context. In the course of our journey, I would find the same shade of blue in the underglaze of the few remaining tiles from Samarkand that are studded on the walls of the Jahangir Mahal in Orchha. So we shall settle for Samarkand blue.) The skies are a brilliant Samarkand blue. I cannot remember now if the spire of the temple is visible from below.

We have a late lunch. Since we won't have to pay for dinner tonight – we have an invitation to one at our homestay – D stretches the budget airily and eats ravioli swimming in cheese sauce, sitting cross-legged on a cushion. It is a sunny restaurant with blue walls, low tables, and flowers hanging from its windows. And it is full of excited French tourists who have been lured by the promise of blue cheese flown in from Provence. The manager, M, is originally from Tamil Nadu and subsequently from Calcutta. He wears an accent that is neither Tamil nor Calcuttan, and an eager overfamiliarity that a few Indians adopt, particularly in places where mainly foreign tourists come; it leaves a strange taste in the mouth.

Then we set out. As we begin to leave the village behind, first, stretches of brown-gold sand. Under a banyan tree children play with bricks and a ghastly doll. A forlorn camel is tethered to a cart. A track runs in the middle. Small eddies of fine sand rise as we walk. Low blue hills on the horizon. Our shadows precede us, long blue blurs on the grey road. Finally, Ratnagiri hill – though that's tautology, like saying Ratna-hill hill – with numbered steps leading up.

In the beginning I am very enthusiastic. This is exactly the sort of exercise that will make me as fit as I was at eighteen. This is exactly the point of the project, of this new life. A trek a day. I hurry uphill, waving to D as she rambles with her camera. But by the time I am halfway up and the tall bare trees seem an arm's length away, their pale chiselled trunks spectacular against the sky, I am already winded. The breath comes out ragged. My chest is burning.

I am worried at who I have become.

The endless blue surrounding the hill on all sides now plunges into me like ice. In the nature of fear, it pulls along the other components: the jobs that we have given up, the money in the accounts that will no longer be topped off at the beginning of the month. And now this – these ragged breaths. It is too late, the fear booms. I am too far from the natural state; every attempt to return to it is mere pretending, the sort of Pinko fad that we have assured ourselves this is not.

I shrug off my jacket, I pause and look at the filigreed branches that stretch into the sky. Beyond the green fields punctuated by golden-brown plots of sandy earth, little white boxy houses merge into each other as though made of ticky-tacky.

A descending tourist stops next to me to rest. He drinks water from his bottle.

'Is better coming down.' He smiles.

'You bet,' I reply, allowing myself to be quickly cheered. We fall into conversation. He's Israeli. A thin young chap, twenty or so. He wears a sleeveless black t-shirt and khaki shorts. Just out of the army, I presume.

We talk as strangers do. He has just finished his military training back home, he'd been in signals, he says vaguely. We arrived last evening, we are at Mayur Guest House. He'll leave tomorrow. We're not sure where we'll go from here.

'Have a good trip,' I tell him.

'Enjoy the view,' he says.

We shake hands. He leaves. D catches up, smiles at him as he passes her, and begins to lead the way.

More and more people are climbing down now. Mostly lean foreigners who smile politely and hurry along, absorbed in themselves. For most of them, the landscapes are an interesting setting, remote and appropriate, for their obsessional inner dialogues. Henry David Thoreau had suggested that 'to be truly free' one must be surrounded by unfamiliar landscapes and strangers. Some take photographs. But without those cues – we will see later from friends we make along the way – the names and particulars of hills and forts and views, the details, are immaterial. They all merge into a blur. The opposite for me: everything I see is invested with meaning. Everything is a version or a shadow of something I know or have heard and want to interpret better. It is *with* these that I stage my obsessional dialogues. And then, inevitably, I carry the burden of their meanings and their failures.

A few local youths with gangly limbs and bright clothes descend nimbly. It is plain they own these hills. The routes are remembered in their bodies. They clamber up and down along the slope. They stare at us freely, yet are surprised when I smile or look their way, and quickly avert their eyes. But the children who run down at great speed like mountain goats are enamoured only of the foreigners. They wave at us half-heartedly but their eyes are on their quarry, and they follow them, shouting out greetings and swear words alternately. After them, old men, in groups of three and four, descend. They are very chatty and tell me they make this trek to the temple every day. They don't mean to be smug, I know. But they are proud of their lives, of their certainties. That, at their age – one is sixty-eight, one seventy-three – they can still climb up the hill and pay their regards to the goddess in person, every day. It means something to them; they like to talk about it.

Savitri, whose hill this is, is a redoubtable mother goddess. Polly Parashar, the owner of Mayur Guest House, told us the local version of the legend this morning. The story of the epic estrangement between Brahma and Savitri, his first wife. Later, we acquire a small booklet, *Pushkar Guide*, authored by the Late Shri Tejulal Nagori, for ten rupees. This gives a colourful account.

The asura Vajranabha was creating havoc on earth, killing people at will. At least so goes the story from the perspective of devas and men. To deal with him, Brahma threw his lotus in Vajranabha's direction. In the Puranic version, however, Vajranabha was doing grave tapasya to bring about the destruction of the devas. The ability of the asuras to conduct arduous tapasya was well known and greatly feared. The lotus that Brahma threw (the Puranic version maintains the lotus was not thrown but fell of its own accord) not only destroyed Vajranabha through the sound waves it generated, but it fell at three places, and fresh water sprang from all three spots. The largest and first of these lakes is the Jyeshtha Pushkar, followed by the Madhya Pushkar and the Kanishtha Pushkar.

Polly also informed us that the word 'pushkar' is a composite of pushpa (flower) and kar (hand). Brahma's hand, that is. After that, naturally, Pushkar became Brahma's spot.

In the age of Chakshusha Manu, Brahma appeared on earth and decided to conduct a yajna at Pushkar. One yojana land was earmarked for the rites and rituals. Invitations were issued all round. Indra came with a large contingent of gods and goddesses. Shiva appeared with an entourage of disciples. Brahma requested Vishwakarma to make suitable arrangements for the gods to stay, and asked Kuber, the god of wealth, to provide money and clothes to whoever asked for these. Vishnu was urged to preach good things to all who would gather. Shiva would be required to protect the yajna along with his ganas. And Vayu, the deity of air, was asked to carry forth invitations for the yajna across all three lokas. Brahma himself created the low hills around the site of the yajna to keep the place secure from asuric attacks.

But it is not the asuras who cause trouble.

When the sage Pulastya indicates the time is propitious, Brahma sends his son Narada to summon Savitri. It is traditional for man and wife to participate in a yajna together. However, Narada, who is some kind of an Amar Singh character on the divine stage, instead of telling Savitri to come at once, asks her to wait for her friends – Lakshmi, Indrani, Bhavani, as well as a few celestial nymphs. Returning to the site of the sacrifice, he informs Brahma and Pulastya that Savitri has decided to come later, accompanied by her friends.

At the site of the yajna, Pulastya is worried that the auspicious moment will pass owing to Savitri's delay. Finally, he advises Brahma to take another wife and perform the rituals with her. Indra is sent to look for a suitable girl and finds Gayatri, who is, according to some versions, a Gujjar milkmaid. However, when Savitri appears at the site of the yajna and sees Gayatri carrying out the oblations along with Brahma, she is justifiably furious. Shri Tejulal Nagori narrates: 'Turning to Lord

Brahma, she cursed him, you have become old and have lost the thinking faculty. Now I curse you, except at Pushkar, at no other place you will be worshipped ... Mother Savitri was so furious that her face turned red black with anger and she appeared as Mother Kali of Kolkatta (West Bengal).' Afterwards, Savitri left to come to Ratnagiri and meditate here.

Meanwhile, Gayatri rose to the occasion and redressed the curses as best as she could. For example, Savitri had cursed the celestial nymphs with childlessness. Gayatri simply told them that they would never feel the desire to have children, and so, childlessness would cause no suffering to them at all. Gayatri's abode on a nearby hill is thus called the Paap Mochani Temple. She told Brahma that though Savitri's curse could not be revoked, and Brahma would never be widely worshipped, no devotee would get the benefits of the Char Dham pilgrimage unless they also come to Pushkar.

⌒

The winter light is pale when it falls on fields in the distance. From high up, the views are spectacular. The hills again. Browns changing to blues that merge with the horizon. On the other side, though, the edges of the western sky are now curling into a crushed pink dusk. Engulfing the ticky-tacky houses. Unreasonably, I am filled with great hope – about the future, about the journey, about revolutions and transformations. About us. The Jyeshtha Pushkar is visible though it seems dry. Apparently, Tejulal Nagori notes, when Aurangzeb had come to wreak destruction in Pushkar, one of his grandfather Jahangir's favourite places, he'd washed his face in the waters of one of the lakes. And his face had suddenly aged. Buddha Pushkar, it began to be called: old Pushkar. Aurangzeb with his prematurely aged face had moved on, the story goes, leaving the ghats untouched. It is said that afterwards, he made a land grant to the Parashar Brahmins of Pushkar.

D calls out now from twenty steps higher and her voice comes on the back of the wind. She asks me to hurry. The crest is nigh.

9

There is a puja at the Parashar house today, to which we have been invited.

This morning, when we were leaving the guest house for the day, armed with our *Lonely Planet* guide and camera, Polly's mother, quite the old matriarch, was sunning herself on a chair in the street outside. She had heard about us already. We stopped to chat. After a few minutes, she asked us to the puja in the evening. Dressed in a purple sari and matching cardigan, a scarf wound around her head from which a thin braid snaked down, she told us to stay on for dinner.

I quickly gather that we are some sort of curiosities to the Parashars. Their guests are almost entirely European or Israeli. Sometimes there are Americans; very rarely, a few Japanese. In ten years of running the guest house, they've never had Indians like us. Poor Hindu pilgrims prefer to stay in dharmashalas close to the Brahma temple while upwardly mobile Indian tourists would naturally choose from a range of posh hotels with TVs, ACs and other such amenities.

While most are backpackers during their gap year, there are a few regulars. Old Mrs Parashar tells us of the fifty-something gora couple (from Germany, Polly tells us later) who spend six months of the year at Mayur. The other six months they run an antiques business back home. I had seen the Germans this morning, when I'd nipped upstairs to the terrace and spent part of the morning gazing at the neighbourhood. The Germans had kept the door of their room open. The lady was in the verandah, pinning clothes on the clothesline with her fair veined hands. The man sat at a small desk, writing, his light hair catching the sun. I had quickly moved past, not wanting to snoop.

Polly was hovering around. Soon he joined us and we ended up talking for a long time, right there on the street. The sunlight fell in pleasant notes on the blue-white walls of the house. A beautiful house; an architectural marvel. A house so lived-in and unselfconscious, it made me sigh in pleasure every time I looked up. Polly's mother told us that one of her husband's ancestors had been granted this plot of land as a royal present. The Parashars are Brahmins – this had come up two or three times in Polly's telling of their story – and the ancestor who had secured the land was a royal pandit. They still have the old firman. However, she added, bringing out her knitting from a plastic packet, this architecture was *nothing*. We should go to her hometown, Bundi. *Then* we would see the glory of Rajputana. Out came my yellow notebook. Bundi, I noted. Children ran past, their shoes thudding on the concrete; endings of conversations drifted in from around the corner in the hard syllables of Rajasthani; we said goodbye and walked on.

In the evening, though, when we walk back from the Savitri temple after having tea in a dhaba full of Israeli travellers, at the foot of Ratnagiri, the luminous pink dusk turns to a brittle unhappy darkness. A sudden column of loneliness arises between us. My feet are aching, my shoes are full of gravel, and I am overwhelmed with doubts. The sunny morning seems such a long time ago. I even begin to wonder if we do indeed have a dinner invitation after all.

'It was only mentioned in passing, wasn't it? Maybe we misunderstood?'

This irritates S. I was positive about the invitation while having the expensive ravioli, wasn't I?

The ennui of evenings provides a perfect foil for recriminations. But this larger trend, I am to map only later. Today, I am too tired to react. We merely walk ahead in a huff.

By the time we reach the guest house, cutting through the bazaar as the sky darkens and lights begin to gleam in shops, S says finally, adopting a conciliatory tone, we should go for the puja, and depending on the situation, take a call on dinner. We could always walk to a nearby place and have roti-sabji if the invitation had been misheard. And perhaps, in that case, we could also stop for cake. We had spotted an old gentleman in the bazaar selling cake in many kinds of flavours: apple-cinnamon, chocolate, coffee-chickoo.

New Chandra Bakery. The old man stood patiently by the street, in a neat white bush shirt, beside his cart which bore its name in tidy

penmanship. Behind him the sky was a dark sheet, decorous, yet with
something in it of shattered glass.

10

The Parashars are a large family. The parents; Polly and his brother;
the two wives; five children. A couple of months ago came the
newest addition, Polly's wife tells me, as I slip out of my shoes in their
courtyard. Behind round black glasses, her face with its soft hazy
features is radiant. They have had a baby boy, after two girls.

The puja, though, has not been organized because of the baby. Today
is one of the quarterly teej days, something the ladies tell me they would
have celebrated anyway. But the scale is perhaps a little more lavish,
another little sparkle in the flush of celebrations the new baby has
occasioned. By the time we arrive at their place, freshened-up but empty-
handed, the pandit has already finished his rituals and left.

The main house has a courtyard in the middle, skirted elegantly by a
verandah. Rooms open onto this. At first we are led into a room on the left
side, where the senior Parashar, Polly's father, is sitting, all muffled up on
the bed, under a blanket, watching the epic saga of Rani Lakshmibai on
TV. His wife is sitting next to him, although unencumbered by blankets
or sheets. They greet us and immediately begin to tell us about the serial.
The room is dominated by the large bed which faces the television, and
on a mat on the floor, Polly sits comfortably, surrounded by pillows
and the children – three girls and a boy. They promptly begin to recite
the story, episode-wise. On regular days, dinner is over by seven-thirty.
The family gathers around the TV every evening. But today, it seems,
the women who have followed us into the room are impatient. When
there is a lull in the initial pleasantries, they whisk me away quickly,
into a little anteroom on the other side of the courtyard: the puja room.

The puja room is small and squarish; its whitewashed walls bear
the imprints of much devotion over the years; handprints in turmeric,
an aum in red, a swastik symbol that was drawn sometime in the past
and is now slightly runny, slightly faded. They sit me down on a mat

in front of the large wooden simhasan where all the deities are placed amid crushed flowers and incense sticks. The silken pleats of their saris swish near my face.

The younger daughter-in-law covers my head with the end of my stole.

'No, no,' the senior Mrs Parashar says, motioning with her hands. She has left the comfort of the bed to join us and sits on a folding chair just outside the room. Arthritis.

'Kaadi chunri na,' she points out. Not the black stole. I am a married girl after all. I need an auspicious colour. The younger daughter-in-law quickly gets me a fuchsia shawl from her room. The fuchsia shawl, warm and soft, smells of Vaseline and naphthalene. The younger daughter-in-law looks a lot like the actress Renuka Sahane, particularly in the role Sahane essayed in *Hum Aapke Hain Kaun*, her head covered with the end of her sari, a tiny stud gleaming on her nose. I think she has modelled herself on Sahane too; her carriage erect and honourable. Her face is lit up with a lambent intelligence that comes from a quiet sense of control. I take a fancy to her immediately.

'Do you never wear a bindi?' she asks me in Hindi, amusement dancing in her eyes; *oof, these modern girls.*

'Sometimes,' I reply. 'When I wear a sari.' The answer pleases her. 'Haan, while travelling of course jeans is good. How will you manage a sari?' She puts a tika on my forehead. Then she pulls my palms in front and puts some rice in the cup they form. Old Mrs Parashar tells her what to do in Rajasthani; led by her translated instructions, I do as I am asked.

There is something primal about the rites. The strange female space. It feels as though I have given over my body to these two women. A very gentle feeling of well-being begins to swirl inside my head. The quiet surrender to memory. A wave of childhood images washes over me. Occasioned either by the naphthalene or the sitting cross-legged before so many gods, in their rough home temple filled with crushed flowers and tiny brass utensils. It is all oddly reminiscent of my grandmothers.

Curiously, both my grandmothers grew up, in very different ways, as Bengal Renaissance women. My mother's mother, Geeta (first Miss Banerjee, then Mrs Mookerjee), was the eldest daughter of a remarkably handsome barrister. She was one of the first girl students to read physics honours at the Scottish Church College. Her father had originally wanted her to study medicine. Though disappointed in her for exhibiting squeamishness about cadavers, he finally relented. Scottish did not have a girls' common room then, and so, between classes, she would walk down to the all-girls' Bethune College to use the toilet and to chat with the students there. She was about ten years older than my other grandmother, my father's mother, Archana (first Miss Banerjee, then Mrs Roy), the daughter of yet another handsome brown sahib who managed collieries in the tribal hinterland and took his wife, my great-grandmother, to occasional parties where the British wives would speak to her in English and she would reply in Bengali. My grandmother Archana was sent off to Calcutta to board in a residential school where she was one of the first to introduce sanitary napkins to her peer group, and though she was not particularly scholarly, she grew up to become the most voracious reader I know, negotiating with great ease the scale from popular magazines and *Rebecca* to the most literary novels that Bengali literature has produced.

But much more significantly for me, both my grandmothers married for love, embraced uncertainties and provincial lives instead of the glamorous if predictable futures far more covenanted Calcutta grooms would have brought. This also freed me, on both sides, from the certainties that accompany growing up in old-money or middle-money families. When my parents moved to Calcutta in the late 1970s, the sort of poverty they faced as young professionals with small salaries has been well documented in Farooq Sheikh–Deepti Naval films of the time. By marrying unconventionally, both my grandmothers had broken the more obvious trends of colonial inheritance that produce a peculiar brand of brash Bengali insiderhood.

My grandmothers had their modest home temples; more like corners in rooms than temples. And it was at their knee, sitting on my haunches, that I was initiated into the mystical art of ritual-making. The devis and devatas were not about religion at the time, but about the narratives that fashioned them, handed down by these old women even as they customized their own pujas from things they had observed *their* mothers do. I can pare down my memories to two abiding ones. The first is Geeta Mookerjee's Lakshmi puja in the rambling old country house in Jharkhand. My mother and I would go there in the Puja holidays. (Lakshmi Puja was about five days after Dashami.) And Archana Roy's Saraswati puja in a sunny corner of our crowded, high-ceiling, rented, fourth-floor flat in Calcutta, where, in my growing-up years, Saraswati was the most cajoled deity. There were no pandits involved; both were personal if poetic affairs.

During Lakshmi puja, every year, I was delegated to gather flowers in a little basket. I picked up the fallen frangipanis from below the tree and washed them carefully. Circumventing rules, my grandmother would agree to offer these fallen flowers. But I was not to smell them. When you offer something to the goddess, you don't partake of it yourself. Suppose you serve a glass of water to a guest, would you take a sip of it yourself? I would follow this rule, though the urge to smell the flowers would be particularly acute since I was not supposed to. I also remember kadma, a unique eggless meringue-like candy that came in many colours and was also offered to Lakshmi. My grandmother would soak rice in a little water overnight and, dipping a piece of cotton in it, she would draw Lakshmi's feet – a charming S with dots to symbolize the toes – on the red floor. Alpana. Selfishly, I am casting this story to include only her and me, though in reality of course there were many others who would bustle around: my aunts, cousins, the tribal maids. My mother.

All the while, her hands busy with the preparations, she would tell me the story of Lakshman Seth, a businessman who had all but been ruined. His several businesses had failed, his children were starving, his wife had sold all her ornaments and the debtors were calling night and day. Things had come to a head. He sent his wife off to her parents' house along with the children. He alone remained behind on the tithi of Lakshmi, to reflect on what was to be done; only a miracle could save them now. It was the evening of Kojagari Purnima. Lakshman Seth sat in his house, in front of his deities, praying to Lakshmi. He drew her feet with great devotion and lit the lamp just as dusk began to creep in.

Saying this, my grandmother would light the brass lamp, dousing the wick in oil. I remember I would look out to see if the red moon was visible from where I sat on the floor.

Suddenly, Lakshman Seth looks out of the window and sees a beautiful girl enter his courtyard. She has long hair and the most gorgeous features. (My grandmother Geeta was never one to emphasize fair complexions. She was not particularly fair while her sister-in-law was; this had led to some favouritism among her in-laws. Secretly, I think, she was liable to equate a peaches-and-creams complexion in Indian women with dumbness.) Lakshman Seth immediately steps outside and greets the parama sundari girl, to quote my grandmother. Recognizing who she is, he quickly improvises. 'Come in, my dear,' he tells her. 'I was hoping someone would turn up. You see, my wife and children are away. I have just remembered a very urgent errand but it is bad luck to leave the house empty today. Just sit here and make yourself at home until I am back. Will you do so?' The girl with long hair and divine features is very gracious. She agrees to house-sit until he is back.

Lakshman Seth closes the door of the house and hurries out of the courtyard. Perhaps he stops once and turns to look at his house one last time.

'Why last time?' I ask this every time, though I have heard the story before, with its bitter-sweet goosebumpy ending. The story is printed in one of those useful booklets with thin pages where rituals and stories are recorded in uncertain grammar and spelling.

My grandmother's face is shadowy in the 50-watt light. She tells me softly, 'Arre, the beautiful woman was none other than Ma Lakshmi. He had been the first to light the lamp. So she came to *his* house. Another name of Lakshmi is Chapala. The light-footed one. She never stays in one place. But Lakshman Seth got her to promise that she would stay in his house until *he* returned. So he knew when he was leaving the house, that for Lakshmi to stay forever, he could never return.'

The original must have said that Lakshman Seth drowned himself in the river. My grandmother would leave it delicately ambiguous. I was no fool, particularly in the matter of tragic endings. I adored them though I might cry copiously later. But there was something about this lack of closure – we liked to think that Lakshman Seth went to a city far away and led a parallel interesting life.

We both knew he didn't.

'Who will run his businesses then?' I demand. 'If he goes away?'

'His wife,' my grandmother would reply. 'She is a very smart woman. And since Lakshmi has been tricked to stay back, their businesses expand greatly. They are able to pay all their debts. The wife does a lot of charity too.' I don't know if the wife did a lot of charity in the original. But I came away with the rather uneasy conclusion that to make light-footed Lakshmi stay, one has to give up everything, including, often, one's life.

Saraswati, on the contrary, was much easier to please. Her day on Basant Panchami falls in spring, when the weather in Calcutta is delightful. All blue skies and crisp cool air and mellow sunlight bouncing off new green leaves. To please Saraswati, one wore a yellow sari and coyly avoided the glances of neighbourhood boys; to please her one did not eat gooseberries till they had been first offered to her (not that I was ever uncool enough to taste gooseberries; they were the sort of things my mother favoured); and of course, ultimately, to please her, one attended to books. My mother claimed that Saraswati would leave *only* if one ill-treated books, unlike Lakshmi, the light-footed, who was always going away anyway.

In S and my life, of course, this has borne out. Light-footed Lakshmi has remained elusive, but our shelves have swelled with books old and new. Or at least had, when we had shelves and walls of our own, the frail fences of our domesticity. At the moment all our books, along with our other worldly goods – a grey fridge, a dismantled garden swing that was the first piece of furniture we bought together and a plastic folder with our degree certificates – lie in Calcutta.

⌣

The older daughter-in-law, by now Badi Bhabhi, extends my left hand and dips the little finger into a small bowl of henna. When I was in school, I learnt about henna at the same time I learnt the word loam in geography classes. To me the two are inextricably linked.

Mehendi is patterned on the palms of all three; they must have been preparing for this puja for a few days. The henna is cold. Its loamy fecund smell fills the room. For the rest of the evening, I am going to be half-conscious of my finger; it is going to be curiously heavy, with the crust of dried-out henna. Then we go up to the terrace, the old lady with some difficulty, each of us holding a brass tumbler filled with water. Under the full moon, we link hands and move in a circle. They sing a song– I don't get the words – and then, bashfully (except the old lady, the rest of us are bashful) we stretch our hands and upturn our tumblers and clear streams of water merge into the middle of the circle, falling on the cold stone terrace, silver in the moonlight. And it is then that I realize, the glint of shattered glass in the sky behind the old man selling cake in the bazaar was just the full moon.

Three

How (Not) to Be Blue

Parvati said: 'O you of a good vow, tell me about the holy places that exist on this island. This island is fashioned by the lord as the king of all islands. O lord, favouring me, tell me about them…'

Mahadeva said: 'The Omnipresent (lord) should be seen in all beings on the earth. Whatever primary substance, with the mobile and the immobile, is seen in the seven worlds, is not seen or heard by me to be without Him … I shall certainly tell you about all the holy places. First is the holy place called Pushkara, auspicious and best among holy places.'

— *Padma Purana*, Chapter One Hundred and Thirty Three,
'The Holy Places in Jambudvipa'

11

Dinner is served in the verandah, which is wide and high, almost like a stage, opposite the main doorway. In traditional fashion, S and I have been served in one plate. Under the tube light which casts a dim blue-white glow on the plinth, we sit cross-legged. The huge steel plate and the many tiny bowls surrounding it are arranged on a low table in front. Perhaps it is a water-conserving device, this thing about husbands and wives (even other relatives) eating from one plate. I don't know if in the past the husbands ate *before* the wives did. In our case, we eat simultaneously, hungrily. The Pushkar cold whets the appetite; in any case, lunch was a lifetime ago.

The food is hot and delicious. There is rice and dal, and a dry subzi and a spicy vegetable curry. Bajra rotis. Curd set in a bowl. The Parashars have eaten already – dinners are early affairs for them. The women send us second helpings from the kitchen, fresh hot rotis, through the beautifully behaved daughter, Badi Bhabhi's eldest. Old Mrs Parashar has carried her chair into the courtyard and urges more food onto our plates. Polly talks. His brother lurks in the shadows behind.

Polly's brother looks rather like him – the same haircut, the same cast of features – but he's taller and thinner. A man who seems capable of fingering discontents within himself, used to holding things inside. Polly is chatty, quite the extrovert. Years of interacting with foreigners has rubbed onto his vocabulary, made it expansive, rich in experience. Through his hospitality, Polly has *felt* the world. It has accorded him a confidence through which he can easily negotiate the modernity that is above and beyond Pushkar; Jaipur, after all, is not far away. Delhi too. Polly talks about trade.

Pushkar has 5,000 tailors; it exports top-quality garments. During the camel fair, room rents sky-rocket. Our room might well go for eight hundred or even a thousand rupees a night. There is no water in the Jyeshtha Pushkar now because the government is having it cleaned, but thousands of fish were left to rot. It was a disaster!

They have three sisters, all of whom are happily married. But the marriages, expensive as they were, have come in the way of renovating the old house. Polly's brother is shy and slightly remote. He smiles politely but maintains a respectful younger-brotherly distance. In that silence one feels that perhaps if we had been *his* guests, he would have told us other stories, shown us other Pushkars; then, we would have talked about other things, big things perhaps. Globalization. The state of the nation. The Delhi sarkar.

After dinner, we wash our hands at a tap in the corner of the courtyard and S goes through with Polly to the TV room. The bhabhis roll out a mat on the verandah. Old Mrs Parashar rises from her folding chair but lingers in the courtyard for a few minutes. She asks me how many years we've been married – and upon hearing the answer, advises me to have a baby now. I murmur something vague about the inopportuneness of our travels and make a mental note to lie the next time the number of years comes up. Three months, I should say. This is our honeymoon. (Hah! I remind myself to put that on the list too. A honeymoon. But S is likely to rubbish it as too bourgeois.) Mrs Parashar then goes off to join the men, leaving us to relax and stretch our feet, and the bhabhis turn to me, full of questions: Where are we going? Did we have a love marriage? Who all are at home?

I chew my lips and rearrange my hair and wrap the fuchsia shawl closer and tell them about the book we hope to write; the books we have written, one each, which should be published sometime; about the anxieties of it all. I tell them about how we met in college. About our families in Calcutta, my nephew, the apple of my eye.

They tell me in turn about the rhythms of their day. They wake up at five and begin the chores; the kids go to school. They tell me the summer afternoons are long and so hot. They tell me about the gifts that must come from the families of the women every time a baby is born. They are brides of the house – 'bahuen' is the word Renuka Sahane uses – they can't go out whenever fancy strikes, to shop or wander whimsically, though last year they had gone as a large party to a pilgrim town somewhere. Planning is important in their excursions; it's almost bureaucratic.

I am utterly taken with the bhabhis. Ever since I read Ismat Chughtai's memoirs – where she writes with great warmth and compassion about her cantankerous aunt who went through life believing, below her bluster, that she was an incomplete woman, and railing against Ismat's mother, the complete woman, who bore her kids, did her politics, wove her web and managed her household with both art and craft, with both guile and generosity – I have learnt to name, and therefore analyse, this crush I develop on women I think are complete. It is a version of the same thing. Instead of Bachchu Phupi's angst, I just have my nice timid longings. Whether it is women who have children and roll rotis effortlessly or my peers in the Delhi circuit who have their apps, investments, stilettos and feminist theory pat, I hero-worship complete women.

One of Renuka Sahane's older sisters is married in the neighbourhood – she comes to visit often. Impressed by the success of Mayur Guest House, they have also converted their old haveli into a homestay. But of course, Badi Bhabhi adds mildly, *Lonely Planet* or *Rough Guide* have not featured it. But yes, they are trying hard. That is good. Business is not the usual profession for Brahmins, of course, but then, what to do in these times? Also, hospitality is not business exactly. Badi Bhabhi's brother is in Jaipur, with his family. They are in service. She is inordinately proud of them.

Suddenly she asks, about my nephew, 'He must be going to a playschool, no?'

Playschool.

The English word sounds strange and foreign to my ears. *Playschool.*

Badi Bhabhi is saying, 'My brother's son in Jaipur is only two-and-a-half. But he goes to a playschool. Very modern playschool.' Then she adds wistfully, 'Jaipur has many facilities.' She is ambitious for the baby. And perhaps, sensing the burden of ambition he must bear, the little creature cries out from one of the many rooms opening onto the verandah. Badi Bhabhi leaps to her feet and with a happy-apologetic smile rushes in that direction. The children are in the TV room.

Renuka Sahane and I are alone. We smile at each other.

Our silence fills up quickly with the quiet interest that can suddenly flower between women. In trains or hospitals or even wide verandahs, as now. Though we don't say anything, the stories spill out like unruly vines. I don't talk about the day we loaded our stuff onto the truck in Delhi and sent it off to Calcutta. I had stood in the large terrace above our tiny home, trying to memorize the twilight. The idea of leaving Delhi with its long spectacular dusks had crushed me. At the other end of the terrace, under the still-blue sky, S might have felt the same. But we were too proud to admit this to ourselves. We had left our jobs for freedom; the price had to be paid.

Renuka Sahane does not tell me how the bluish-white walls of the beautiful house can sometimes fail to absorb the everyday sorrows that creep up like walls between women who are married to kinsmen; she does not tell me about all the beautiful bluish-white walls that can become prisons in these parts.

And then, finally, after a quarter of an hour, because it is late and time for us to leave, and Renuka Sahane must respond now to her husband calling her upstairs from the shadowy end of the verandah, we both know that something must be said. She tells me. 'The next time you must visit in monsoon. The hills are green and so lush then. All the rituals of saawan are performed. I'll take you to my peehar. It is more beautiful than Pushkar.' And then, Badi Bhabhi comes out from her room, holding the baby. Renuka Sahane cuts across the courtyard, her payals tinkling faintly, and takes the stairs. I can hear S beginning to take his leave, though I cannot see him.

Badi Bhabhi settles down next to me, our feet dangling from the edge of the plinth, and I admire the baby. The children return and begin to play noisily on the verandah, clapping their hands and reciting something. The little girl, Badi Bhabhi's second daughter, only around three-and-a-half, is waddling around happily, holding a doll. I observe for the first time that her gait is slightly awkward. Badi Bhabhi leans in. 'You know, this little one was born with a congenital disorder, her feet were turned inward. We had to get several operations done to have it fixed. But by God's grace all the operations were successful. Now there *are* scars but the doctors have promised that those will heal. Only after everything was done did I take a chance again.' She smiles beatifically at the baby in her lap. Turning to me conspiratorially she says, 'We don't believe in sonography and all that. Many people in Rajasthan do, of course. But I just took a chance. And we were lucky. Turned out to be a boy.'

12

Later at night, in my pyjamas, I sit shivering under the quilt in our room. Damn, I forgot. I had meant to ask Polly for another quilt. Next to me, S is busy: sucking Internet. His face is craggy in the blue hum of the laptop. I can see the familiar grey and white horizontal stripes of his favourite forum page. How I hate that forum for defence geeks. I reopen the notebook where I have been sanctimoniously making notes on the day. It's been a long day.

'What is going on in the world?' I finally ask.

'Usual,' he mutters.

'Can we *please* go to bed now?' I say, laying my head on the pillow and stretching my legs. 'I thought we were supposed to correct our cycle. Go to bed early and wake up at dawn. And you haven't even made any notes,' I point out primly.

'You've made notes,' he replies, 'should be enough.'

'Oof!' I sit up again. 'What about the times you were alone with Polly and his parents? What about the stuff you talked about with them?'

'Hmmm,' sighs S. 'The India–South Korea FTA will be signed by the end of this week. I think the Japanese will have to move quicker on the trade front with us now.' He switches off the laptop, rolls up the charger and packs it away in his bag. He turns the light off and dives under the quilt.

He says, 'I heard some pretty interesting things.'

'What?' I ask, though I had been planning to ignore him.

'For one, Polly told me about Neki Mohammad. He is a wood merchant by profession, but is actually a famous tantrik. His relatives Salim and Nizam run the Honeydew Cafe. Remember the one opposite the restaurant where we lunched?' I nod. *Lonely Planet* recommended its pancakes. 'Neki can cure diseases and solve problems and fix matters. But apparently he does not accept a single paisa in payment. Not even a stick of incense. Once, one of Polly's uncles was possessed by a spirit. Neki managed to cure him.'

'Wow!' I turn towards him. 'And?'

'And that's all I know. But when Polly first set up the homestay, it seems he was quite the ladies' man. There were several angrez mems who were eager to marry him. He could have emigrated. One girl was particularly keen; she was even quite pally with old Mrs Parashar. Had managed to mollify her and get her consent. But finally he didn't. He married Badi Bhabhi. He told me, quietly, just as we were coming out for dinner, "A white woman is like a cat. You can never fully domesticate her."'

I burst out laughing.

'Doesn't seem like you are having much luck with your brown woman either,' I say.

For a while, there is silence. Then we hear the familiar sounds outside: a cow lowing softly; the scooter with a faulty silencer; far away, the strains of a TV channel.

I have almost surrendered to sleep, my back to S, when he taps my shoulder and speaks softly. Through the skin of dreams I hear his words. 'The most interesting thing Polly said was this. Every Kartik purnima, it is said the Gaya kund visits Pushkar. So for those who cannot go to Gaya to pray for the solace of ancestral spirits, Gaya travels to Pushkar once a year. On that day, if you go to Gaya, the pandits will tell you, "*Aaj puja nahin hogi; aaj toh Gayaji gayi hain Pushkar!*"'

Sometime afterwards, I fall into a deep sleep.

Saurav

Six months before my mother died, I had the dream. I was twelve. By then, the cancer had metastasized to her pancreas, after spending a decade in different lymph nodes in her body. On good days, she sat up in bed reading Mills & Boon romances and made me chicken sandwiches at midnight when I awoke and wandered hungrily to the fridge. On bad days, she would fling her medicines away and thrash on the bed, crying bitterly. My father would make us noodles in sauce for dinner, look for the medicines crouching on the floor, and hold her hand. Very bad days were a blur of doctors and hospitals.

Six months before she died, I had the dream. There was a room in a house. It looked like my room but was not. I was outside the room in that half-familiar house, standing at the edge of sleep. I knew instantly my mother had died. Even in the dream I was not surprised. My brother and I, though we never talked about it, had lived with the certitude of her impending absence for years. An abiding presence in the dark corners of the verandahs, under the awning of the kitchen, in the guest bedroom, gathering dust. I must have tossed in the still airlessness of the room that was not my room, must have tried to shake off the dream I did not want to see. But the dream had not ended. I saw further that my father had died. Even then the dream would not go away. I saw I had become the boy with a stone for his heart.

It was a Russian story. In left-ruled Calcutta, beautiful children's books by Raduga Publishers were readily available in independent bookstores on College Street, and during the book fair every winter, long before book chains had mushroomed in the city with their coffee shops. I would pore over these books. Olegs and Vasillys and Annas were my friends. The mathematician Nikolai Lobachevsky, my hero. In one of these books was the outcast boy, the boy with a stone for his heart. I can't remember now what happened to him.

Around six months later, her stomach filled with water for the third time and the doctors suggested, in accordance with her wishes, that we bring her home from the hospital.

Afterwards, people came to visit and sat on the sofa and sipped tea. With voices heavy with concern, they said they feared most for my father. In all such cases they had seen, and in their time they had seen a few, the spouse did not last beyond a year. They then wiped their faces with big square handkerchiefs and went home.

Stiff white cards were printed. They listed my brother and me as bhagya-heen. Luckless. The words curled like black ants on the card above our names. The luckless brothers invited everyone for lunch on the eleventh day of their mother's passing to pray for the peace of her soul.

I remember reading one of the cards when the batch was delivered home and saying to my brother in some surprise, 'Look, Dada, they have called us bhagya-heen.' How can anyone be bhagya-heen? Without destiny? 'But that is what we are,' my brother had replied. His Bengali was always better than mine. In any case, he was nineteen and very tall. He went to college; he even topped. He had friends to rally around him. He had a knack of dealing with things; fighting stupid luckless things with a maniacal pursuit of success. For example, he had dealt so much better with the Bengali/non-Bengali minefield that was the lot of our family: what sort of strange creatures were we anyway? We had a Bihari surname but we had been speaking Bengali for generations, and my aunts were known to look down upon 'Hindustanis': Biharis and UPwallahs. Exactly like the Bengalis, who always complimented us on the fluency of our Bengali and with their compliments fenced us outside Bengalihood.

I waited for the rest of the dream to come true. Every single night, for months, I would wake up in panic. The memory of the dream would enter my head and stand with its feet firmly planted. But I never *saw* that other room again. Fearfully, I would look for my father. Invariably, he would be pacing in the hall. I would return to bed, satisfied that he was alive. It was enough. It was even plenty. Sometimes, if he saw me, he would follow me to bed. Other days, I would look out of the window. The walls of the next house were unpainted, shabbied by the polluted air. The street-lamp cast a yellow beam on the road. The trees would catch a sliver of light from some angle and project furry shadows on the brown walls. Sometimes dogs would bark all night.

When I went back to school the next session, summer had returned to the city. I glittered in the gaze of the students; an anthropological specimen. Everyone knew why I had missed the finals. The teachers looked at me with sorrow. But I had no use for their sympathies. I was finally settling down into rage and outsiderhood, both of which fought all night with the shadows against the brown walls.

I also became wiser in the ways of the world. Mother tongue and father tongue were all irrelevant nonsense. In a classroom full of boys who came from two-parent homes, from *families*, who is a greater outsider than the thirteen-year-old boy who has lost his mother?

13

The days in Pushkar are blue and airy. Their memory rings still like a sharp sweet bell announcing the end of school day.

In the mornings, I run upstairs to the terrace. And invariably hop from one foot to the other, shivering in my pyjamas, wistful for a cup of tea. The season has injected an icy sheen into the full-bodied Pushkar sky, which is a vivid but cold blue and one can almost feel the ceramic touch. And so cloudless and optimistic that I begin to fear for my inner neurotic self. It could be the 1950s here and one wouldn't know.

There is a network of terraces surrounding ours. But at different levels. It breaks the sky into a playful unevenness. A young bride dries her long hair in the terrace to the right, chatting softly with an older woman. On the terrace behind, a thin elderly man sits hunched over an almond-brown desk in a precise square of sunlight. He is reading what appears to be a holy book. The *Ramcharitmanas* perhaps? The old man rocks gently, backwards and forwards, and is probably singing. Though I strain my ears I can only make out the empty shapes of musical words in the air. I have no idea what they are about. But in front of the house, past the street where a motorcycle is parked, past other flat-roofed houses with their whitewashed fronts and unpainted brown sides, and then past yellow, brown and olive-green fields, there lie the snaking low hills that Emperor Jahangir had loved.

We walk a lot. On our comings and goings, we run into the Parashars and stop to chat. We trudge past the poorer parts of Pushkar to the hill where Gayatri's temple is.

The sky is cut into shape-shifting oblongs by kites flown from the roofs of shabby houses. The boys who fly them – and one or two girls – have clear loud voices that send out ungrammatical, unapologetic English at us. Much waving occurs. There is a rocky lip and then, standing rugged, rich-brown, is the hill, in a landscape that after all the prettifications of Pushkar is unmistakeably desert-like. Loose stones fall as we climb past huge cacti. The direct sun dazzles the eye.

Other days, we ramble in town, along the ghats. The Queen Mary Zenana Ghat, with its white arch and portmanteau summation of Indian history, is my favourite, and I like to sit by it in silence and watch devotees, both very rich and very poor, being led by priests into what is left of the lake. Men and wives stand in little pools of water, sometimes accompanied by children, and faithfully carry out the rituals. Then we walk through the bazaars – with their rows of carved wooden boxes, mounds of colour, racks of sparkly bangles, bright hippie-chic clothes undulating in the breeze, incense shops and, finally, the intoxicating gali of halwais – to the Brahma Mandir. The donations of devotees to the temple are recorded in cold marble tablets on the walls and the floor. Several of these are in Arabic.

On the way back I buy picture postcards.

Apparently, it upsets the budget completely.

⌣

'Sixty-seven rupees for lunch!' I have just mopped up the last of the chana masala with my thick roti.

'And sixty-seven rupees for dinner if you decide to eat here and not in one of the firang places. We can try one of the subzis instead.'

'But that means, for the first time, we have money to *spare!*' I say.

'Not spare exactly. Remember we exceeded the budget by fifty bucks in Jaipur.'

I pretend not to hear this. 'We can visit New Chandra Bakery too.'

'Not so fast,' he continues, now rapidly devouring the pickle that had come free with a bit of roti. 'You have to send your fancy postcards. God knows how much that'll come to.'

'Oof!' I reply. 'The Indian postal system is very reasonable. It will barely cost us anything.'

'Please don't make sending postcards your new fetish,' he says meanly, counting with his left hand the postcards of Pushkar that I have written out painstakingly: one to my grandmother; one for my nephew (who can't yet read); one for a young cousin, J, who never quite forgave me for getting married and sort of becoming a grown-up. He grumbles like an old husband, 'Anyway. Send only four postcards to each. One from each corner of India.'

⌣

That night we dine in the hole-in-the-wall but rather famous Honeydew Cafe. Chocolate pancake for me; (vegetarian) French toast for S. Pushkar, like several other temple towns, is vegetarian only. The brothers Saleem and Nizam, relatives of Neki Mohammad, wood merchant by day, tantrik by night, have invented a fine recipe for vegetarian French toast. We have a guessing game running about the key ingredient which is used to replace the eggs. It is a tiny restaurant and the brothers are chatty. On the third day, Saleem finally tells us what his substitute is. Bananas. Oh. So *bananas* induce such clever sweetness into the savoury? We recount our journey. I look through the notebook.

'We need to move on,' S says, finally.

'Fine,' I can almost hear myself glowering. 'Fine. Yes. We must, I suppose.'

'Go to Jodhpur,' Saleem tells us, joining the conversation from his corner, behind a curtain.

'Should we go back to Ajmer and take a bus from there?' S asks.

'Naah,' says Saleem, 'don't bother. Take a bus from Pushkar to Merta City. And from Merta, you can take another bus to Jodhpur.' He blushes boyishly and says, 'My missus is from Merta. We take a bus from here only.'

'Aahaa,' I say, 'so Merta is your sasural!'

And as we are about to leave, Saleem says, 'Oh, and you do know that Merta is where Mira Bai came from? Her father was the ruler of Merta.'

Merta: city of Mira.

We had not known that.

⌒

Just before noon the next day we leave Mayur Guest House with our red and black rucksacks. The bhabhis come to see us off. 'Next time, in saawan, come with one like this.' Renuka Sahane nudges me, pointing to the baby in her lap. I laugh and say, 'If you put conditions like that, I don't know, Bhabhi.'

'Oho.' She cuts me short with a laugh. 'Saawan will be green and lovely. We'll look after it, okay?'

Then it all gets hopelessly mixed up.

Renuka Sahane stands waving at the threshold of the whitewashed house with the arched doorway. The sunlit courtyard is visible. The sky is beginning to whiten at the edges as the sun gets hotter. A little ahead there is the dull gold of sandy earth. We get into the bus for Merta.

One of the central themes in Mirabai's songs is saawan. The rains come with her dark lover; the rains come and her fickle lover, the dark one, does not; the dark clouds gather from all sides, shivers of lightning cut open their bellies, and tiny cool drops stream across her face. It is time again for *him* to come.

I was always gripped by her poetry: by the imagery of longing. And yet, until I travelled to Rajasthan, I never quite understood the exact contours of a cry for the monsoon that might emanate from a dry, dry land; I am from Bengal. Green and moist and full of ponds. So fertile that people say it's made us lazy.

Mira occupies the messy grey zone that appeals to me so greatly. Feminist. Author of such perfectly female, perfectly natural sentences that Virginia Woolf would have held them up as examples. So centred in her own space. So cleanly refusing to be torn by husbands or rules or children or empires. And simultaneously, so anti-feminist. So full of waiting. So much crying for a fickle lover. On one hand, she is utterly feminine. The eros of her poetry inscribes her body as the chief site of play. Of meaning. On the other hand, so anti-feminine. The ungendered yogi who circles the town with other bhaktas, in a nakedness of clear enlightenment that she herself fashions as asexual. When she roams naked with the other saints, she does not want to be seen as a woman at all.

The bus moves. I sit by the window and look outside. I do not process a single thing I see.

Since the previous night, ever since Saleem mentioned Merta, I've been in an odd sort of agony. I am trying to remember one of Mira's songs from a selection I once read for a term paper. And all the time, since last evening, I'd been getting distracted. The packing and the paying off, this and that. Now, finally, I sit down, my bag squashed on my lap, my hands bunched together, and I close my eyes as the bus begins to move. I focus on the lines that begin to appear in little flickers. I have to work to remember each line. So I hear nothing of the discussions that keeps S rapt in the bus; there are heated arguments between Kangressis and Bhaajpaayees, apparently. Much discussion about an honest collector, Shri Sumit Sharma. The notes in S's scrawl indicate that there was an idealistic young man called Ram Dayal Jat in the bus that day, a small neat chap with his hair parted in an exact straight line on the left, who was a fan of said district collector and on his way to take a mid-level government exam. I heard none of this. There was only the invitation of monsoon mid-winter. A word, a phrase at a time.

> *Baadal dekh dari main, Shyam! Main baadal dekh dari.*
> *Kalipeeli ghata umdi, barsyo ek ghadi*
> *Jit jaun tit paani paani, hui sab bhoom hari*
> *Jaakaa piya pardes basat hai, bhinju baahaar khadi.*
> *Mira-ke prabhu Hari abinasi, kijo preeta khari.*

(I saw dark clouds and was filled with fear, Shyam!
Dark clouds saw I and paled.
Black-and-yellow, the skies broke open,
For hours after, it rained.
Water, water, wherever I go,
All the earth has turned green.[1]
Drenched to the bone, standing in the street
The forlorn girl is seen.
My lover is away in far-off lands.
Mira's lord is Hari-Indestructible.
Pristine is her love for him.)

⤚

The bus pulls into a stand. Merta City is the prototype for hundreds of places we shall stop at the hinterlands in future to change buses or drink tea or look for filthy toilets. A cluttered littered dustbowl with unpainted concrete buildings and thriving businesses and piles of trees and dull-green bricks. Men in mighty orange pagris or white skullcaps go about their business or loll in the shade. Women favour magenta, sunflower yellow, pink and red when it comes to dupattas and bangles. Or they wear black burqas.

---

1   'Hari' is both 'green' and the lord's name. The duality gets lost in translation.

14

I have spoken to Mr Joshi of Cosy Guest House about a room. According to the *Lonely Planet* guide, Cosy is a 'five-hundred-year-old blue house with several levels of higgledy-piggledy rooftops'. The eccentricity of the description appealed to me instantly. I called Mr Joshi, told him about the book we had in mind – emphasizing the budget bit – and he agreed to give us a discount. 'Three hundred rupees. Okay?' He spoke through the crackling on the line before the phone got disconnected altogether.

Hopefully the room will be ready for us when we reach Jodhpur.

The land turns burnished copper while we are still in the bus, about 20 kilometres from the city. When we near the urban sprawl, with large stores advertising furniture and gemstones, the sun has set and the birds are going mad. The solid bodies of old T-55 tanks lined outside the military base and billboards announcing Java/Oracle/C++ classes still retain a brief phosphorescent orange glow, steady beacons in the twilight. By the time we reach the bus depot in Jodhpur and dust our bags and stretch our legs, a curious dusky film tints everything we see. When we walk out of the bus station, we are assailed by a snarl of rush-hour traffic; honks, beeps, squacks, screeches and long low purrs that surround the crossing like a magnetic orb, absorbing into the din every other sound – our conversation, for instance. We engage an autorickshaw, shouting, and throw in our bags. We haven't eaten all day. I am now craving sugar; S is impatient and snappy. He begins to recite facts. Something he always does when he is exhausted. 'Jodhpur is the second city of Rajasthan.' 'A great node for trade.' 'It almost became the capital of the state.'

The auto enters the old city through the arch of Jalori Gate. We go past the congested bazaars and S clutches on to my bag. Apparently, I am giving off my dotty am-about-to-float-out air. But then, it's true. There are those who like the seas and those who love mountains, but give me a busy Indian bazaar and I am giddy with delight. I shall remain transfixed all day.

The autowallah manoeuvres through the chaos of narrow tube-lit lanes. There are tiny stairways by the streets which lead to boxy blue flat-roofed houses. S shines his phone on the maps, looking to make sense of the turns that come upon us every minute. I gaze outside, my nose sticking out from the auto, and old Jodhpur, obliging and quirky, tumbles into my startled lap. It is so charming that my heart begins to ache with strange longings. I am already reminding myself to hold on to the details; already half-hysterical, since I know I will have to leave soon, long before the place settles into me and brands my bones. I tell myself edgily that I will come back again, and the *next* time, I will remember everything. S grumbles and blames himself for not taking directions. The auto zooms around in the blue web, lost in that maze.

Eventually we get to Navchokhiya Road.

It is deep within the intestines of clustered blue-laned Brahmpur. A quiet lane climbing up between two buildings bears the sign of Cosy. Our autowallah ejects us there with the baggage. He collects an extra twenty for the twists and turns he had not accounted for and vanishes. We wear the bags, count the mufflers and caps, and start walking. Ahead, there is another board.

We follow the signs through frightfully steep up-and-down galis. Cows, however, seem undeterred by the climb. They ramble along in their fashion, and in the darkness, we have to stop and flatten our bodies against walls to let them pass.

Finally, we stand before Mr Joshi's blue haveli.

Strains of guitar. Snatches of conversations in strange languages. We take a narrow flight of stairs to a grungy foyer/family room/ reception where a man with dreadlocks is playing the guitar. Behind him are built-in shelves full of books. Mr Joshi is out for a walk and his brother, a youth with a squarish face, who is filling out a passport application form, is iffy about the three hundred. But eventually, after speaking to Mr Joshi on his mobile, the brother signs us in, collects the money for one night. This is standard procedure. Backpackers are not considered particularly reliable. He asks us to follow him up the narrow blue stairs.

One level up, there are rooms. Two levels up, there are more rooms, and a rooftop cafe filled with travellers. Almost all are foreigners, chiefly goras. They are eating, drinking, chattering and smoking ganja aloft large cushions. A couple sit on a swing, studying the menu. It is all very relaxed and neo-hippy. The final flight brings us to our attic.

It is tiny. But the room is clean and friendly. There is a narrow wedge by the door with a table and one chair squeezed in. Three steps to the rest of the room, with barely enough space for a bed. The bed is fat and comfy (I sit on it and bounce once or twice). It is pushed against the sky-blue wall upon which an amorous couple have been painted. The bathroom is tinier still but it has a proper geyser. Hot water. I immediately feel the need for hot water. The bus from Merta to Jodhpur was jam-packed with people.

'Come and see *this*,' S calls from the doorway. 'Come now. What are you doing?' Rubbing my forehead, I go and join him, thinking disconnectedly that I could do with some coffee. Below us, on the terrace, the revellers are busy.

But I follow his arm and raise my eyes. Only then do I see. Straight in front, across the hotchpotch rooftops, the skyscape is dominated by a shadow. The fort. Mehrangarh. It's strange that neither of us noticed it while we were climbing up. Lights glimmer along its ramparts. Even in the darkness, when we can only see a rough shape rising from the dim cobalt in the distance and can only *guess* its scale, it is spectacular.

My phone begins to ring. I turn around and scrabble in my bag. S ventures down to investigate the affordability of sandwiches. It is my mother.

15

Phone conversations with my mother, even at the best of times, is an intriguing affair. For an eminently practical person, my mother introduces dancing eccentricity into our telephone relations. 'Hello,' I might squeak, just waking up to her long-risen-and-been-shining-for-hours voice. 'Remember the paper I was co-writing? On the application of principal component–minimum variance technique in gene prediction?' (Oh, and by the way, my mother is currently doing a PhD. Only for the love of the subject, mind you, not for any career reason or anything. She is due to retire in a few years.) I have no recollection nor had knowledge of said paper. 'They asked for an online submission. The website wanted me to upload it page by page, which I have done. But the final submit button is not working. What does it mean?' 'Umm-hmm,' I might say, now swimming rapidly towards wakefulness. 'Maybe it's your connection?' But by then she is saying briskly, 'I have to go now. The police are here. Two of my lecturers have filed complaints against each other. See you Sunday.' 'Bye,' I say weakly after the line has already gone dead. Did I just agree to see her on Sunday?

When the going is good, this can be fun. When the going is what it is, it can be, truth be told, taxing.

This criticism is, of course, a bit rich coming from the likes of me. Not that I have ever been a model daughter myself, telephonically speaking. Or otherwise. Not by a long shot. It has always been high drama or surly moodiness, slamming doors, recriminations and/or presenting of fait accompli, only sometimes softened by tears.

At any given time my mother – justifiably some might say – can be any of the following on the phone: busy and bossy; just busy; just bossy; loving and money-plying; happy and travel-enthused; worried and antsy. Ever since the grand experiment has begun, the unemployment, the plans of travel, the whole *opting out*, she has mostly been flourishing her final 'Do-What-You-Like-But-Let-Me-Tell-You-Your-Father-Is-Extremely-Worried' card.

Now, instead of beating about the bush regarding her call that evening in Jodhpur, let me just come out and say it straight. Has anyone heard of a more pompous phrase than *opting out?*

Opt: it's such a casual verb.

It sounds about right in a muted restaurant with starched waiters and sparkling tableware. I'll opt for the fish. Or, in similar environs, I can as easily imagine some of my super-sophisticated friends adopting the same tone about theory. I'll opt for the Menshevik dissensions over the Bolshevik mainstream for my paper, thank you very much. But ever since articles have flooded the glossier sections of Indian newspapers, about forty-year-old corporate honchos and advertising stars who have quit their well-paying but soulless jobs to live in villas in Goa and pursue writing or cooking or inner selves, and smile smugly at the camera, wearing a hessian skirt they hand-made themselves along with blind schoolchildren, this phrase has firmly entered urban middle-class vocabulary. Along with assisted reproduction, time-sharing at resorts and SIPs.

Opting out.

Except, that's not what *we* are doing. In any case, we have neither savings to speak of nor a villa in Goa.

What is it then we are doing?

It's a tough one.

⌐

When S returns, eating a sandwich and bearing one for me, I am unpacking feverishly. 'Thank God I did not listen to you,' I say, 'and brought my princess top along.'

'Why?' he asks. 'Are we going to dine with royals finally? I didn't know Mummy knew the Rathores.'

'Well. Not exactly, no. But at least we are going to Harimahal.'

I pause and narrow my eyes. I can be quite foxy when I choose to. 'You can have that sandwich,' I add magnanimously.

'Harimahal?'

'*Taj* Harimahal. We are going there for dinner. Mummy would have called my aunt, my aunt would have instructed my cousin, and sometimes, it must be said, my mother does indeed ace these chain phone calls.'

'Your cousin R?'

'My cousin R.'

Two decades ago my cousin R had introduced the novel stream of 'hotel management' to the extended family. In a way, he was the pathfinder. Because he did hotel management then, I am doing the opting out now.

And so, a couple of hours later, we sit by the pool, a flickering candle between us, parsing fish tikkas that come in giant platters from the kitchen along with the chef's compliments. Afterwards, my cousin R will give us the grand tour of the premises. We will walk through the marbled corridors, my good shoes clicking smartly and then, even better, through the clean clean *clean* kitchen with fifty people working away diligently, to laundry rooms in the basement from where dumbwaiter-like chutes send clean sheets upstairs. Apparently, the hospitality managers pick out sheets at random to check if they're spotless. We will have far more fun than might have been possible, I'll have you know, at some sit-down dinner with royalty.

Saurav

According to some schools of thought, the foundation of Jodhpur was the third grand event in the reign of the Rathores, after they left Kanauj and travelled on to Rajputana.

Jaichand was the last great Rathore ruler of Kanauj. In popular lore, he is invariably cast as the Amrish Puriesque father-in-law to Prithviraj Chauhan, king of Delhi. By all accounts, however, the power and prestige of Kanauj under Jaichand was unparalleled at the time. The glory of Kanauj has been attested to by even the enemies of Kanauj, the Chauhan bards, and later, the Muslim annalists of Ghori's entourage. However, in AD 1175, the star-crossed swayamvar of the princess of Kanauj, Sanyogita, changed everything. Jaichand had a golden effigy of Prithviraj Chauhan strategically placed in the swayamvar sabha as the 'poliya' or porter-of-the-hall. The insult backfired since Chauhan was able to spirit away his beloved Sanyogita from that very hall. Battle ensued between the Rathores and Chauhans, with most of the assembled kings joining issue with Prithviraj Chauhan. Taking advantage of the severe dissension that followed, Mohammad Ghori, who had been kept at bay till then, finally marked a permanent route to India. Delhi fell in 1192 and so did Kanauj, in AD 1193.

Twenty years or so later, the grandsons of Jaichand, Siahji and Setram, left Kanauj forever and along with two hundred retainers made their way westward. Some say they had intended to visit the shrine at Dwarka as pilgrims but ended up in the desert. Others contend they had merely decided to find a new home elsewhere and re-establish their clan. Under the leadership of Siahji, and through exploits (both valorous and treacherous) the Rathores became rulers of Marwar. The name Marwar itself is a corruption of Maru-war, originally Marusthali or Marusthan, the region of death.

If Siahji's re-establishment of the clan should be considered as the first grand event, doubtless the acquisition of Mandore from the Parihars by Prince Chonda might be considered the second grand event in the Rathore timeline. Within 300 years of their arrival in the desert, the Rathore lands were spread across 80,000 square miles, and their numbers had swelled, in spite of continued war and famines, to 500,000. Rao Jodha, grandson of Chonda, was the architect of this glorious third grand event.

Rao Jodha ascended the throne in AD 1459, and upon the advice of an old ascetic decided to shift his capital from Mandore to 'Bakharchiriya' or 'the bird's nest', a hill about four miles south. It was then renamed 'Jodhagir'. It was, of course, a sound suggestion, not merely astrologically but also strategically. The fort would be almost impregnable. The rulers would command excellent views such that on clear sunny days they could glimpse the very edges of their sandy dominions. Jodha's engineer, however, in his circumvallation, ended up taking over the ascetic's humble hermitage too. In consequence, it is said, the insulted ascetic cursed the Rathores that the new fort would only have brackish water. This turned out to be so. Many efforts were made by later princes, including the blasting of rocks, but it seems better-quality water was not to be had. Arrangements were then made to pump water up to the garrison from a lake at the bottom of the fort. Fortunately, the lake was propitiously located and since the walls of the fort overlooked it, it is reasonable to assume that it could not be easily cut off by the enemy in case of an attack.

⸺

It is late afternoon. On a day that began very late, after the five-star excesses of the night before, we find ourselves standing by this lake. All morning we had dilly-dallied. D had found a trove of books that tourists had left behind. She had read on the deserted rooftop, ordering not one but two coffees with a desi macaroni. I had caught up on some work over egg sandwiches: an article on the Kaiga nuclear plant that had to be sent off by afternoon.

It was after three that we finally set out. Owing to the fortuitous location of Cosy Guest House, we found we could cut through the blue lanes of Brahmpur and quickly reach the edges of the fort area and cross the low wall which marks the outer rim. But we are in no hurry today and the waning sun feels warm and pleasant; on the sandstone walls it casts a net of spun gold. We discover that instead of going all the way to the front entrance of Mehrangarh, if we like, we can go round the lake, climb up the cheek of the hill and enter the walled area from little openings among the stones, slipping into what were formerly the stables of the castle. We walk back afterwards and decide to just stroll around on our own. We might as well go to the fort tomorrow, enter from the main gate where tickets are sold.

The lake is greenish with tree shadows. Every now and then there is a splash. It is invariably a young boy on the other side of the lake. Running on the narrow path between the lake and the dark walls of the fort, the boy vanishes behind the ruins, and the stone he throws disappears underwater. The dimpled lake quivers for a while, each ripple catching a shard of the smashed-up sun. We watch the circles continuously expand and then disappear before the lake comes to silence again.

16

Past the low walls marking the outer area of the fort, across the bare sandy fields dotted with boulders, there is a hill with a temple. After Pushkar, we are always looking for hills to conquer. 'Perhaps that is where the ascetic relocated,' I reflect, 'after his hermitage was bulldozed.' S does not know. Whether or not, the views of the old city are sure to be spectacular.

The sun is slung low in the sky. Halfway up the stairs – a proper cemented stairway has been built on the hill for the benefit of temple-goers – we find a couple of reed-thin Israeli youths, taking photographs at great speed. 'Mossad,' I mutter darkly. I nod at them briefly and march on, climbing briskly until I realize, much to my annoyance, that S has gone right up to one of them, and is saying, 'Hey! How are you?' The boy has a ponytail. I retrace my steps. 'Hey!'

the boy replies, coming closer. He shakes S's proffered hand. I observe the exact flicker of annoyance that had switched on in my head now light up his companion's face.

That's the thing with S. People know me as the nice one, the chatty one, the neither-take-nor-give-offence one. But truth is, it can be quite the opposite. When we travel, he is the friendly one. Always willing to intervene in conversations that circle annoyingly around Indianisms – nobody is as bad as our politicians, nobody is as sold out as our corporates – and then take flight to become, well, quite interesting.

There is a formula to these proceedings. On train journeys, for instance, he'll usually instruct me before getting in, 'We'll just keep to ourselves. Right? *Right*?' I nod. I carry two books per overnight journey. In case I finish one by the morning or the train is late, I like to keep a backup. So naturally I'm not partial to chattiness. But S? It's happened every single time. I go to the bathroom, leaving him with his magazine. I return and find him discussing the GDP in detail with the bearded guy. How the China model is not right for us at all, with the Marwari businessman who has returned from Shanghai, all impressed with their development. Or Delhi traffic with Calcutta Aunty in crushed cotton. Once, there were four clerics going to attend an all-India imams' meet and after non-stop talking for the whole duration of the journey, they invited him to the jamaat. The only non-cleric to be invited apparently. Another time, a wedding planner told him how at the latest posh wedding her company had organized in Istanbul, the groom's uncle got drunk and peed in the pool. The company had to pay sixty lakh rupees to the upscale hotel as compensation. The groom's family is absolutely refusing to pay up since it is not in the contract. So now the wedding planners have had to add a new clause to the usual draft contract: the company will not pay compensation in case of guests doing toilet outside toilets.

Anyway. I am not in the mood to chat. I squint sourly in the sun.

'We met in Pushkar,' Saurav turns and explains to me finally.

Oh yes. I now remember.

'Sorry...' The boy smiles. 'It took me a moment to recognize you. This is...'

'Your brother?' S asks, helpfully.

'Clevery custard,' I mutter under my breath. 'Who said *brothers*? People travel with friends, not brothers.'

Nevertheless, I look up at the other guy. While our friend has his hair neatly pulled back in a ponytail, the brother (?) has a shock of curly hair surrounding his face.

'Whew!' the guy says. 'You're right. We're twins actually.'

I am looking at both boys – the other has come forward and now that he has been dragged in, he nods at us civilly. I am still searching. And then, suddenly, my synapses click in. It's like one of those optical illusions. It's a castle, it's a castle, it's a castle, and then boom! It's also a face. Once you've seen the face, it can never be that confident black-and-white castle any longer. I grasp the likeness.

Oh yes, oh boy, save the hairstyle, they are *identical* twins. Peas in a pod.

By now the brother doesn't look annoyed any more. He extends his hand and says, 'Hi. I'm Zvika Hillel. And this is Motty.'

We begin to introduce ourselves.

And then we begin to climb together. Suddenly, just like that, we are a group of four. Four travellers. The twins and us. There is such a nice ring to this, I'm now overcompensating for my former lack of enthusiasm.

Initially, our conversation revolves around the names, carefully enunciated for each other's benefit. The names are rolled around like unfamiliar wine in foreign mouths. Zvika means deer. Motty is short for Mordechai. 'Like Mordechai Vanunu?' S asks. The boys are surprised for a second. I see their eyes narrow. 'I write on geopolitics,' S clarifies. 'And nuclear matters.'

'Ah,' Zvika says, his face clearing. 'Like a journalist?'

'Something like that,' S replies.

'Yes, that's right,' Motty says. 'That's why I call myself Motty. I don't want to be like that Mordechai *at all*.'

I find myself rolling my eyes furiously. 'Will someone *please* enlighten me? Who is this other Mordechai dude?'

We have ascended the hill. Zvika has a fancy camera and is pointing it this way and that, quite battily. Motty tells me on the side.

'New camera. There is *nothing* he is not clicking. In the morning when we walk, there is a truck filled with sand going. Zvika running and running after truck to take photo of sand.' We laugh, and then the three of us take off our shoes and enter the small temple. Later, S leaves a small offering in the box. The pujari in turn gives us an apple. Then, on second thought, he takes the apple back, finds a knife, cuts it into four quarters and returns the prasad to us. We sit outside and munch and chat. Their travels thus far; ours.

'Mordechai Vanunu was a sort of whistle-blower in the Israeli nuclear programme in the eighties,' S tells me finally.

'He was a spy, yes,' Motty adds.

'He was in London, waiting for his story to be fact-checked and published by *The Sunday Times*, when Mossad executed a classic honey-trap operation on him,' S finishes.

Zvika joins us briefly to claim his piece of apple. He asks, 'So this book thing that you are travelling for? Does it pay? Or you have to have jobs and all?' I see Motty raising his eyebrows at Zvika; probably to check the plain-speak. 'I mean,' Zvika shakes his head apologetically. 'Since you are married, you have to have jobs. No?'

'We had full-time jobs,' I say. 'But we've quit those now. To travel. We did get a small advance for the book. But then, we plan to travel on a tight budget.'

'Nowadays it's freelance work that brings in the money,' S adds. '*Much* less money than the jobs.'

'Ah, yes...' Motty and Zvika nod their heads vehemently. 'Freelance, we know,' Zvika says. 'Is good. No boss. Sometimes, there is no work. Sometimes, lots of work.' We laugh. Motty adds, 'You see, our father is a tour guide. We know all about *freelance!*'

'Which part of Israel are you guys from?' It's my turn to ask.

'Holon.'

'So are you Sephardis?' S asks, in his characteristic manner of raking up strange anthropological questions out of nowhere, rudeness be damned.

'Yes.' The twins nod in unison. 'Actually,' Motty says, pointing to his prominent nose, 'you know what this is? It is a classic Baghdadi nose.'

Jews are ethnically divided into three broad categories: the Ashkenazi, Mizrahi and Sephardi. The Ashkenazi come from central Europe, comprising a large Yiddish-speaking component, and are genetically similar to Europeans of that area. Ashkenaz, after all, is the name in medieval Hebrew for what is now Germany.

The 'Mizrahi' or the 'eastern' are native Jews of West Asia and North Africa who have a lot in common with their Arab neighbours. As do the Sephardi, whose name seems to suggest an origin in the Iberian Peninsula (Spain) since 'Sefarad' is medieval Hebrew for Hispania. But Sephardis have not migrated to Israel directly from Spain. After being expelled from Spain in the fifteenth century during the culmination of Reconquista, many migrated to Baghdad where they came to speak a dialect of Arabic strongly inflected with Hebrew elements. Hence the name 'Baghdadi Jew'. A key identifying marker being a certain prominence of the nose that some Muslims and Christians of Baghdad also sport. Although seemingly culturally assimilated, the Baghdadi Jews witnessed persecution when the Ottoman Empire held sway over what is modern-day Iraq. This led to waves of Baghdadi Jews emigrating to India, which in time gave rise to some very eminent families such as the House of Sassoon. India's Baghdadi Jews have also provided famous film personalities such as the actor Nadira. Once the state of Israel was created, Baghdadis, from wherever they might be, mostly moved to Israel.

As Sephardi Jews, initially their father's generation had faced discrimination from the Ashkenazi majority. However, Zvika adds hastily, 'Now things have changed. There is no discrimination any more.'

'You guys don't look that different from my Lebanese friends in JNU,' S says.

'Yes, yes...' Zvika smiles. 'We are cousins after all. Arabs and Jews! In Israel, there is always competition about whose shops make better hummus. Actually,' he lowers his voice conspiratorially, 'the Arab shops do.'

Cousins eating the same sort of food; an important point some would say. Unfortunately the descendants of Ishmael and Isaac disagree deeply on this point: we leave S and Motty to such reflections.

They speak in low voices out of deference to the pujari who has begun the evening worship. The light is rosy and strangely fragrant. Zvika leaps up again. He shows me how to adjust the lens of my camera, and I too manage to get some beautiful photographs in the bargain. We balance on the edge of the platform. Then Zvika takes off his shoes and climbs down to a ledge, where he takes pictures from precarious angles. The huge orange sun bobs at the edge of the sky, about to fall off, and in the altered light, the blue houses of the old city seem like crazy china scattered in a generous arc.

S and Motty signal to us that they will descend, and we should follow. I wait for Zvika. He ties his shoelaces. Then he points to blue specks in the distance, the houses enfolded in the velvety dusk. 'You know, Dippy, our father is a tour guide. He has taken so many people on tours across Israel. But he has never travelled abroad. Our mother once went on a trip to Europe. But not our father. He has never stepped out of Israel.'

17

According to the shastras, if you walk three steps alongside someone, you become his friend. And here we are, climbing up and down hills together. The matter of friendship was a foregone conclusion.

By the time Zvika and I come down the hill, after several interruptions for photos, the other two are far ahead. We can see them in the distance, Motty's dark brown t-shirt, Saurav's beige jacket, in the haze of twilight. We follow in that direction. Zvika is telling me about their family. In addition to their parents, they have two elder sisters. Both married. The eldest sister has three kids. One boy. Then twin-boys. Twins run in the clan. Their second sister, a graphics designer, has one little girl. Letta. 'Her husband has travelled to India eleven times, you know?' Zvika tells me. 'He is a biker. You know the Shiva Riders?'

'No,' I say.

'They are a group of bikers. They go everywhere on motorcycles. From the Himalayas to the seas. Hundreds and thousands of kilometres on the road. He has biked with them.'

'Wow!' I sigh jealously.

You know what happens if you are an only child growing up in the city? You never even learn to ride a cycle, let alone a motorbike.

'Our sisters also travelled through India after they finished their army service. It's like a tradition in Israel. Like a growing-up thing. After you finish army and before you go to college, you visit India. When we were planning our trip here, everyone told us, "Oh, many countries have great views and great places, blah blah blah. But India has some magic. Something extra."' He grins at me.

We near one end of the low walls that ring the larger fort area; we had crossed the wall elsewhere. A strip of grey road is on the other side; a thin trickle of traffic on the road. Saurav and Motty are waiting for us there, talking intently about army training. I interrupt the discussion on the IDF, which I gather is the Israeli Defence Force, and wonder about the plan of action.

The boys have planned to leave for Jaisalmer tonight. They arrived this morning and spent all day inside the fort. They have to collect their bags from their hotel somewhere near the Clock Tower. 'Let's go to our hotel,' S suggests. 'There's a nice rooftop cafe. We can eat something.'

'I need some coffee,' Motty agrees.

Zvika, however, hems and haws a bit. He fishes out a card from his pocket. 'But before that, can we find a telephone booth? Let us call the manager of our hotel once,' he says, 'and tell him we will be a *leetle* late. We have already paid and everything. But they said they might want to give the room to someone else. What happens to our stuff then?' S produces his mobile, squints at the card and dials the number. Zvika remains next to him, instructing him in what needs to be said to the manager. I turn and find the fort looming in the dark, propped up on the ridge, through the silhouette of huge cacti that dot the land. The sky behind is purple but for a red band at the bottom which meets the earth somewhere behind the ramparts.

In a perfect inversion of the walk so far, it is Motty and I who jump the wall first and head towards Cosy. Then, because he asks, I complete the arc and tell him about our families.

⌐

Caffeine makes us boisterous. We laugh loudly and chatter, sometimes speaking diagonally across the table to one twin. The boys sit opposite us. We share a pizza. S is buying. A contingent India–Israel friendship fund has been instituted. Zvika becomes Zohan of *You Don't Mess With the Zohan* and I am happy to note that the smug goras from yesterday evening, the ones who were drinking life to the lees and not sparing us a glance, are now looking over at us and envying all the mirth. *They* don't have a Zohan. Zvika has us in splits with all his mimicry.

Afterwards, Motty tells us how the brothers had actually begun travelling separately, with their *own* friends from the army. Motty came via Nepal, while Zvika had plans to get to Delhi straightaway. Motty and his two friends had a bit of a shock in Nepal. One of the friends suddenly complained of a terrible pain in the stomach. They were in Pokhra. The hotel guy got them to a private nursing home though they said a hundred times they wanted to go to a government hospital. Not only was it rather shady, there was no power when they got there. The doctors (who seemed polite but inscrutable to Motty) brought the friend to the OT to examine him (the OT, unlike the OPD, had power backup) but the friend freaked out massively. He thought it was an organ-harvesting racket that they'd been dragged into. He jumped off the stretcher and streaked out of the OT, screaming.

The two friends were in shock after this. Fortunately, the stomach pains disappeared. Motty did his best to convince them that it was probably not what they thought anyway. In the light of day, the place didn't even seem that shady but was full of genuine-seeming patients and nurses. The other boys, however, would have nothing more to do with the holiday. They didn't even go to Bangkok. They simply went home. Zvika, meanwhile, had already spent a few weeks in India, and was more than happy to lose the group he had attached himself to. After Motty arrived, the boys began travelling together. 'You know,' Zvika says, 'you guys will understand this. Being twins is a little like being a couple. You fight a lot but you also stick by each other. And it is easy and comfortable. You don't have to try and seem smart and funny all the time. Unlike a group of tourists. That is a lot like a summer camp. You have to make an effort to stand out. It can be tiring.'

⁓

The rest of the evening, we walk around the chaotic lanes of old Jodhpur, first looking for the Clock Tower, and then for Motty and Zvika's hotel. They'd left it in the morning and in the sunlight everything had looked different.

Not that the rambling is a problem. The bazaars are noisy and dirty. Full of life and people and cows and bicycles and autos and motorbikes and charm. Great dollops of charm. The narrow lanes are lined with houses, the filigree around the scalloped balconies making one pause and point. There are temples where women crowd in bright saris and then, further ahead, a mosque with imposing minarets. The shops are full of customers. Tailors who make jodhpuris; little jewel-box rooms with scarves and stoles and handmade paper notebooks where foreigners attempt to strike bargains; more mundane stores stocking utensils, grocery items and sports equipment; pharmacies. Motty and I eat jalebis and talk about college. The boys will go home and start preparing for college entrances while working part-time. There are specialized institutes across Israel that train people for these exams. Motty wants to do 'something with my hands. Mechanical or electrical stuff. Maybe.' S and Zvika are walking just in front of us, devouring kachoris and talking about tantra. It all began with Zvika's description of some strange rites witnessed in Rishikesh. 'There was a baba sitting by a fire all alone at night, drinking something strange, with a dog sitting calmly beside him. He was talking to the dog.'

'Perhaps he was an aghori,' I say, from behind.

'Do you know what an aghori is?' S asks.

'Like a bad baba?' Pat comes Zvika's reply.

'There is no good or bad baba, only fraud baba and capable baba...' S begins to offer a detailed philosophical exposition on tantra.

Motty and I hang back in the vegetable market to ask the rate of potatoes and onions that day.

According to my notes, potatoes were twelve rupees a kilo and onions, twenty rupees a kilo.

⌐

After a couple of hours, Motty and Zvika Hillel finally recognize their hotel. It is a decent-sized house built in the traditional way. When we follow the boys up to their room, we are flabbergasted. For three hundred rupees – which is what they paid – they have a large airy room with tasteful furniture and ethnic orange draping. Gorgeous lampshades. There are windows on all sides and a TV. 'Super bargain, boys,' I tell them, my eyes widening. Motty smiles and says, 'We haggled.' Zvika says, 'We told them, "Hey, see, we're poor Israelis. Not Europeans. We have less money. One shekel only eleven rupees. Not like dollar or euro or pound."'

They strap up their bags and check the drawers. We troop downstairs again. Very conveniently we find an auto outside the guest house. And as lightly as it had begun, the evening is over, and we are back to our original couplings. S and I stand aside. The twins push their bags into the back of the auto.

The street is dark. 'Maybe we'll meet again!' I say brightly, trying not to behave like a sentimental fool. 'We might as well go to Jaisalmer next. Right?' I look at S. 'Yes,' he nods in assent. 'Sure. We'll mail you guys.' Zvika makes us pose for a photograph. The rest of us complain but secretly we are happy. There is going to be some trace of this evening somewhere.

'If there is karma,' one of them says, 'we meet again.'

The boys are off.

We begin to walk back to Cosy. It's a long, long way. My feet are aching and I feel exhausted. The markets are winding down and the place seems strange and forbidding, the Clock Tower slightly eerie, and I want an auto. I *need* an auto. But apparently we have spent a lot of money already and cannot afford one.

'Look, if you hadn't had coffee after coffee, you could have taken your rick,' S grumbles, walking as fast as his long legs can carry him.

'The boys got such a fabulous room for three hundred rupees,' I grumble in turn, sprinting to keep up. 'That's the market rate. We should have bargained more. It's your fault. You *never* haggle. Always playing posh.'

'No, no,' S says, looking at me. 'Think of our *view*. That's why our room is for three hundred. It's right next to the fort.'

'Anyway,' I say, 'let's just hurry up and go to the room now. I'll take a nice hot shower and read my book. I am tired of talking. For the rest of my stay in Jodhpur, I'll simply keep my mouth shut and soak in the blue. *Okay?* Okay.'

Half an hour later, the old man stops us.

The old man is sitting in his shop. He is large with white hair, in a cream sweater-vest and white pyjamas. The shop is a bright little room, carved into his house in such a way that one couldn't walk into it from the level of the road. It is like a stage, a plinth lit up by a fluorescent tube light of generous wattage. The shop stands out in the dark lane, its counter lined with jars full of toffees and mini-tubs of Vaseline. By this time, the lanes of Brahmpur are quiet. 'Namashkar,' calls out the man, his voice ringing in the night, his white hair gleaming like a halo, when we walk past his shop at the mouth of Navchokiya Road.

'You must be from Bengal,' he says. 'I heard you speak in Bengali when you were going to the fort this afternoon.' We stop and smile and begin to explain the backstory of our Bengal roots. But the notion of Bihar/Jharkhand underpinning our Bengaliness delights the man immensely. (Other than S's dad, the three other parents grew up in Jharkhand when it was still Bihar. They all considered themselves Bihari.) His family, though originally from Jodhpur, had migrated to Madhubani in Bihar a couple of generations ago. It was only in *his* late twenties that he moved back to Brahmpur, to Rajasthan, but it is Mithila that he longs for. The fertile soil, the lush green, the hush of rain, the musical language. 'You see,' he tells us, 'I lived with a large number of Jhas. And since I have a bit of an interest in genealogies, I used to track families as they spread out across India. Do you know where your *mool* is? Have you been to Mithila?'

'Tarauni,' S replies, though he confesses to not knowing more about the place. Perhaps, in the course of the journey, we'll go to Mithila, we tell him. And then, naturally, we have to tell him about the journey.

There is another man in the shop. A fair bald man in a smart cardigan and trousers, glasses perched on his nose. He is reading the newspaper. A neighbour. He emerges from the slight crackle of the creased day-old paper, to be introduced to us. Also a resident of Brahmpur, we are told he belongs to a unique community of Brahmin goldsmiths. 'Mahech is his name,' the shopkeeper tells us. Mr Mahech is in the gemstones business, and after we have chatted for an hour or so, offers to look at our palms. He examines S's closely and finally remarks, 'But you have no attraction to money. Money will come and go and come and go and come and go.' Then he looks at mine. 'It is perhaps just as well that Madam seems to have a good Jupiter. Money will come.'

'Speaking of money coming and going,' the shopkeeper says, 'do you know this conspiracy theory? Indira Gandhi's people did a great deal of digging in these parts and truckloads of gold coins were carried away from Marwar. The national highway was closed to the public for three whole days! I am talking about the seventies, of course.'

We laugh.

The shopkeeper then looks at Mr Mahech and rubs his palms together. 'Instead of discussing it obsessively, just the two of us every night, why don't we ask these travellers?' He looks first at S, and then at me. 'We hear India is going to be a superpower. Is that right?'

S opens and shuts his mouth. I roll my eyes. They might as well have handed him a mic and a podium. He begins to speak.

It is one o'clock in the morning when he stops. The cold has crystallized into lozenge-like slabs that drape the houses and coat the streets, making them glint soberly in the clear night. Mr Mahech's son has joined us in the shop. 'Water?' he asks, without any trace of irony, though it makes us burst into peals of laughter. S accepts the bottle from him. Mr Mahech promptly organizes bowls of kheeran – a rich creamy dessert of boiled rice and milk with saffron and raisins – to be delivered to us on the street, in steaming hot bowls. It is a tradition after all. You never give just water to a traveller. You ought to offer something sweet.

Four

How to Write in Indian

The trouble is our lives are polyglot,
to write them down we have to
cheat a lot.

– 'Tonguing Mother', Editorial, *Civil Lines 4*

18

We were global and opinionated. We were conscious of what we had earned.

A few of us could pull off the sharpest of short skirts. Others might invent the most stinging of put-downs. Several loathed their bosses, a small number ran popular blogs on company time, all took particular preferences seriously: pepperoni with no mushrooms meant *no mushrooms*, okay? A few clung on to the 1970s' ideas of love and marriage. But the rest of us pitied them deeply. We were that generation.

Our successes too were built on the foundations of a few words losing their meaning altogether; bleeding out to become cold curiosities like five-paise coins and pagers. Consider lakhpati. When we were children, lakhpati was such a sparkly word, glamorous and debilitating all at once; it was powerful in our mouths, expanding between tongue and palate to mean cars and factories and garish drawing rooms filled with large marble vases. Lakhpati was Juhi Chawla's father in *Qayamat Se Qayamat Tak*.

By the time we entered our twenties, those of us who went to top B-schools became lakhpatis in the first month of our jobs. Those of us who studied the arts and social sciences, and remained at university to pile on degrees, obtained an arch tone about this lot. Some of us who studied medicine and spent our twenties in protracted agony punctuated by raucous boozy pharma parties and impossible examinations merely glowered. But we would have our day in the sun. If we became surgeons and joined those private hospitals which looked like malls, we'd get a lakh per operation. We could do about six operations a day by the time we were in our mid-forties though our spouses might complain about the frequency of sex.

The culture guys call us the children of globalization. But really, we were lip service givers to global warming. Globalization meant global warming, but we could not do without our globalization. We paid more for our bras and floaters than our parents had earned in their very first jobs. We whittled our profound anxieties down to perfect apps that kept our fingers twitching all day, and to blue anterooms of the mind by night, where nightmares battled with furniture wish-lists. Sometimes we would wake up in panic at 3 a.m. But on the whole, we were reasonably sure we would survive. The house with the three bedrooms and the heated swimming pool downstairs at the clubhouse would be ours; on the honeymoon in Mauritius, champagne would gleam in cold flutes by the window.

We would spend our lives pursuing happiness since the American Constitution had asked us to.

⌣

And then there were the younger or more fortunate among us, whose parents too had ridden the liberalization boom.

Sometimes we let them take us to fancy restaurants. When the cheque arrived, we saw how the ageing skin beneath their eyes registered the mildest of flickers. Though naturally they had come prepared. They knew what fine-dining meant. They were learning the ropes. Their fingers would rub sharply at the friction generated by the crisp thousand-rupee notes. It was still so new to them, this Indian plenty. We observed, and in all our love and protectiveness, were a little pitying in our hearts. We spent thousands *far* more casually. In any case, what is a thousand? Film and popcorn over the weekend.

Foreign travel – whether on company money or on academic grants (for many of us still believed in the West) – made us smooth. We learnt to distinguish between types of beer and complain about airlines. We saw white people begging and felt vaguely embarrassed.

The real innovators among us, though, the ones who truly pushed us into a new age, were those who brought to cleverness that sense of democracy. The cleverness of old boys' clubs – beginning in posh boarding schools, honed at old-money universities in England, and then served up with bitters in clubs – was old hat. It didn't matter where we came from any more; or if we were women. We would read the *Guardian*, follow Manhattan's hippest blogs. We would learn the language. It only mattered how quickly we caught on. But then again, balance was important and we negotiated tightropes. Too much cleverness, and you became a cynic; too little, and no one would retweet you ever.

We were so glorious and so connected, it never really felt that in a nation of a billion, we were so very few. And so we forgot that if practised in appropriate amounts for too long, cleverness could take the place of life.

Saurav

'I will speak to you afterwards,' is what Mr Mahender Joshi had said. 'At dusk I climb up to the Chamunda temple next to the fort.' We nodded because we knew the temple. 'Every evening, I go there without fail.'

We wait for him in the deserted rooftop cafe. D reads. There is a French couple in the corner. The girl snoozes on the swing, her legs tucked under a patchwork cloak. The guy smokes softly; grey rings surround his head. All day, we have walked. Making our way through litter and friendly old people, past a solemn procession of donkeys carrying baskets followed by angry dogs howling in their wake, old Jodhpur with its pleasant swathes of sunlight on streets and houses, and later, on the sandstone walls of Mehrangarh. Golden parallelograms through which we passed as grey shadows.

We entered the fort from the main gate this time, and inside, D had spun around the grand spaces, the large open courtyards and gigantic corridors, rapturous over the columns and arches, everything in royal proportions. A couple of musicians in traditional garb were singing in a corner of a courtyard. In the museum, we marvelled at the weaponry – shields and daggers, guptis, matchlocks, helmets. The elaborate howdahs for kings and paalkis for queens. There was a carved wooden palanquin with pink and gold silk covers and a European-style carriage-shaped palanquin, again wooden, with tin plates and peacocks on either side. The most intriguing was a very English phone-booth-style paalki, upholstered in severe Victorian fabric.

Walking around the display were these Japanese tourists. They held in one hand their fancy cameras. In the other, they held aloft the relevant pages of *Lonely Planet India* (in Japanese) in a spiral-bound folder, each page laminated. Phew! They must have sat in their homes, packing for the trip, and systematically pulled apart their fat *Lonely Planets* to arrive at these convenient slices. At midday, we found ourselves veering from the museum area to a large terrace. Rao Jodha must have seen the bluish edges of his dominions from here. It was noisy and full of tourists. I observed the specific happiness of ample Indian grandmothers when their rosy grandchildren, perched on the slim jean-clad hips of their NRI mothers, called out to them in accented Hindi. Their faces brightened.

And then the spectacular views darkened in my head and the light began to dim. We sat downstairs, exhausted. There was a museum shop where thousands of tourists were jostling and jabbering, many more tourists than had been at the museum. D averted her eyes and began to scribble in her notebook. A guard came and sat next to us. 'You don't want to shop?' he asked us. 'You should shop.' I ended up talking to him about the project. I am always garrulous when I'm hungry. 'Good, good,' the guard told me, 'I like people who write. In my village, we have this proverb: *jahaan na pahunche ravi, wahaan pahunche kavi.*' (The poet reaches those places where even the sun forgets to visit.)

'Coffee or tea?' asks Mr Joshi, striding to our table. He is wearing a navy-blue sweater and a woollen cap. His beard glistens. He is a stocky man. He takes off his cap and sits down. He is followed by a young lackey who is despatched with our requests, tea and coffee, and milk for him. He has just returned from the temple and has a prominent red tilak on his forehead. While his brother has an uncertain aspirational whiff about him, that scent of wanting to go places and get ahead, not so Mahender Joshi. He's very contained in his deportment. One might conclude that, all said, he is a happy man. On our comings and goings, we have spotted Mr Joshi's wife in bright saris, and his charming little girl flitting about the house. In their presence, amid his guests, Mahender Joshi becomes slightly shy – they have that kind of beauty – and therefore a tad brusque. We tell him about our sojourn to the fort. He tells us that unlike most of the other forts in Rajasthan, Mehrangarh is still administered by a trust controlled by the Rathore royals. Most scions of princely states had not believed it possible that after Independence the Indian government would actually take over their forts and titles, and so had been caught napping when that came to pass. The Rathore king had quickly felt the political pulse. He had formulated a private trust to administer the fort well in time and the arrangement continues.

'They are a bit like banias,' Mr Joshi says. 'Rather than like kshatriyas. They understand business well. They run the trust effectively. The hotels too. I mean, you know Umaid Bhawan is very popular for foreign weddings.'

The drinks arrive. Mr Joshi now warms up and begins to tell us his story.

Brahmpuri of old Jodhpur is a Brahmin cluster, and Joshi's ancestors, like several of their neighbours, had been retainer priests in the fort. Some say that there is a secret tunnel that connects the fort to Navchokiya Road. In case of attacks or exigencies or coups, the royal heir might have had to be smuggled away with the family deity and hidden. Ten-odd generations ago, the Joshis settled on this plot of land – what is now Cosy Guest House. The family still has a copper plate – a taamra patra – that recognizes the gift. Mr Joshi lowers his voice to tell us that he keeps the taamra patra in a bank locker.

Mahender's father was a learned man, a professor at the local college. But as for him, he tells us apologetically, his heart had never been in studies. He dropped out of college and started doing freelance work – sometimes in hotels, but mostly as a tourist guide. For two years he even worked as an assistant to the maharani of Jaisalmer. But he had always wanted to be self-employed. The economic liberalization of the 1990s, when the inflow of Western tourists to India increased manifold, marked a turning point in Mr Joshi's life.

The goras discovered Jodhpur – and how. They began to trickle in, in a steady stream, the rich zeroing in on Umaid Bhawan and other converted havelis, while others would hunt for local hotels and sigh at the blue lanes and the old fort. Mr Joshi made friends with this one angrez, a real angrez, that is, from Britain. He was a friendly guy, and he found Mahender entertaining. He invited Mahender to his room one day, just to chat and have chai. He was staying in a hotel the goras favoured for its proximity to the fort. (Mr Joshi can tell us the name of the hotel, of course, it's still there, but he's a good man and would rather not.) So that afternoon, he arrived to meet his angrez friend. He parked his bicycle and went past the reception to the stairs. 'Oy, oy,' the owner shouted. 'Where the hell do you think you are going?' Mr Joshi was wrong-footed for a while. The hotel owner knew him well enough. He came back to the reception and said that he was going to room no. so-and-so to meet, let's say, Scott. 'Meet Scott!' the owner mimicked. 'Who do you think you are?' Mr Joshi still did not lose his cool. 'Arre bhai, I am lying or what? Scott asked me to come and meet him in the room at three o'clock.' The owner looked at his cohorts (the oily bunch I can see trooping in from the kitchen when they hear their master shouting) and then addressed Joshi. 'Of course you're lying. Do I sit here and eat grass all day that I have to now believe that a gora has asked you to come and chat with him?' He turned to the cohorts. 'And his English is also laughable. Hah!' he said. One thing led to another and the young Mahender Joshi found himself thrown out of the hotel, his bike hurled after him, his forehead bleeding. But Mahender Joshi got up and brushed the dust off himself and wagged his finger at the owner. 'Mark my words, you *ullu ke aulaad*, one day I will be where you are. But better. Much better. And I will be *surrounded* by gora-goris.'

Mere aas paas sirf gora-gori hi honge!

Mahender Joshi can afford to smile now, as he recounts this story. It is an object already attained, even if he says so himself.

'It's a bit like the Gandhi moment in reverse,' D whispers.

But, Mr Joshi continues, *that time* had not been a time for smiles. He was like a man possessed, a man with a mission. He would have to do *something*. No longer this kowtowing to hotel owners for a spot of guiding. Enough! It was winter. He cleaned out one room in the house. The best room, which had a view of the fort in the distance. He bought the frame of a bed for 140 rupees and found a spare mattress. He began to pace up and down in the railway station, promising a home-style holiday experience to arriving tourists. On 12 January 1995, two girls from Spain agreed to come and try out the homely experience. They would pay forty rupees for a room and use the common facilities.

With the two giggling girls renting his room, Mr Joshi's gaadi began to inch forward. Others began to come. On 17 January 1995, a couple from England arrived, taking the total number of tourists staying with them to nine. The family had huddled into fewer rooms, moving out of their own bedrooms to accommodate more guests. Mahender Joshi remembers he had to run out that night to hire five blankets from a decorator at two rupees each. As spring crept in, he brought his guests to the Mehrangarh tank for their bath. It was exactly the sort of thing they enjoyed.

'The Blue House' became a word-of-mouth success. And then, pretty soon, *Rough Guide India* included 'The Blue House' in their recommended budget options. But Mahender Joshi suffered another blow. A clever competitor stole the name 'The Blue House'. He had not registered it and from the legal standpoint there was nothing he could do. Business suffered badly. But he prayed and worked hard and eventually added the two floors on top, so that the views remained unparalleled. 'It is very cosy, very cosy,' all the gora-goris used to say to him, so he went one day and registered his ancestral house, finally, as Cosy Guest House.

Now of course, thanks to guidebooks and grace, business is booming. His brother helps him out – though he is trying to go abroad – and they have acquired another property in old Jodhpur. To give customers home-style experience that is slightly more discreet; a notch higher. Every room has an individual courtyard or terrace with it; the rooms are large and airy. In fact, just this morning, he has made the final payment. It is all quite stressful.

Mr Joshi's brother joins us now at the table, bearing ledgers.

'Do you ever meet that man any more? The one who had you thrown out?'

'Of course. All the time. That is, whenever I go in that direction. He is quite respectful now. Maybe he thinks he deserves a little credit for my success.'

We laugh. 'I think we'll leave you to that now,' I murmur, pointing to his books.

'Thank you for your time,' D adds.

⌐

We walk up the narrow flight of stairs to our room. When we turn and stand, wedged tightly in the doorway, we can see him hunched over his ledgers. And all around Mahender Joshi, talking, ordering drinks, smoking joints and reading menus are his guests, the goras and goris. The night is smoky and the dark shape of the fort teeters over their heads. I look around, somehow disappointed, until I spot two dreadlocked African Americans in a corner and one South Korean girl climbing up tidily from the lobby. Not one African *from* Africa naturally. The luxury of world travel, even on a budget, is yet another first-world perk controlled by the economics of currency arbitrage. Oh, and there's a Baghdadi nose, I add, aloud. At least, it's not *literally* all gora-gori.

'Stop being so p.c.,' D orders.

'I never thought of myself as politically correct. Gee. That's an awful insult,' I reply.

'Not *that* p.c. Nobody would ever think that of you. Post-colonial, p.c.,' she clarifies. 'I mean, if this were one of my JNU term papers I'd be writing about the desire of the once-colonized for whiteness and the great problems this poses to our national psyche. The intimacy of enmity. Falana falana falana. But in *this* context, it's also kind of sweet.'

Her eyes flash as I open my mouth. I am not allowed to be ponderous this evening. Not today.

'Tomorrow is fine,' is what she says. 'I'm too tired to talk about serious stuff tonight. My cousin R called. He'll drop in after work. Apparently he has a surprise for us. Also, we ought to finish packing?'

19

It is afternoon and we are sitting in a bus bound for Jaisalmer. We were the first ones to buy tickets mid-morning – along with an old Muslim couple – and so we have been allotted seats in front. I am by the window. S is trying to sleep. He rests his head on the iron railing in front, and later, long after the incident, after we have reached Jaisalmer and found a hotel and eaten dinner, at night I will smell the sour iron smell on his forehead and wake up in panic. The old couple are sitting behind us. They are going to Pokhran.

Last night, my cousin R arrived at eleven. It was so cold that his breath misted in the air when he spoke. He brought an extravagant offering. The pastry chef at the Taj had handcrafted these gourmet chocolate affairs for us. Gigantic slices of a multilayered cake, lined with generous layers of chocolate ganache, steeped in syrup, and topped with a dark chocolate slab. Arranged artfully on each of the four rectangles were a strawberry, a cherry and a milk chocolate cigar. Individually, they were certainly worth more than the room rent. We shared one last night, squabbling like children over the strawberry and the cherry. And now, the remaining three in their cardboard box sit delicately in a thin cloth bag on my lap, along with my jacket and cap. It's quite hot in the bus. My handbag is stuffed in the sliver of space between the two of us, along with a fair amount of annoyance. These seats have been designed for midgets. In the canvas bag, we are carrying a jacket that another guest, an Australian, had forgotten in his room at Cosy. We have his number, he has ours; he'll pick it up from us at the bus station in Jaisalmer. Our rucksacks are crammed into the spindly racks above.

The bus is already very full. But people are still buying tickets and bustling in, though there are no seats left, flush with that resolute Indian hope for adjustment. Mostly it's men in pagris who tumble to the back and slither into spots where there is something to hold on to, hoping to get seats later. The engine thrums, that hefty asthmatic sighing, and we have been ready to leave any moment now for the last half hour.

In a last-minute scramble a bunch of women climb in, trailed by children. They are all reed-thin and the women wear colourful synthetic skirts with bright dupattas wound around their torsos and covering their heads. The little girls wear frocks and scuffed sweaters. They have several sacks with them and the conductor heaves these in. There is no place for these sacks to be stowed, so they are left to sit, all misshapen and lumpy, fruits and vegetables popping out, in the aisle. The women and children scatter, a few squatting on the floor of the bus. At some point, trouble begins. One passenger points to a sack and says something. Immediately, two other passengers chime in. The conductor takes it up. 'Kathal? Kathal?' he asks, looking this way and that. Jackfruit. One of the sacks is stuffed with jackfruit.

Commotion ensues.

In many parts of India (including Bengal) there is this notion that one should never, like never ever, carry any of the following on journeys: jackfruit, pickles or very ripe bananas. The no-no lists often have minor cultural variations, but jackfruit, it seems, is a common factor. Or bad things will happen. My mother, that very sensible science-minded person, has her own reasons for believing this. A year or so into their marriage, my dad and she were once going to attend a wedding in Asansol. On the Howrah Bridge, their taxi broke down. They ran all the way to the platform only to see the train leaving in front of their eyes. Fighting with each other over the apportioning of blame (this bit I assume), they returned home. Later they realized that the sealed brown package they were supposed to deliver to someone in Asansol (my dad is a great one for volunteering for such things) had contained jars of pickled jackfruit. At this point in the story, my mother's voice would rise an octave or two. 'You know how we found this out? The oil from the aachaar leaked through and ruined all my best saris which I was taking to the wedding!'

Years later, I gathered the reasoning behind this odd no-no from Robert Svoboda's *Aghora*. Apparently, the only sense spirits employ is that of smell – the reason why across cultures incense is employed to show respect to ancestors or household gods and goddesses. Now, overripe jackfruit and bananas and strong oily pickles have a fecund musk that attract spirits – mostly naughty ones at that – to themselves. And with naughty spirits at play, cacophony ensues. Bad things might happen.

S is roused and looks around sleepily. We assume that after all the chattering in Rajasthani, of which we understand only a few words, the bus will begin to move. But matters quickly deteriorate. The conductor, goaded by several passengers, is asking the girl to reconsider. To leave behind her jackfruit. The girl in the pink dupatta, whose jackfruit it is, naturally begins to protest. She shrieks shrilly. And then, from somewhere in the middle of the bus, a young man rises and begins to fume. He is short and belongs probably to the newly citified, newly prosperous classes, all faux-leather jacket and Salman Khan haircut. Sure enough, he comes forward, claims he's in the police, and kicks the sack of jackfruit. It skids. The girl in the pink dupatta rushes forward to protect her sack, and then the chap raises his hand.

In a second, fog descends on my brain. A lone flare, red and acid, begins to singe the thin skin of my palms and armpits at being thrust, woefully unprepared, into the sort of incident that happens to other people: riots and muggings and molestations. But S is already there, exactly in the middle, between the man and the girl and, shamefully, very shamefully (for I have been schooled in feminism from an early age and it should have been me in the middle), I feel *thankful* that he is big like a bear and that odious man, police or not, will not stand a chance.

But (much as he would have liked to, one suspects) S does not need to fight. As suddenly as this matter had flared up, it gets defused. The policeman (?) draws back immediately and returns to his seat. He sits down next to an old lady. He continues to roar though. I give the girl my water bottle and assure her that we will join her in protecting her jackfruit *till the very end*. The old woman behind us pipes in with her support. Her husband, his dentures juddering slightly, agrees. She drinks some water and then continues to tell me her story in Rajasthani, beginning probably at the moment the jackfruit tree had been planted in her village. The man who had raised his hand to strike her is reciting angrily to the people clustered around him the influential positions his friends occupy in local, state and finally, the Central government.

S tells the conductor that he understands the feelings of the other passengers. But the fact is that jackfruits *do* travel from villages where they are grown to cities where they are sold. People must have transported them, no? The conductor nods matter-of-factly though a few passengers in front still grumble. They are not against the girl, the conductor translates in Hindi, not at all, but they are against the jackfruit. But it is her property, S reasons patiently, while I bristle in my seat. Finally, he says to the conductor, now sitting down, there are so many of us. Right? Even if there is any trouble, it will get equally divided into so many parts, that what befalls us individually is sure to be minimal. 'That is right,' says the conductor, now shaking his head in assent, 'that is how these things are,' and after he confers with the driver, the bus begins to move.

The man who had kicked the jackfruit is travelling with his mother. That odious woman – who had done nothing to stop her headstrong son – now begins a long, slow fight with the girl in the pink dupatta across the aisle. Both give as good as they get. I cannot follow most of it. At one point, I hear the old woman tell the girl, '*Tu toh raand hai.*' That word I understand and it makes me start. Whore. I hear the girl give a low voluptuous cry at this allegation and screech something stinging in reply, but I do not understand what it is.

S rests his head on the iron railing again. I shed some hot, meaningless tears on the box of cakes sitting prettily on my lap.

20

The girl in the pink dupatta and the man (policeman?) who attempts to strike her. The man's mother, shrill voice supporting her ugly-Indian son, and girl in pink dupatta's little sister, kajal crusting her eyes and bright necklace of plastic beads. I see them frozen in the bus. I see myself, in my blue stripy sweater, sitting with a box of cakes on my lap, shedding tears copiously over what has just happened, the fog in my brain still and tremulous. Pasted on the window, there is a frame of a dirty, busy bus station that could be anywhere in the country. I close my eyes. I can see my friends in the city, in a tasteful drawing room in south Delhi – though the drawing room, like the bus station, could also be in any Indian city. Instead of a box of cakes, though, my friends have other things on their laps: a pile of pink papers, a fat manuscript, an i-phone, a copy of *The History of English Literature*, Vol II, by David Daiches. I can see their faces, smooth, the distinct shades of brown flattening into an even skin tone, as though they are sisters: the investment banker, the editor, the mommy blogger, the lecturer – I can see them and they are shedding my tears. They are angry, exasperated, darkly ironic, depending on their style. We talk and talk and talk; coffee cools in our cups and the two who are mothers call and tell their nannies they will be late. The state of women in real India, our cross. (There is always this mild sting of guilt that banking, blogging, publishing and lecturing are not real India, not really.)

To them, I can open up and say the stuff that I only *suggest* above, circuitously, for fear that in the mouths of others, people who do not read Indian, they will get twisted to mean something else. I can tell my friends that the stocky man *must* be from a Thakur-type caste. That it is totally a caste and gender and class thing, his assumptions that he could kick around her stuff and hit her in rage. What would have happened if we, the Delhi couple or whatever, with our rucksacks and running shoes, had been carrying a jackfruit? Would he have said anything to us? The girl is probably part-tribal; certainly, working class. My lecturer friend now begins to rant. Against a system that allows such things to happen, to continue. No country for women, the banker, youngest VP in her bank, shakes her head and says. The *very* worst. The editor immediately fishes out her tablet and shows us this powerful article she'd bookmarked in *The New York Times* about women and real India and shame and stuff. And something about this annoys me – just as much as the passengers in the bus obsessing about that sack of jackfruit had – and I begin to argue loudly, against myself, because in these cosy sessions the five of us, for a while, become one central self with the impressions of character lightly layered on, like a smudged oil painting. It's not that those Americans treat women – or other races – very well. Who has given *them* this arrogance of high moral ground?

'How is that even relevant?' one of them asks.

'Because,' I glower.

The more I sulk and behave rudely, the quicker I separate from that central self, and the more my friends ply me with food and indulgences. I am the youngest after all, and with the most uncertain means. Privately, they often wonder exactly how we make ends meet. *If only I could write in Indian*, I mumble.

'What do you mean?' they ask, kindly.

I tell them, looking specifically at the editor, 'Remember how we got to Pushkar? Where we got off from the bus and stepped into mud? While writing that bit, I had erred on the side of cow dung. "We disembark at the wrong stop near Pushkar, and in our hurry step right into cow dung," I wrote initially. "Was it cow dung?" S asked, revising that part later, his brows beetled together. And then, I re-imagined the scene in my head, jogged my memory, recreated the exact squelch, remembered the smell as best as I could, and finally I thought it must have been mud. We've had too much of this shit clogging our writing anyway.'

The lecturer is unsure where I'm going with this. The mommy blogger is quiet; the banker has excused herself and is speaking to a client in hushed tones in the corner. My editor, with her slim fingers woven together, is always very patient.

'What I mean,' I continue, 'is that I doubt if any Bengali writer *ever* – whether humourist or serious novelist – has had to break her head over a splatter of cow dung on the road. Gobor, they would say, matter-of-factly. Photik slipped on it and broke his crown. Full stop. And when *they* say it, the Bengali writer or the Malayali writer or the Marathi writer, cow dung is simply cow dung. But in English, it can quickly become something else. If it's wielded by the foreign correspondent, it is definitely something else. In this age of connectedness, these articles enter our inboxes and timelines in India so airily, far more democratically than, say, Katherine Mayo's *Mother India* could ever have done. And like eavesdroppers who never hear any good about themselves, we hear what they have to say, and squirm or chime in agreement. If I could write in Indian, the jackfruit incident would be the jackfruit incident and cow dung would simply be cow dung. And I tell you, come Mathura, it's going to be one big cow-dung conundrum.'

⟶

S taps my hand and asks me if I know where the Photon is. The scene unfreezes. He takes one look at my face, the odd mix of tears and sleep, the strange smell of mixed-up timescapes, and tells me, 'This isn't over yet. They're all getting off at Pokhran and I bet the woman will have the rest of her family waiting there.' He speaks with relish. 'The guy is *sure* to get beaten up.' He takes out the laptop and balances it on the bag. Our bus has just hit the highway and is beginning to pick up speed. Simultaneously, several women vomit. In that interval, the girl and the mother decide to stop fighting. People protest about the smell. The bus stops. The local solution is to bury the vomit in sand and mud, scoops of which are sourced from nearby fields. The conductor oversees operations. The bus moves again.

I cannot sleep any more. Outside, the grey road is sunlit and one can go miles without seeing a soul. At intervals, attempts have been made to green the land. Apparently an Israeli variety of grass had been introduced some years ago and it adapted very well to the climate here. There are mustard fields and trees full of rust-orange flowers. But ultimately, these are just interludes. There are long sandy stretches dotted with black thorny bushes. I try to memorize that desert smell; it is a dry, aloof brown. I stick my nose out of the window and the tears dry up quickly. Later on, when I get off the bus, fine grains of sand will rain around me. And when I try to recall the journey to Jaisalmer, it is only that peculiar hurtling sensation – the rushing towards the edges of the land we know as our own – that remains.

At Pokhran, about half the travellers line up to disembark. The odious man lurks at the back but his mother comes in front and stands near the conductor. The women are sharing the weight of their sacks, the little girls trying to help. The girl in the pink dupatta and the ugly-Indian mother are talking again. The girl is grim. The old woman tries to make nice. I finally hear her say, before they all troop down, '*Arre, tu toh hamri beti hai.*' The whore becomes the daughter in the space of a couple of hours? It's probably the fear of numbers at work here, at a strange stop where the woman may have a whole group of her men waiting, and the mother-and-son, removed from their big contacts, are just one pitiful cowardly unit. 'There has to be something there – about agency that these women too possess? No?' I tell S. 'The guy should be beaten up,' he replies.

I spot deer, peacocks and peahens, blackbucks and goats. At six o'clock, the sun goes down. And later, when the sky looms pink and mauve, S looks up from the laptop, 'I finally have a signal. The twins have sent an e-mail.'

Saurav

If you are a true Bengali, there is one thing on your bucket list, between No.5. *Seeing Sunset from Tiger Hill* and No.7. *Wearing monkey cap on trek from Kedarnath to Badrinath*. That one thing, the number 6, secretly more special than either Tiger Hill or Kedar–Badri, is to get a glimpse of the golden fort when Jaisalmer's dramatic sunset is enacted in the deep bowl of that endless desert sky. A concave sunset.

Ever since Satyajit Ray made *Sonar Kella* in 1974, a cult film featuring Ray's Calcutta-based private investigator Feluda, generations of Bengalis have made a beeline to Jaisalmer. While in Jaisalmer, they have woken up at dawn to see the ninety-nine bastions of the fort gilded in mannerly splendour. While walking past mighty havelis inside, through the warren of narrow cobbled lanes, they have imagined past lives when instead of being pen-pushers or code coolies or researchers in cold American labs, they were warriors or merchants. All the Bong women with their spectacles and large bags remembered princess-hood, the hundred retainers who polished their skin with milk and honey and smoked their hair dry. 'But isn't it tough being a Rajput princess?' I ask D conversationally, as we get off the bus and she reports an immediate déjà vu (it seems she instantly recognizes the scent of evening here). 'One has to always be prepared for violent wars and self-immolation. Take the case of Jaisalmer. The city was sacked two-and-a-half times; thousands of women jumped into the fire.'

'Well, that might be,' she replies archly, turning her nose up, 'but if that's what the code was, so it was. The past was a bloody violent place anyway. It would have given an edge to life.'

The bus station is noisy and the smell of roasting peanuts fills the air.

'But what makes you a pacifist in this life then?' I ask her as our eyes scan the crowds.

'The proof of the pudding is in the regretting,' she says, her eyes twinkling. 'Naturally that might be the response of someone who's seen the pointlessness of violence.'

Her black eyes look brown in the half-light.

At that point, Steve, the Australian who is waiting to collect his jacket, emerges from the crowds, reeking of alcohol, and we hand him his stuff. He is a handsome man – and goes on and on about how his friends call him Stavros because he is part-Greek. D is charmed and chats pleasantly and I feel stabs of jealousy. For an instant, I want to punch his Grecian nose. We find an auto. We head to the hotel.

I note that she neglects to ask me how a city could have been sacked two-and-a-half times.

⌐

Jaisalmer was founded in AD 1156 by Jaisal, a prince with a dubious track record. He swore allegiance to Muhammad Ghori who had, by then, overrun Multan and Sind, and acquired a force to attack Lodhruva, the capital of the Bhattis, which was now ruled by his nephew Bhojdeo. After Bhojdeo was slain in battle, two days were given to the subjects of Lodhruva to escape with whatever goods they could manage to carry off. On the third day, the city was sacked and many valuables were carted off by the forces of Muhammad Ghori.

Afterwards, Jaisal decided that the location of Lodhruva made it vulnerable to attacks, and determined to move his capital elsewhere. About five kos away, there was a rocky ridge that he found suitable. In a lonely spot by the fountain of Brahmsar, Jaisal found an ascetic sitting in deep meditation. Jaisal approached him in all humility and asked him if the spot was indeed an auspicious one for his new capital. The hermit, it seems, was almost expecting him. He pointed to the three-peaked hill or Trikuta Parvat and said that in the Treta Yug, this had been home to a celebrated rishi called Kak – or Kaga – who had sanctified the place. To attend a sacrifice here, the Pandava, Arjun, and the Yadu king, Krishna, had come to Trikuta Parvat. According to the hermit, Krishna himself had prophesied that a descendant of his would come here one day and establish a castle. Arjun pointed out that the water, as far as he could see, was brackish. Most unsuitable for a new site of settlement. Apparently, Krishna had cast his discus at the rocks and through the cracks that emerged, sweet water had bubbled forth.

The hermit foretold that the new capital would be sacked two-and-a-half times and rivers of blood would flow. For a while, all would be lost to his descendants. And yet, Jaisalmer would survive.

In AD 1156, on Ravivar (a favoured day for the commencement of auspicious projects), the twelfth of Shravan, shuklapaksha, the foundation of Jaisalmer was laid. Soon, the inhabitants of Lodhruva began to abandon the old capital and migrate to the new one.

Exactly 853-and-a-half years later, D and I have reached Jaisalmer. According to the Saka calendar, it is Shanivar, the nineteenth of Pausa.

⌐

We stow the luggage in our room – the hotel has been recommended by Mahender Joshi – and decide to set out and find the twins. Their final email had read as follows:

motty_hillel_87@walla.com   1/9/10

To me

Heyyyyyy how are you ?

Nice to hear from you

We staying in Temple View guest house.

We all ready booked a camel safari trip for tomorrow morning, for 2 nights and 3 days, starting tomorrow morning 7 am 10.1.10.

So we will probably meat you in 12.1.10 evening time.

If u are here, this 9.1.10 evening, you welcome to join us

I'll check your comment in about 1 hour

Well Come to Jaisalmer

Cheers,

Motty $ Zvika

21

The night is cold and we are exhausted. Just as we are about to step out of the hotel, the manager calls out to us and hops over, interrupting his conversation with a group of three beautiful Mediterranean women. He is a clever-looking tall chap with light eyes, a pronounced air of when-I-drink-I-chase-girls-in-my-open-jeep, a handlebar moustache and a turban perched cockily on his head for effect. He gives us some directions to Temple View. It is inside the fort. Among tourists, he hates, no, absolutely *loathes*, Koreans and Bengalis. And then, before returning to the beautiful women, he warns us. We ought to turn left outside the hotel. A cow has died on the street to the right and nothing can be done about the corpse tonight. A dead cow is a huge thing; special arrangements will have to be made to remove it.

We step out of the hotel; we turn left. We have, however, already caught a glimpse of the animal, pale and gigantic in death. Other cows are clustered by the corpse and flies hover above. We walk in silence. No detail of the roads or the skies or the cold seems to register. So it is *only* after we have entered the fort area, oblivious of the sandstone gates sporting the colour of wild honey in the fuzzy yellow fluorescence cast by electric lights, that we see. Only after we are already embedded in the network of little lanes.

The lighting is inconsistent. There are lanes of shimmery darkness through which shapes of balconies with lace-like jharokha loom. The dark patches are interrupted by bright shops full of clothes with mirror-work and other touristy stuff. It is *then* that we literally take a step back and realize we are in a magical land. Its charm is of the extravagant sort that makes one say extreme things like, 'If you have not seen Jaisalmer, *what* have you seen?'

We have stopped and turned, so now we are facing each other. We look around, our heads swivelling, slightly hysterical. I hear S draw his breath in sharply. 'Wow,' he mutters under his breath, for you do not talk loudly in front of such beauty. 'Wow,' I whisper back, the soft 'o' ballooning between us and then drifting over his shoulder to wander into the louder bargaining of tourists and shopkeepers close by. Here, on my right, there is a little bookstore built into a haveli that is several hundred years old. There, behind S, I can read the hectic signposting – hotels, restaurants, desert safaris – advertisements on a grainy golden sandstone wall that is resonant of genealogies and histories, going back centuries. In the street corner is an old Jain temple. We begin to walk again. It's like striding through a museum. But a lived-in museum: piled clothes, masses of papers, the colliding smells of lust and dinners cooking. It is a peculiar kind of awesomeness, possible, perhaps, only in India. Anxiety flares in me instantly: how on earth will we ever do justice to this place?

Anxiety is a strange but not uncommon response to beauty. It is mostly exhibited by people with a talent for stress. My head begins to throb. My eyes feel tired suddenly, and I take my glasses off and rub my eyes. S, meanwhile, has popped in and out of the bookstore, and got directions to Temple View Guesthouse.

We walk along a street of shifting shadows and street lights on golden walls, S very garrulous. 'Can you *believe* this place?' he says, again and again. We arrive at a busy chowk where someone points out Temple View, but before we cross the lane and get there, we hear voices with familiar inflections. 'Dippy! SJ! Hi.'

We have an excited reunion with Motty and Zvika Hillel on the street. They'd just stepped out of the hotel to go to the cyber cafe – to check if we'd mailed them about meeting up – and we troop towards each other joyfully. Zvika has sprouted a new pimple. Motty's hair is neatly tied in a ponytail and he smiles shyly. Instantly, around us, there rises a billowing circle of hellos and hugs and what-have-you-been-up-tos that buffets us and carries us on to dinner. Even in this age of connectedness, there is something spectacular about meeting the twins again in these ancient streets with the new licks of paint. In a whoosh, my anxiety abates. We are starving. The last meal was in pre-jackfruit Jodhpur.

The boys take us to a tiny restaurant they've been frequenting. We order from the menu that is, for the most part, a compilation of stuff backpackers across India seem to favour. Chocolate pancake for me, a mango lassi and cheese paratha for Zvika ('Cheese-cheese or paneer-cheese?' he asks the young waiter, who assures him it is cheese-cheese), a macaroni for Motty. S, wherever he gets one, picks the thaali.

'You know, that day, when we left Jodhpur?' Motty says, after thanking the waiter politely for bringing us water. 'We didn't get a bus. So we went to the railway station and took a train. We reached in the early morning. It was beautiful. Zvika went totally mad.'

'Yes, yes, I took about a thousand pictures of the sunrise. But now I am excited about the real thing. Mwahahaha,' Zvika says. 'We have booked a camel safari for tomorrow.'

'Oh?' I reply, and look at S. The camel safari is something we have been arguing about. 'When do you want to go on a camel safari?' was the second thing the hotel manager had asked us (the first being the nature of our relationship. He too was disappointed that we were not 'friends'.) 'Let's also go.'

'No,' S replies firmly. 'It's *way* out of the budget. You know that. We'll have to do Jaisalmer on a lot less and move on to Barmer.'

'Also,' Zvika deflects mildly, 'I don't think they can add two more people at such short notice.'

'What's Barmer?' Motty asks.

'Ya, what's Baaaarmer?' I ask, mincing my voice and making a face. The boys laugh.

'Barmer is a trading post from antiquity, which is now a wildcatter town of sorts. Of course, *technically* we can't say wildcatter because it's not independent bounty hunters looking for oil but two large corporations,' S replies seriously. 'But it'll be interesting. Also, we've been in Rajasthan for almost eight days now. We have to be on the move. Hurtling pace, remember?' He snaps his fingers.

'Hurtling pace, remember,' I mimic.

The food arrives, and I begin to wolf down my pancake.

⤸

Afterwards, I reminisce moral science classes from my schooldays, in the course of which we were taught graphic stories from the Old Testament: the heroic Israelites on the one hand, the cold-hearted

Egyptians and the battle-ready Philistines on the other. In the Calcutta summers, the classrooms would be still in spite of forty tweens in crisp white shirts and maroon skirts modestly covering their knees. Outside in the gardens, the flowers would wilt in the strong humid heat; within, the seas would part for the Israelites to cross over into the Promised Land while the Egyptian army would drown.

The boys are surprised that I remember the exact details of the travails of Samson and Delilah, Job, Noah, the sacrifice of Isaac, Jacob's feud with his brother Esau and his love story with Rachel. Ours was a missionary school – chapel in the morning and nativity plays before the Christmas holidays. Once a year, a bunch of American missionaries would come and distribute Bibles and ask us, after a happy singing session in the school auditorium, if we believed in *the* God. All the girls in their maroon skirts and white shirts, irrespective of family faith and general knowledge, would all raise their hands dutifully. The Americans were guests after all. It would not do to be rude.

The twins had no religious training in school, though they see themselves as Jewish. In Pushkar, they stayed in the Chabad House – it is free for Jews – and they did not particularly mind joining in for prayers. After Jaisalmer, they plan to go to Rishikesh where the Kumbh Mela is on. A second round of coffee arrives.

Somehow – I have no idea how, but I do remember it was over coffee – we get to numbers. I have before me a loose page where one of the boys has written 1 to 10 in Hebrew. I remember labouring over the pronunciation. And then, in my precise hand, there is 1 to 10 in Devanagari. 'Teach us to count in Indian,' they'd said. 'Indian is twenty-four languages,' I'd exclaimed, 'and counting!' And thus, next to the Devanagari, is written in Bengali: Motty Hillel, Zvika Hillel.

⌐

After dinner, the twins have made vague plans to meet another group of friends (also Israelis) who are supposed to come to Jaisalmer. They are likely to check into a hotel in the fort. Which hotel, the boys do not know, but it is near the first Jain temple. 'Right,' S says. 'Girls in the group? Or a certain girl?' Zvika blushes violently. His pimple turns puce.

Motty says, 'You are exactly right, SJ. This is the group Zvika was travelling with before I came from Nepal. I think he blames me for losing that group.'

'Nothing like that, nothing like that,' Zvika protests.

'Methinks the lady doth protest too much,' I sing.

'Come, come, see our room,' Zvika says.

We walk with the boys to their hotel. It is an old house with many rooms beside a long verandah. The boys have one on the ground floor, a small square with pitiless lighting, but clean enough, with an attached bath, bright bedspread and a picture of a camel on the wall. They have got all their clothes laundered; these are stacked in many piles on the bed. The hotel guy comes to us and offers camel safaris and rooms at very reasonable rates. S keeps his card. I get my hopes up again.

The twins are now behaving mysteriously. They collect a plastic bag kept in the corner of the room and speak to each other in rapid Judaic; Motty, it seems, does not entirely approve of the plan. Zvika is trying hard to appear in control. It is quite funny. They finally lock their room and we step out together. Near the first Jain temple, rather regretfully, we leave them floating around. I would have liked nothing better than to observe them go to every one of the hotels in the region, looking for *their* group of friends who may or may not have checked in this evening. With the girls. 'Bye,' we say, after the customary handshakes and hugs and maybe-we-will-meet-after-twenty-years. Motty lingers shyly, even after Zvika has walked a few steps ahead and Saurav has crossed the road. 'Keep in touch, Dippy,' he says. 'I hope your book is a big success. Then you can come to Israel and write a book about our country.'

'Thank you,' I say. 'I hope you have a fabulous trip. And next time, come live with us in Calcutta.' And then, both Zvika and Saurav, their faces at once open and craggy in the uncertain light, call out goodbye and wave.

'Your packet is tinkling, Zvika,' is my parting shot. 'What's in it?'

'Oh, that?' Zvika sparkles, and his smile, clean and toothy like a child's, spills out of his face. 'Just water.'

22

The big fight begins lightly. And in the first few minutes, there is the possibility that its comic possibilities will triumph.

That at seven o'clock or so, when the sky is probably a quiet eggshell blue, the birds are barely cheeping and I am stirring in the deepest depths of somnolence, if he insists unreasonably that I wake up and get ready, I shall not respond at all. It's hilarious he'd even expect it. I'm exhausted; we'd trudged around the bloody fort till midnight; in any case, morning is when I get my restorative sleep. I might open one eye and crack a joke, lumber out of bed and bite his ear and return to sleep. Better perhaps, I should figure out, for I love him and we are married, that it has nothing to do with waking up in the morning and rushing to the fort – doing Jaisalmer – at all, but that, really, he is worried about money and the future. And that worry – for anyone who has embraced uncertainty on the flimsy optimism that the pursuit of art or knowledge is sustaining in itself will know – peaks and ebbs with the regularity of tides. When it peaks in flood, restlessness is a symptom, snapping is a symptom; and there is only the relief of a long sweet brawl. An avoidable one, since its signs are so textbook. He has not slept well at night and that sour iron smell has transferred from his forehead to his tongue. I will understand all this in an instant. I will be funny and wise.

But what happens in Jaisalmer that morning – as in love and marriage, frequently – is not any of the above.

S leaves the bed at around six. He is jittery, annoyed. He goes to the bathroom. After coming out, he begins to clear the mess in the room noisily. We had unpacked in a hurry last night, in our rush to meet the twins, and things are strewn all over.

I loathe this thing: this cleaning up of rooms at the crack of dawn before I have left the bed. It fills me, unreasonably, with guilt. I am always in a state of precarious hysteria about anything that might be perceived as a slight on my general way of living. Unfortunately, I live in constant mess, lurching through mismanaged episodes. So if someone is cleaning up showily, on a bad day it hits me as direct – not to mention very cruel – criticism.

Dum, doosh, bam, blim. There's the swish of a flying coat. The splat of a chappal hitting the floor. The wlooozz of a bag being zipped up. The noises wake me up fully; guilt floods my gut. And then, because my years of feminism have built in me a Pavlovian response to this (very female) guilt business, anger takes over. I cannot reconstruct the conversation exactly but here's what is likely to have happened.

'Why are you cleaning up at this hour?'

'Because things will start getting lost. I could not find the Tata Photon, for example. It had got misplaced in the tumble of your clothes.'

'Stop blaming me,' I say. 'Anyway, I'll put the clothes away when I get up.'

'What do you mean *when* you get up? You have to get up now.'

'What? Why?'

'What do you mean *why*? I will keep everything packed and ready. Get dressed and give me your pyjamas. After we spend the day at the fort, we can take a bus to Barmer. We are haemorrhaging money in Rajasthan. One day in Barmer, and then onto Gujarat. We have to move on. We've barely covered any territory in these last few days.' The red rucksack lands on the bed with a mighty thump. Shloop, shloop, shloop, the t-shirts land in them.

At this I sit up. 'Are you *insane*? How can we leave tonight? What about the desert safari?'

'I have told you again and again and again that we cannot afford it. The cheapest safari will be something like 3,000 rupees. We have the budget to monitor. I'm the one having to keep an eye on the finances. You are in your la-la land. We don't have money pouring into the accounts every month. It's just getting depleted. You know what they say – money talks? It's usually saying goodbye. We spent quite a bit on dinner yesterday. Please get up and get ready.'

The anger that has been swirling in me gets a new force of life. 'Do not talk about money like that, okay?' I say this bitingly, knowing well that there is some truth in what he has just said. He is responsible for fund allocation. And yes, our resources are low. Even so, my fury has reached the tongue. 'Stop ordering me about. I cannot get up. I am exhausted. We can't leave today. What if I had my period?'

'But you don't. When you do, we will stop and take a break. But now we have to keep moving. You know the deal.'

And on and on.

At some point, it seizes to be a civil back and forth and turns into an uncivil volley. The sun rises higher on the horizon. The windows shimmer. There are breakfast noises outside, people walking in the corridor. And then, when S wants to wind down, I do not let him. What we do in Jaisalmer seems to become a metaphor for the rest of our lives. Are we simply going to go hurtling through – without taking my obsession with details into account? What if we never ever come back to Jaisalmer? Then all this beauty will be lost to us and I will have to live with that regret *all* my life.

What if our money runs out, he says, before we are any closer to completing the project?

What if unhappiness is all we shall ever have?

It becomes an all-consuming squall. The fury in the room heats up the air, it expands and drifts to the upper reaches, to the decorated ceiling with its pretty cornices, above the large paintings of full-bodied girls in traditional ghaghra-cholis, past the shimmery orange curtains, leaving us breathless with fear – the truth that runs below the rivers of dissonance and breaks onto the surface like this: fear. The nameless fear that we will be crushed by the risks and *they* will *win*, all those people who predicted this failure, all those who have savings and investments and EMIs and stuff.

In the resulting vacuum, I shout and rage and cry bitterly, bashing my head against his chest. We had fallen in love during a hot Calcutta September eight years ago, the sun beating down relentlessly on hectic noisy streets; something of that weather persists in our relationship. The last two years of impecunious existence; the reinforced co-dependence of living as writers together; the truth about marriage in the fine layers of knowing and not knowing; the heady mix of too many books and too little money; the everyday anxieties this journey throws up – there is enough hurt below this bedrock to offer a steady supply of material for cruel accusations to be flung at each other for an hour or a day, depending.

It takes the better part of the day.

By the time the original quarrel breaks down into vicious little eddies, each circling in one corner of the room, generating its own narrative of melodrama, I use my final weapon. '*I hate you.*' And at that moment, I do. I relish the words. At that moment, everything is already ending. I cannot comprehend a future, two hours/two days/ two weeks later, when I am calm and happy again. I narrow my eyes with hatred and the words shine like polished knives. 'In 2006, you did *this.*' I am unstoppable. '*That* day, in *that* season of *that* painful year: how could you have said the thing you said?'

'2006? You want to bring up the past *again*?'

Now that there is no hope of retrieving the morning, S surrenders to the luxurious extravagance of the fight. Things are said. Things are hurled.

At one point, I heave on the bed. He sits with his head buried in his hands. There is a turn in the wind: a hesitant allocation of blame elsewhere. 'It was yesterday's awful incident in the bus,' I say. 'That is what has depressed me.' He murmurs something in consolation.

But then something leads to something else and we are off again.

Noon arrives. Noon departs.

'If I've made you so unhappy, why don't you go away?'

The light outside seems post-meridian. Sobbing, I pull on my jeans, throw my coat over my pyjama top, grab my purse, take my three add-on credit cards (no bank in their right mind would have issued credit cards to me) and throw them at S. 'You'd better call the publishers and tell them this is off. Or,' and here my voice quivers, since, as you know, this had been *my* idea, 'you can do the journey yourself.'

I hoist my already packed bag on my shoulders and storm out.

Five

How to Sell Reproductions of Old Masters in Europe and Other Stories

Whatever celebrity Jaisalmer possesses as a commercial mart arises from its position as a place of transit between the eastern countries, the valley of the Indus, and those beyond that stream, the Kitars (the term for a caravan of camels) to and from Haidarabad, Rori-Bakhar, Shikarpur and Uchh, from the Gangetic provinces, and the Panjab, passing through it. The indigo of the Duab, the opium of Kotah and Malwa, the famed sugar-candy of Bikaner, iron implements from Jaipur, are exported to Shikarpur and lower Sind; whence elephants' teeth (from Africa), dates, coco-nuts, drugs, and chandan, are imported, with pistachios and dried fruits from Bhawalpur.

– 'Annals of Jaisalmer', *Annals and Antiquities of Rajasthan*
(By Lt Col. James Tod and Edited and With an Introduction
and Notes by William Crooke)

23

I storm out and push the door behind me. The finality of the slam is empowering – for about a second.

The corridor is deserted. Afternoon plays out on the stippled orange walls. Dust motes dance in a funnel of sunlight. Our room is on the ground floor. From the corner of my eye, I can see that the door of the next room is ajar. I can feel a pair of eyes watching as I march along. It is difficult to affect a dignified posture while sobbing. 'A-*and* she's off,' I hear a clipped British accent.

Outside, as I emerge from the darkened corridor, the sunlight blinds. I trudge along for a few feet, eyes flickering, in the direction opposite to where the cow had died. I turn left and there, just across the dusty road, the fort looms, radiant in the sun. I increase my speed, annoyed with the fort and its beauty – I have nothing to do with it now – and turn into a side street, where I find a large stone to sit on.

I sit and sit and nurse my injuries. In spite of the rage boiling inside me, something in the quiet warmth of that sunny spot begins to play tricks on the primary cortex in the brain, and the rush of fear abates. A supremely healthy cow ambles along and stops next to me. It flicks a fly with its tail smartly. Without the powerful sea of fear buffeting the rage, it loses steam.

I know, of course, that I will return to our room and we will travel on. He knows I will return. One time, I'd stormed out of his room in the hostel – that sad little room with a broken window and dirty corners – after a similar fight. When I returned exactly two minutes later, he'd laughed and said, 'I was doing a countdown. You returned at fifty-three.'

The bitterness in me begins to abate. In the clear pool within myself, I can see the reflection of his face. Not as it is now: for now it is greyer, thicker at the edges, marked with tired lines, dark circles under the eyes. But as it used to be when he was nineteen and we had first met and he filled my head with ideas. In the curious light of memory, I can see the seasons recede until it is the light of late September in Calcutta, eight years ago, and the clunking sound of trams linking with overhead cables fills College Street. Another time, perhaps, we shall get to know the golden fort; we shall return in that future, older, greyer, only to remember how we had been so afraid of time and its consequences when we were still young and foolish and full of love.

A quarter of an hour later, the British gentleman will be heard reporting to his wife, '*And* – she's back.'

Afterwards, we will walk through sun-dappled streets. We will climb up to a rooftop restaurant and even at this curious hour – after lunch, before tea – the friendly waiters will agree to serve us. We shall sit in the terrace that affords stunning views. We shall wait for the food, eyes riveted on the glorious golden fort perched on Trikuta Parvat; tiny windows and latticed balconies jutting out from a height. The sunlight, already texturally transformed by the sandstone walls and pillars it has encountered on the way, will fall on the burnished copper urns kept on ledges and decorative tables in the corner, and bounce off in a honey haze. We will link our fingers under the table. A hundred pigeons shall mill on the ramparts of the fort, grey fluffy balls pecking at grains, and behind the fort, the blue sky will begin to mirror the white of their breasts in larger and larger patches. One hour later, appetites sated, chins apologetic, we shall walk the streets again as the sun dips west. We shall laugh about the names of hotels: Laughing Camel Inn, Mr Desert Hotel. At Gadi Sagar, which Motty and Zvika had recommended heavily, we shall line up to hire a boat. Since the camel safari is off, S will allow the boating. That's where we will run into the couple.

24

We had met Yam Shaham and Tally Prozanski in a tea shop at the bottom of Ratnagiri in Pushkar. We'd chatted with them for a few minutes. Yam was busy taking pictures of the owner of the tea shop. The old man, after posing, instructed him to email the snaps to his son. The tea was milky and very sweet, and in the late blue of dusk, it had felt very travellery to sit in the dhaba and talk to other backpackers.

Tally reminded me a little of my friend Zarine from university. Tally was thin and chic, loose-limbed in the hippie clothes she preferred. She gave off the air of someone trying things out. Unravelling, if temporarily, the skein of her privileged upbringing through this whole India tour of cheap hotels and ganja shared with dirty strangers, long winding bus journeys and people with funny English. (In Zar's case, her posh bungalow in south Bombay and holidays abroad had given her a certain sureness in her skin, something we admired but never could get our pulse on exactly. The rest of us had all been twenty and awkward. But Zar strived to override this cloud of privilege in the shabby hostels where we lived, with their shared loos and fixed hours for water, where a few girls washed clothes obsessively and hung them in the corridors to dry.) In an impetuous moment, Tally Prozanski and I had exchanged email IDs. We'd even sent one-liners to each other – 'It was nice meeting you, hope you have a lovely trip,' stuff like that. Yam Shaham, her companion, was tall, muscular, and sported the Israeli army shaved head. He had a bit of a mysterious salt-of-the-earth thing about him. He hadn't cared much for our conversation in the tea shop, the questions posed either way – on their Israeli armed service and the nature of our English. And now, several days later, S has spotted them from far away; even before we have neared the shore.

Gadi Sagar is a stately tank surrounded by small temples and shrines, and it used to supply water to the fort. It is a sparkling blue bed of water with horizontal striations of glitter. The sky above is mostly blue too, though in the western corner a handful of red vermilion seems to have been carelessly strewn. But it is the sandstone structure in the middle of the lake, the small neat observation post perhaps, now golden in the fading light, which ultimately makes it so charming. There are many people around, both locals and tourists and the flavour is that of a mela.

Finally, I am able to see Yam and Tally. Tally is sitting on a stony ledge that looks over the water. Next to her is an old man in a pink pagri and a bunch of kids. Once again, her bearing, her warm open restraint, reminds me of Zar. She is humouring everyone; smiling at the old man and allowing the kids to play with her shawl; but the core of her is elsewhere. Yam stands next to her but he is facing the lake. He's taking photographs. We walk towards them. And after a moment, because that is what it takes for our faces to separate from the sea of brown Indian faces that have surrounded them all these months, to become familiar, they come forward. Yam is surprisingly chatty today. 'You know,' he says, after the initial pleasantries, 'old people everywhere are *just* the same. In Israel, we have people of my grandfather's generation. Always complaining how everything has become worse. This old man too has been saying the same thing. Everything was fantastic in the past. Everything sucks now.' He indicates the old man in the pink pagri who is now looking mournfully at the water. A bunch of people are clustered in a corner. They are feeding the fish there, where the water is brown and laps against the shore and the fish perform cutely, slapping their tails and bobbing up and down. 'Broken English goes a long way.' Tally laughs. 'Many deep meaningful things can be said.'

There is, of course, another problem here, and she tells us as we walk. The frank male gaze she has to bear. Something sticks in my eye and I begin to rub it. The children always ask her if they can touch her. Not the men. They never ask. But there it is – the unnecessary handshake, the casual hug, the clammy skin forced upon her whiteness, which is seen as licence. We stop walking. 'But hey,' Tally says, 'I am a big girl.' She can take care of herself, she says. She understands the context. It makes us blush, apologize. But Tally and Yam now suggest the lake.

We stand in the queue for boats and get tickets. It's the second time this afternoon for them. We rent small paddle boats shaped like swans; and the first ten minutes are great fun. S paddles away happily and I take pictures. We sluice through the water and there is the shadow of fish glimmering below. There are races with Yam and Tally's boat; improvised games as the boys try to ram the boats into each other's and I stow my camera safely in the bag, away from the cool spray that rains on my face. Then both boats get stuck in the shallows, though some distance away from each other. All around us is the blue lake. The sandstone structure close by, now catching the red sun. Hundreds of pigeons suddenly take flight; the simultaneous flutter of their wings detonating on the ground – and for an instant we are blindsided and our boat rocks. Before the rescue boats arrive, there are several minutes when it is just us and the red sky and the blue lake and the birds.

Afterwards, we walk through the lanes inside the fort, and in the post-fight phase of extra courtesy towards each other, we buy a book each from a quirky bookshop run by an old gentleman who had walked from Karachi during Partition. He tells us how the Ahmedabad–Hyderabad (Pakistan) rail link undercut the importance of Jaisalmer. I cannot remember which book S got for himself but I do remember the memorable first line of the novel I bought: '*My mother told me I would cut off my nose to spite my face, and when I was thirty-three, to prove it she died.*'

We enter a restaurant– just to check out the prices – but then we see Yam and Tally there, again, and we go straight to their table. They see us and scooch over. I sit next to Yam, S joins Tally. 'Children,' I say, 'I think we are meant to spend this evening together, so let us not fight it.'

'Yes, ma'am,' replies Tally, and offers me her plate of spaghetti. I eat a forkful and order a cup of cinnamon coffee. She looks at the books we've bought.

The restaurant is owned by the Bhatias, a Marwari couple who have Australian citizenship. Something like that. There is a map of Australia hung over the counter. There is a large sign that says: 'This Restaurant Is Run by a Permanent Resident of Australia'. They come and chat with us intermittently. The subject is mostly the many splendours of Sydney. In between, when the Bhatias leave us, we talk about our lives and travels.

My hunch about Tally is correct. Her parents are both doctors and she's grown up in the capital. She went to a posh school, at university she studied graphic design, and these days she speaks to her parents once a week. 'Do you need money?' is the first question they ask. 'Are you doing drugs?' That's the second. Like Indian parents, they do not want to know too many details though – lest they hear something they cannot file away in a proper folder. Yam Shaham's grandfather had fled to Israel from Transylvania, with only his wife and the clothes on his back.

'We *have* seen him in the sunlight, so I suppose it's okay,' S says seriously, nodding at me.

'That's what I checked when I met him first!' Tally squeals in mirth. 'Those days I used to keep garlic in my purse.'

'Ha. Ha. Very funny. Very funny,' says Yam good-naturedly. 'See, that's the only thing I know about my original homeland,' he adds, shrugging. '*Dracula!*'

The grandfather had held down three different jobs and worked like a maniac to build himself a new life. It was the phase of hungry nationalism in Israel. Jews from across the world had gathered there, most getting away from persecution of one sort or another. (It was only while travelling here that Yam learnt how India is possibly the only country in the world where Jews have never faced discrimination.) In the Israel of Yam's grandfather's time, there were North African Jews who looked black, Bene Israelis who looked brown, and Kaifeng Jews who were yellow. Yam's grandfather joked that had he not been married before his escape, he'd have made a colourful marriage. With the stories of the Holocaust branded into them and their own individual exile stories recounted again and again, it was a generation of warriors masquerading as men. A direct parallel to this is perhaps post-Partition India, when traders from western Punjab flocked into Delhi, having lost everything they had, and started from scratch to build large business empires that, post-liberalization, have put their owners in a different league of wealth altogether.

And yet, though there is the overarching theme of pushy innovative entrepreneurship in the context of Israel, there has also been the kibbutz. A unique institution that offered an alternative model to society, providing possibilities outside the world of commerce. Thus, while it is likely that Yam's grandfather might still have understood the life *his* son chose – Yam's parents lived in a commune where work and property occupied a strange grey zone – one doubts if he would have understood the life Yam has chosen for himself. He still lives in the same place he grew up in, though the commune is no longer current. The land was divided up between the original members and so there is a small house he now owns. Yam never went to university. He studies at his own pace, he does a lot of manual work at minimum wages, and he has a large number of Arab friends. Labourers, with whom he's shared countless smokes and sorrows. He has seen their poverty up close. That has made him dubious about Israel's politics, its king-sized nationalism. Yam is Israeli alright but distances himself from Zionism. He has made his peace with the violent history of his people.

'Both of you did army service though?'

'Oh yes,' Yam says, laughing. 'Long ago. We are not that young.'

'Is there no way to get out of it?' I ask, persisting.

Tally thinks for a moment. 'See, there are some who go abroad immediately after school. The understanding is that they won't come back to Israel ever. If there are valid medical grounds, psychiatric reasons maybe, one can get out of the army. But for the rest of your life you will have to explain to employers why you did not get drafted. Not good for the CV. But though I have been in the army, later on, when I was in university in Tel Aviv, I went to peace marches and signed petitions.'

I smile as I remember my phase of peace marches in college.

'What were you marching about?' S asked. 'Nuclear weapons?'

'I seem that type, no?' She laughs. Then she looks earnest again. 'We were mostly protesting inequality. The state of Arab Muslims in Israel is, how shall I say, not very *worthy*. They are not given access to many kinds of jobs. It is humiliating.'

'Access to white-collar jobs you mean?'

'That's right. That's not the only form of inequality though.'

'Aren't they 15–16 per cent of the population?'

'Yes, and that too is a big concern with many Israelis. They are afraid Israel will get swamped by Arabs. Arab women have three or four children each while the Jews maybe have one or two.'

'Jewish women, very clever,' Yam says. 'Unless you make at least 7,000 shekels per month, they won't marry you or have your kids!'

'Yam,' says Tally, looking at me, 'is full of shit. But what I was saying is that the fertility rates of Bedouins in the Negev and Sinai are very high. So I actually know of some Jewish groups who are actively converting them to Judaism.'

It is around ten-thirty and the Bhatias are getting antsy. The clatter of utensils from the kitchen is getting louder by the minute. The restaurant has cleared out, and the cheque has been lying on our table awhile. We get up and, after one or two final anecdotes about the beauty and nobility of Australia, we are allowed to collect our change, leave a tip, and walk back to our room where dessert awaits.

The orange walls of our room hold the light in a way that makes it seem expensive and warm. The dessert is unveiled – it draws claps of delight from Tally – and divided up. (For some reason, during the fight, when we were both starving, neither of us had remembered the gateaux.) And then, over the next few hours, we eat the chocolate bombs and trade stories. They are narrated, like stories are told at night, with breaks and corrections and liberal doses of drama. Half a story here, then some personal anecdote, a bit of 'we-are-not-a-couple-but' on the part of Yam and Tally, and then the rest of someone else's story. At one point, S insists on checking three facts on the laptop since his story is packed with historical detail. Yam demands a personal mystical story and suddenly my mind draws a blank, so I root around my in childhood closet and tell him the one story that my mother would tell me, and every time she finished, her eyes would be bright with tears. It is impossible to recreate that conversation or the effulgence of that night here. I am not even going to try. What I am going to do is simply tell the four stories here.

Saurav's Story or How Jaisalmer Was Sacked Two-and-a-half Times

The first part of the story goes back to AD 1294, when Rawal Jethsi was on the gaddi of Jaisalmer, and Alauddin Khilji reigned in Delhi. Jethsi's brave sons heard rumours of a great treasure caravan passing via Bakhar, 1,500 horses and 1,500 mules, laden with valuables. This was actually the tribute of Tatta and Multan to Delhi, but en route, the sons of Jethsi ambushed the convoy and made off with the treasure. Alauddin Khilji was furious at this and his army marched upon Jaisalmer. When Rawal Jethsi heard that the army from Delhi was camping at Anasagar, Ajmer, he sent the children, elderly and sick, together with some troops to a safe haven deep inside the desert and applied a scorched earth policy to the countryside surrounding Jaisalmer. All the small towns were laid barren. The Rawal, with his two elder sons and 5,000 warriors remained inside the fort to defend it from inside, while his grandson Deoraj and great-grandson Hamir, a mighty warrior, led an army that would deal with the attackers outside. The sultan, meanwhile, remained in Ajmer and sent a great force of Khorasanis and Kuraishes in steel armour, who, according to the bards of Jaisalmer, 'rolled on like the clouds in Bhadon'. A fierce battle ensued. There were casualties on both sides.

The siege of Jaisalmer lasted eight years.

During this time, Ratansi, the younger son of Rawal Jethsi, formed a friendship with one of the prime leaders of the adversaries, Nawab Mahbub Khan. Every day at dusk, they would meet under a khejra tree, between the advanced posts, and play chess. Their heroic courtesy towards each other is the stuff of legends. After the death of Rawal Jethsi, Mulraj ascended the throne. Skirmishes escalated into a renewed attack, and this time, the besiegers had sufficient reinforcements at hand and were able to impose a complete blockade of the fort. The Bhattis, facing certain defeat, decided there was no alternative but to perform a sacrifice or sakha. The brave queens did not hesitate and gave instructions for a giant pyre to be prepared. Approximately 24,000 women took their lives, most on the pyre, while many embraced the sword. The brothers, having borne witness to this unimaginable horror, now prepared to die in battle. They bathed, prayed, gave gifts to the poor, wore the salgram around their necks, and along with 3,800 warriors awaited dawn when the sultan's army would arrive.

Ratansi had two young boys, Gharsi and Kanar, the eldest not yet twelve. He wanted to protect them from the terrible fate of Jaisalmer and so he appealed to his courteous foe. Nawab Mahbub Khan sent two of his most trusted servants to receive the boys, in trust, and appointed two Brahmins to take care of them. (Many years later, the brave Gharsi would, through services rendered to Delhi, win a grant from the then sultan, as well as permission to re-establish Jaisalmer.)

In battle, every one of the Rajputs fought like a hero and every one of them embraced death at the hands of the enemy.

The royal garrison kept the fort for two years, after which they blocked up all the entrances and abandoned it. It remained in that state for several years until reclaimed by a Bhatti chief, Duda, who was later elected Rawal. Duda was aided by his brave brother Tilaski, who quickly extended the sway of Jaisalmer over its neighbours. It was Tilaski who carried off the prize steed of Sultan Ferozeshah from a camp in Ajmer, and this led to another disastrous attack on Jaisalmer. The siege led to the second sakha of the prophecy, the suicide of 16,000 women and the death of Rawal Duda and Tilaski, together with 1,700 warriors, only ten years after coming to power.

The half sacking of the prophecy occurred in the sixteenth century, and is arguably the most tragic. An Afghan chief by the name of Amir Ali obtained Rawal Lunakaran's permission to let his wives visit the famous queens of Jaisalmer. But it was a ruse. Instead of Afghan queens arriving in the retinue of palanquins, there were hundreds of armed warriors. This took the guards of the fort entirely by surprise, and a skirmish broke out. When it seemed to the Rawal that he was fighting a losing battle, he chose to kill the women with his own hands as there was no time to arrange a funeral pyre. In an instance of extreme tragic irony, immediately after the deed was done, reinforcements arrived, thus snatching the men from the jaws of death, and Amir Ali was defeated. This was the half jauhar of the prophecy.

And that is how Jaisalmer was sacked two-and-a-half times, and thousands of women embraced terrible deaths voluntarily.

Yam's Story or How to Sell Reproductions of Old Masters

I will tell you a story from our life. You have been asking, Devapriya, how Tally and I met? This is how. After my army service was over, I drifted for a while. I did some manual labour, saved a little money. But not enough to get away and travel, like I am doing now. Then a friend told me about this agency that was looking to hire new people for a gig in western Europe. I liked the idea of being able to travel in Europe. My friend had worked there. Apparently, the job was very simple. He did not give me too many details. I went for the interview, it did seem reasonably simple and I joined up. The company had one branch in Berlin and one in Dublin.

Now let me tell you what the job was.

Paintings of old masters – Breughel, Botticelli, Titian, da Vinci, etc., were shipped in bulk from China very cheaply. Painters in China, art college graduates as well as talented street artists would make these oil paintings on standard-sized canvases. Our job was to read up on art so we could talk about it knowledgeably. We then walked around the city, one or two canvases slung to our backs. We went door-to-door and told people we were poor artists from Israel (it was important we highlighted the Israel/Jewish bit) and had come to study at the local art college. Things are so expensive that we could not make ends meet; so we were trying to sell some paintings. Would they at least take a look at our work? Even if they did not buy anything, we would not mind. Sometimes just talking about art is enough for us. One canvas is for 100 euros. After all, I am an artist. I am not selling a poster or something mass market.

Every time we made a sale, out of 100 euros, we kept 70 euros and gave 30 euros to the company. Business was not bad. We grew into our artist lives, added many details. In Berlin, you know, in most households, we were invited inside and then apologized to. On behalf of the family, the city, the country. They apologized for what had been done to us.

After a while, this job got to us and we quit. But apparently the company is still in business. This is the story of how a globalized chain can work efficiently, once it identifies pressure points in people. Right?

Tally's Story or How the Courtesan Made the King Bow

I'll tell you this lovely little story I heard in Jaisalmer. We had a nice guide. Once, I asked him, 'Why is India so dirty?' He said, 'Oh, very simple.' (This guy said 'very simple' a lot, as though all questions put to him were from an examination paper.) 'In the past, people used to eat on plantain leaves and drink in mud glasses. They would throw these away, and no problem. But now, plastic plastic plastic everywhere. Not bio-degradable like leaves and mud so you see so much rubbish.' Anyway, this is just an aside, not my main story.

So, opposite Gadi Sagar, there is a beautiful arch, right? You must have seen it today. It was built by a famous courtesan of the city. When she first planned to have it constructed, the king refused permission, saying that he would have to bow his head under the arch to go to the tank and this would not look good since she was but a courtesan. When the king was away, the courtesan had the arch constructed anyway, and had a statue of Krishna installed on top so that the king could not tear it down. This is the true story of 'Tilon ka Pol', and the arch is still there for people to admire.

D's Story or How to Conquer a Fear of the Forest

Once there was a poor little boy who lived with his mother in a tiny house by a forest. The father had died, and mother and son had no one but each other. The mother worked all day as a maid in people's houses to make ends meet. She had to leave home at dawn, before school time, so the little boy would have to find his own way. Now that he was six years old, he was supposed to go to the main paathshaala in the village on the other side of the forest. And though in the afternoon his mother would pick him up from school and walk back with him, early in the morning he would have to cross the forest on his own. It was a harrowing experience. The forest, thick with undergrowth after the rains, was dark and gloomy even when it was a bright sunny day. Strange sounds assailed him from all sides: crickets whistling all day long, mad unfamiliar birds shrieking, the cry of monkeys and the silent roar of dangerous animals he could hear in his head. Even the waterfall was scary. It seemed to rush down at great speed and call out to him like a siren. He screwed his eyes shut to conquer his fears and then banged into trees. Only he knew how his heart pounded heavily as his footsteps creaked on twigs, and the sounds of shadows chased him from all sides. Every evening, the boy would beg his mother to not let him go to school alone. The poor single mother had greater worries than imaginary fears. 'You'll get used to it,' she kept telling him. But after ten days in a row, when the boy cried bitterly that he was so afraid he could never cross the forest alone, she gave in. She told him, 'Okay, tomorrow, when you are in the forest and you feel afraid, call Madhusudan Dada.'

'Who is Madhusudan Dada, Ma?' the boy wiped his eyes and asked.

'Oh, he's a very kind man. He is a friend to those who need him. Call him and he'll come.'

Silently, the mother wiped her eyes and cursed that husband of hers for having died and left her alone, so needy. And the boy – oof, the boy – but at that thought she bit her tongue and stopped herself.

The little boy, however, reached the forest skipping the next day. Who knew in so many years that he had a relative? A *kind friendly* relative?

But he didn't call the man immediately, of course not. Now that he knew he had someone, he did not cheat. It was only when he encountered one of those cold spots in the forest, when the blood in his veins seemed to cool rapidly and an icy wind blew in from nowhere, did he close his eyes and call out loudly, 'Madhusudan Dada, I am not cheating. I am really afraid. Please, please come. I am alone.'

Madhusudan, of course, was none other than Lord Krishna. The slayer of the demon Madhu – Madhusudana. And one of the things about Krishna is, if someone calls out with such faith in him, Krishna must come.

A warm hand held the little boy's palm. But the little boy was not afraid. His eyes were shut, he ought to have started and jumped, but somehow he knew his cousin had arrived. Every morning, from that day, Madhusudan Dada would traverse the forest path with him. They would chat, they would laugh. Sometimes the little boy would hope that Madhusudan Dada would accompany him all the way to school, but that never happened. At the edge of the forest, Madhusudan Dada took his leave.

Every evening, while walking back together, the boy would regale his mother with stories of Madhusudan Dada. If she was worried about his new imaginary friend, she did not show it. At least he was happy.

Seasons turned. Autumn became winter when the animals slept, and then, soon, spring was in the air. Over the months, the boy had learnt many lessons. He had become the keeper of forest secrets and lore. The forest was now his home. Every leaf, every flower was familiar to him. Madhusudan Dada had taught him to communicate with the animals and birds and trees. He understood what power was hidden in the waterfall's rush and rumble that smoothened the pebbles on its sandy bed until they gleamed like precious stones. The boy had forgotten fear.

On the day of Basant Panchami, the schoolmasters planned a festive gathering. Every boy in his class of twenty was to bring something from home to contribute to the feast. Some would bring fine rice, some would bring specially flavoured dal, the rich boys had volunteered to bring enough ghee to cook for everyone, and vegetables too.

Once again, the little boy and his mother were in a quandary. It was the end of the month and she had no money to spare for such frivolities. She cursed that absent husband of hers silently, and when the boy whined about his prestige in class, she told him in her anger to ask his Madhusudan Dada.

Fortunately, there were still two days to the grand affair. When the boy told Madhusudan Dada about the festivities – and the food he had to take – Madhusudan Dada paused for a minute. Then he smiled and said, 'Okay, I'll manage something tomorrow. Don't worry.' That day, while walking, both were pensive. The little boy seemed to feel they were coming to the end of this camaraderie; he felt angry that his mother had made him complicate this perfect friendship with a stupid demand. Madhusudan Dada too was unusually quiet. But then they had traversed every inch of the woods together – there was nothing new to say.

The next day, the day of Basant Panchami, Madhusudan Dada was late for the first time. The boy sat by the waterfall, waiting patiently. The animals came out of their corners and waited with him. The birds were quiet. Finally, almost when the boy was about to give up hope, Madhusudan Dada arrived. The boy's face lit up. 'Oh no,' Madhusudan Dada said, 'I wasn't going to let you down. And yes, I've got your thing.' They started walking together, footsteps in tandem. 'You aren't afraid of the forest any more, right?'

The boy looked at Madhusudan Dada in consternation. 'Why do you ask?'

'Because I think you've grown a little older now. You can understand what the sounds of the forest mean – when the earth is hungry, when the animals are scared, when the trees at the outer reaches of the forest are afraid that cruel people will come and uproot them from their homes.' They had reached the edge of the forest. Madhusudan Dada handed him a little mud container, a tiny thing, filled with sweetened curd. The boy's heart sank. This little thing? He would be laughed at for sure. He wanted to run away home immediately. He felt terribly embarrassed that Madhusudan Dada had even thought of bringing this. Oh God, this meant Madhusudan Dada was just as poor as them.

But Madhusudan Dada was looking hard at him. 'Don't worry,' he said. 'This will be enough. And always remember, I am with you even if you can't see me.'

In school, the cruel children began to point and chuckle the moment they saw the boy entering with his modest mud container. The teachers too had no kind words for him. After they had eaten to their fill, they jeered at him and a teacher said nastily, 'So every boy brought enough food for everyone, but this cheapskate could only bring enough for one person. Have it yourself then!' He upturned the entire sweetened curd on the boy's banana leaf.

After he lifted the mud container and made to throw it away, he saw it was full. In a state of shock, he upturned it on the next plantain leaf – and this time, even the others saw – when he lifted it up, it was full again.

There was great cacophony. 'Who has given you this? Who has given you this?' the masters cried out, and the students scattered in fear. The teacher caught him by his neck and began to scream about black magic and tantra. Suddenly, there was a flash of light and in one clear instant, everybody saw Madhusudan Dada in his royal regalia, the chakra in his hand. The master fell to his feet.

The boy ran out of the school and into the forest. All day he sat by the waterfall. Silent tears ran down his cheeks. One by one, the animals came near him and sat around his feet. When evening began to creep in, he wiped his face and began to walk back home. He knew now who his friend was. He also knew he would never be able to call Madhusudan Dada with the sort of faith he had six months ago – the faith of a child afraid of the dark forest. He had grown up.

This is the story of Madhusudan Dada and the boy. I do not know the source – perhaps it was handed down by my grandmother. My mother would tell me this story, often, because, as a child I was fearful of everything and everybody. I cried in the school bus every day, the moment my house vanished from its view. I cried in school where everything was strange and extremely difficult for me, the studies, the friendships, the large rooms in the hundred-year-old buildings which seemed full of cold spots and ghosts. I know this is not the sort of story you wanted, Yam, but somehow it is this story that you get. In India we say about food that every grain has the eater's name on it; I think it is true of the stories we hear as well.

Six

How to Survive Madna

Dhrubo exhaled richly out of the window, and said, 'I've a feeling, August, you're going to get hazaar fucked in Madna.' Agastya had just joined the Indian Administrative Service and was going for a year's training in district administration to a small district town called Madna.

...

... Menon picked up his papers from the table. 'Have you read this?' He handed Agastya a large green book, Ruth Prawer Jhabvala's *Heat and Dust*. 'I borrowed it from the Collectorate Library because I was told it was about an Assistant Collector's life in the British days. But it's not really about that.' Agastya flipped the pages. Many passages were underlined; all of them seemed to be about an Assistant Collector touring in the early morning to avoid the title. Comments in red ballpoint in the margin: 'Not necessary these days to wear sola topee. Relic of the raj. The bureaucracy to be Indianized,' and 'Difficult question. An officer's wife *should* mix with others, but without jeopardizing the dignity of office.'

'Someone's been scribbling in the book,' said Agastya.

'Yes, I thought I should put down what I feel strongly about so other readers have at least a choice of opinion. Otherwise, they might think that even now this is all that goes on in an Indian district.'

–Upamanyu Chatterjee, *English August*

25

Can I go to the German Bakery?
What?

It's just across the road. There. Beyond the cows crossing. You can see it, right? I'll just rush there and be back in two.

The bus is going to leave *any* minute now.

Uff. It's *the German Bakery*! I must go there once. You can ask the bus to wait.

You know it doesn't work that way. What if the driver doesn't understand my Hindi? We'll be in a pickle. The rucksacks are locked up so I can't even get down from the bus. Why don't you wait a bit? We can buy cake in Barmer. I bet there's a fancy bakery there. You might even get Dundee cake.

Dundee cake?

Well, yes, there's the whole Cairn Energy angle. The Scots are all over Barmer.

26

If you must reach Barmer on a winter noon, you will see, on the way from Jaisalmer, slim dry trees and dark scrub on either side, the sere vegetation cleanly outlined against the sky.

The bus will stop several times en route. Whenever a melee of sheep, goats, buffaloes and donkeys take over the road, you can only shut your eyes and try to recall a map. *Where* is Barmer? And then you remember seeing it on that large map of Rajasthan in Bikaner House, a tiny dot very close to the border.

Barmer doesn't show up on a regular India map anyway; it's neither large enough, nor special enough. The start-stop-start-stop bus makes you sleepy. You haven't had any breakfast; you are annoyed because you have been cheated out of your desert safari (and your cake). You look out of the window the whole way, and the cold makes your nose sore. You see large windmills on the horizon, gigantic contraptions of steel, and then you hear a brief lecture on base-load generation from your co-traveller, who you thought was fast asleep. You spot a shop called 'New Kheteshwar Fancy Store And Mobile Centre' and you get this overpowering urge to stop the bus and get down and buy a keepsake from there; butterfly hairclips, a little tin of face cream. A large party of local men sit outside, in chairs and khatiyas, drinking tea. (New Kheteshwar also advertises tea, coffee, tiffin and sweets made of desi ghee and Bengali mawa.) All the men seem to be in their forties; most favour white turbans, though one or two wear bright yellow and dull red ones; a jaunty sort wears a blue skullcap; there is only one young chap without headgear but his leopard-print earmuffs are arresting. You get a fleeting impulse to do something to shock them – but it passes. You are, in general, a respectful sort.

Past Kheteshwar, you suddenly observe the sand turning pale gold, endless patterns running through it. Perhaps you could rent a whitewashed little room somewhere nearby, you begin to think, one side opening on the bazaar, the other opening on to the sky and the fine gold sand. You could write. He could write. You would have nothing in the whitewashed room but the iron frame of a bed and one writing table each.

And then you see the thin women by the road. Buying robust vegetables with their husbands, accompanying schoolchildren with pigtails, carrying five pots of water on their heads; all of this with their faces carefully covered with the ends of saris or dupattas or hijabs. In one sweep you move the whitewashed room with the piercing sky in the window to the outskirts of Pushkar. After all, Pushkar also has bookstores. *And* that ravioli place. Then you give up the idea altogether. Too precious.

At one point, you start when he suddenly gives a low growl of joy next to you and snatches the camera from your hand. You hadn't even realized he was awake. He rushes to the front of the bus where there is a flower-filled altar and returns after a few minutes. You are about to say something cutting about his drooling on your sweater when you notice the thing on the road he must have seen.

'What *is* that?' you ask.

He looks at you, stunned. As though it is supremely weird you don't know what it is. 'It's an M-46,' he says, finally. 'Isn't it *beautiful*?'

You are confounded by the choice of word. Blocking the way is a giant olive-green mechanical device with humongous tractor wheels and barrels that stick out. It's manned by several military men. The military men sport an air of great smugness atop their vehicle while a bunch of rustics surround it, petting its surface as though it were a large domesticated elephant.

He looks at your face and says, his voice turning fractious, 'It's a 130 mm Soviet-origin artillery gun. Don't look at it like a *Guardian*-reading peacenik would. Learn to see it with geopolitical eyes. Tech-loving eyes.'

'With the eyes of boys viewing toys, you mean,' you reply darkly.

Finally, the bus enters Barmer. The conductor, pen stuck behind his ear, flops into the first row, raises his feet on the iron bars in front and begins to count the money. You observe the government buildings – pale yellow two- or three-storeyed structures, built to last, and with some sense of symmetry. You know that exact copies of these buildings appear across India; everywhere, they are cool in summer and warm in winter and the fight against dust can never be completely won. You know the square rooms with large ugly furniture still sport fridges (unplugged) where files are stacked and walls with calendars feature folk dances from different states of India. You allow yourself a smile.

The mai-baap of Barmer also live on this street, which is well laid out and free of garbage dumps, a minor version of the Civil Lines of, say, Gorakhpur or Allahabad. The bus rolls down this street slowly, in deference to its mighty residents – several haunted-looking supplicants disembark here, clutching cloth bags and old files – and the bus turns into the haphazard madness of town. It deposits the last few passengers near the railway station. With that slightly hollow, slightly acidic feeling in your stomach that precedes hotel searches, you alight and queue up to claim your bags.

Afterwards, as you walk towards the central business district, you realize you've been had. This is Madna. The likelihood of a fancy bakery – or any bakery for that matter – here is dim. You glower at your co-traveller. He attempts to be conciliatory, and leads the search for a hotel. You need a bathroom soon. If one were to go by the formula, he is thinking aloud, next to you, the hotels ought to be here. In every town like Madna, the station is fairly close to Civil Lines, and the hotels are near the station. So there. The mighty and the seedy are separated by a factor of one.

The shops are cramped and shabby – full of furniture and utensils and general stuff people buy – and they merge in your head into a general picture of the India of newspaper stories and growing-demand reports. On either side, the street fades into very dusty stretches. The litter does not bear any logic of distribution, it is everywhere. There are cars, autos, rickshaws, handcarts, trucks and a couple of camels jamming the street; stray dogs and thin men skip through this traffic with remarkable dexterity. Their faces are impassive. You see the dust rising in fine clouds as you stomp in their wake, the weight of your rucksacks making your tread heavy. Even now, in January, you can imagine the heat that will bake these buildings and streets in summer, when the sky is stretched white and taut. You know that this is what your big project is all about – the heat and dust that the goras have written about for decades and every mention of which these days makes your skin crimp in rage. Here you are; and all you can think about is cake.

The street with hotels on either side is indifferent to tourists. There is no attempt at prettification anywhere. Barmer, now a boom town itself, has no aspirations to Rajasthan's usual employment bonanza: tourism. Yes, there is a fort tucked away somewhere on the outskirts. True, there are artisans who do some sculpting and furniture design. But Barmer has no truck with the sort of goras who go gaga over forts and sculptures, and want to wear hardy cotton and make their pounds or euros last for long months. The only goras you find in Barmer come to drill oil – they have money and they do not hesitate to throw that money around. The off-licences in these parts stock the priciest of whiskies for them from Islay. Barmer has no tools to classify you either – a couple who do not look married, wear distressed jeans and rucksacks – and frankly, Barmer does not particularly care for your attitude to life, all this book business.

If you came fresh out of engineering school, hired by L&T and

Cairn, well, that would signify something. You would wear that newly minted look of having made it. After serving time here, you would be posted in Africa and paid in hundreds of thousands of dollars. Along with other sensible chaps, you would come to Barmer, flush with new salaries and post-college freedoms, hire the best rooms in these hotels, the suites with ACs (always pronounced soots, as in Madna) and TVs which beam two hundred channels. But bedraggled and slightly vague, you come across as non-serious people. Barmer hotels do not have a policy for you.

You walk down the street, pop into each reception, suffer some degree of slight somewhere (though the spouse thinks you are being oversensitive), feel revulsion at least in three of the five toilets you see, and finally, you double back to the first hotel you had left in a huff. It has an egregious government look. Seascapes in the lobby and a plastic slab lined with a thin sponge cushion passing off as sofa. It is very expensive. Four hundred plus taxes. You have no choice but to accept their surly room. The room service menu offers a variety of flower dishes: flower pakoras, flower parathas and chilly flower. You cave in and order flower parathas apiece.

'There's one strange thing,' the spouse tells you, taking off his shoes. 'There's no signal on my phone at all.'

You sigh and begin to fiddle with the phone, getting it to manually search for network. The gobi parathas arrive with a very ugly cup of coffee after a quarter of an hour, but the mobile signal continues to be elusive.

Saurav

After we have walked in the pitiless town for an hour, though not as far as the low hills in the distance, I ask a passing autowallah if he will give us a tour of the dunes. He agrees promptly. 'Rupees one hundred and fifty for everything,' he says. I do not argue. D has been glowering for a day and a half now over the desert safari we could not have afforded at all. She hesitates, wavering between holding on to her injury and embracing this, the second-best option. Smartly, I tell her, 'If you hop in right away, we might even make the sunset.'

27

Whatever romantic notions I might have had about gambolling in the sand vaporize once we get there. The desert here is a succession of tall sand mountains. Make no mistake, it's phenomenal. But just the sight of it makes one's back sing like a canary.

Our autowallah leads the way, striding up the sandy slope casually. He is Ramaram Mali, son of Motiram. This information was printed in neat letters behind the driver's seat, along with his address and phone number. White letters on calf rexine. He had played tourist guide pretty efficiently, offering trivia on the various highlights of Barmer. Except for an elaborate ear stud, Ramaram is dressed formally, like an office-goer. White shirt and brown trousers. He has a slight paunch, so his brown belt sags though the silver-coloured buckle has been polished lovingly. He wears formal oxfords, and as he clambers up almost effortlessly, I can see the dark brown socks that cover his ankles. S follows, competently if not effortlessly, looking back from time to time, affecting concern. I flail in the sand, wavering and sinking, my bag and jacket pulling me down, first this way, then that. I struggle in my beloved desert and I swear at S under my breath, until finally, I learn the trick. You just have to be light on your feet and slice through the sand to keep walking. Don't stop. Power on. By the time I climb the first dune, the full red sun is hovering on the horizon, ready to drop. I stop and try to catch my breath. Ramaram is talking expansively.

'My father was basically a farmer though he worked as a chowkidaar. We are many generations from a village close to here. By caste, we are the same as chief minister Gehlot-ji. Many people voted for him from our place. When I was young, we were poor, though we never thought of ourselves as poor, and neither were we the poorest in our village. We had a little land. In those days, my mother had to walk for two-three hours every day at dawn to get water. All the women used to go together, in a group, to fetch water. When we were children, we used to run along with them. In summer, you see, dawn is the most beautiful part of the day. It is cool, and when first light breaks through the night, you feel lucky.

'The water situation is better now. In summer, we would remain in somebody's house all afternoon, talking, talking, talking. We used to go to the *rait* after sunset, before it became dark. There was no electric lighting in those days. When it was dark in the desert – and no moon – it was, like, fully black. You heard spooky stories. I went to school for a few years. From school, we'd come and play in the sand for hours. The dunes began at the edge of the village.

'Now Barmer has grown so quickly, like a teenage boy, always hungry and shooting upwards every night, so quickly that some land I had bought near the village many years ago for five hundred rupees is now inside proper Barmer. And its price? I can't say for sure, because I am never going to sell it, but going rates for land in Barmer are three lakh for a bigha. This is where I live now, with my wife and three children. I have built another house on this plot, a nice two-storey house and I've given it on rent to L&T. Two of the L&T officers are from your Bengal only. I will put ACs in this house soon. Then the rent will go up two times at least. I get 10,000 rupees now. Ever since these oil people started coming to Barmer, we've struck silver, sir. Anybody who had *any* land has become a somebody. There is great demand for houses on rent.'

S discusses other details of the boom economy – inflation, how the land grab is taking over whatever few green fields there are, social implications thereof ... I begin to walk towards the doughty thorny trees that grow here, mainly as small shrubs, but sometimes growing so tall that you can actually sit below them. There are several of these trees. Roeda, Ramaram tells me the name later. The wood is used to build doors. It is soaked under water for a year. I sit under a tree. All around me is a sea of sand marked by undulating patterns of wind. The sky is slate-coloured and the setting sun has torched an entire swathe to the west. Under that half-red, half-slate sky, it is possible to feel alive and humble in a way I have never felt before. I skip back and request Ramaram to take a photograph of the two of us.

Afterwards, Ramaram asks, 'Sir, you must be rich, no?'

We laugh. We tell him the bare idea of the journey.

'Okay, so you are not rich but you are educated. That's the thing.'

We begin to walk. He tells us about his eldest, the daughter, who is very bright. The boys are younger, not yet very serious about their studies. But he has plans for his children – big plans.

And then, he suddenly turns to us and says, 'Why don't you come to my house for dinner? I'll call my wife and tell her to expect guests.'

'Oh, well,' says S, unsurely.

What's there to be unsure about? I think. This is India. People are always inviting people over to their houses.

'We'll come,' I say brightly. 'Thank you very much.'

Ramaram walks away a few steps to call his wife.

'What the hell do you think you are doing?' S hisses at me in Bengali. 'We don't know him at all!'

'That's not true. We know his name, his father's name, his phone number and his permanent address. That's more than we know about, say...' I cast about for an appropriate example.

S interrupts me urgently. 'Don't joke about this. It could be dangerous. The phone is not working either.'

I say, 'Why are we on this journey, if not to meet people? Get to know them? Observe their homes, their family members. All writers must take risks. Plus, he seems such a nice man.'

S looks annoyed. 'I do not want this book to descend into these neo-anthropological studies that people turn India-books into. These long, detailed conversations with people, pegging them as interesting sociological categories, recounting their stories. One way or the other, it's anthropological. We have to be careful about this.'

'Uff,' I reply, 'first of all, this is going to be a book in the tradition of travel writing in the Indian languages. Those have such anecdotes all the time. Bengali travel writers are particularly keen on free meals. And this is a straightforward invitation to dinner. That's all.'

⟶

A couple of months after my MA finals, my friend Jiya and I were invited to present a paper at the American University in Paris. We planned feverishly for weeks and finally, one very windy summer morning, a couple of days before the conference, we found ourselves in a tiny room on Rue Denouette in the fifteenth arrondissement. The view from its small window, between two houses, was a sliver of Paris, all cobbled pathways and flower boxes. We were operating on an extremely tiny budget, chiefly on my account. Jiya is an heiress.

After we checked in, we decided to go for a short walk in the neighbourhood and procure a crepe bandage for Jiya who had sprained her foot while we were dragging our suitcases around, looking for our hotel. There was some dispute over the exact reason for the sprain. On a bench on the cobbled sidewalk were two kids who could not have been more that twelve, blue in the cold air, the girl in a short summer dress, the boy in a cotton t-shirt. They were kissing languorously. I continue to hold that it was from the shock of witnessing this that Jiya tripped.

There was a supermarket close to the hotel, the owner said. We walked there. At that hour, there were no other customers. The Algerian owner was thrilled to hear we were Inde and, though he had no crepe bandage, he babbled wildly for a couple of minutes and rushed out of the store, leaving us all alone. Now, Jiya is one of the prettiest women I know. She is also a very careful and law-abiding sort, given to quadruple-checking passports every other minute. She was most uncomfortable in these circumstances, and her fair face was getting redder and redder. I wandered around the shop, marvelling at the price of wine. A whole bottle for a euro and a half? Wow. Jiya stood stiffly at the door, praying fervently that no one would rob the store on our watch. Finally, the Algerian returned with a middle-aged Indian, his close friend. The man was tall, unshaven, and slightly heavyset. He shook our hands delightedly.

It turned out that Anil Mehra was a Dilliwallah, from Safdarjung Enclave. S and I had just moved into the first of our rented apartments, in Green Park. To Mehra, that made us practically neighbours. We chatted pleasantly and Jiya relaxed. Her face reverted to its natural colouring. Mehra had an import-export business selling bric-a-brac: bronze statues, cushion covers and other Indian exotica. His brother managed the India end of affairs from Delhi. He'd been in Paris almost fifteen years now. We asked him where we could find a pharmacy nearby. Unfortunately, Mehra told us, the crepe bandage would be difficult to secure since all pharmacies were closed on Sundays. However, what he *could* give us, because it's not every day that one meets one's Delhi neighbours in Paris, were a couple of passes to the Louvre. 'They're at home. Why don't you come with me? I live exactly one minute away.' Jiya had hobbled a few steps to stand behind Anil Mehra and was now signalling to me with her hands and eyes that I should immediately say no. Over the years, she and I had developed an elaborate telepathic code. I shot back, with my eyes, 'Oh c'mon, Jiya. It's the Louvre. Do you know how much tickets to the Louvre cost?' Jiya's hands and eyes now began to do a coordinated dance of death but I ignored her. 'That's a kind offer,' I said. Anil Mehra prattled on, oblivious to all this gesturing behind his head, 'Actually, a nephew and his wife had come from Delhi. I'd got these passes for them. But they were not too interested in the museum. I'd be very happy if you use them. Do come over. My son's visiting at the moment. He's thirteen. Oh, excuse me a second, I have to get some juice for him.'

'It's fine,' I say happily, slipping into Bengali. 'Let's go. *Nothing* will *happen.*'

'How can we trust him, D?' Jiya replied. 'It could be *exceedingly dangerous*. Saurav would not have allowed it.'

'That's why I have come with *you*,' I say, trying to seem all larky. 'No, really, it's fine. He's a decent man. His son is at home, didn't you hear?'

We followed Anil Mehra down the street, Jiya wearing an expression of pure horror. It was a nice respectable building. Mehra input the numbers of the security system and the large door swung open. There was a small lobby inside and we got into the narrowest elevator we'd ever seen. 'My son visits me on weekends,' Anil Mehra was saying. 'His mother is French. But she and I separated some years ago. You know, there are many cultural differences that cannot be overcome. In one's youth it seems easy. But later on, things change.' Jiya held her phone in her hand like a can of pepper spray. I tried to seem comforting as Mehra fumbled for his keys. 'Don't worry, Jiya,' I said in my trust-me voice. 'It'll be *fine.*'

We entered the hallway of a lovely Parisian flat, compact but elegant, overflowing with assorted junk jewellery and, in many different sizes, bronze statues of Nataraj, Ganesha and the Buddha, dancing girls and amorous conjoined couples. We sat in the drawing room, also overflowing with more of the same, where Mehra's son, a thin, pale boy was playing video games on TV. He nodded at us perfunctorily and poured himself juice. Mehra offered us juice, and this time Jiya took no chances. 'No, thank you,' she said, before I could open my mouth. Mehra busied himself looking for the passes. He looked through drawer after drawer, stashed with papers, while we stared politely at the TV. Secretly, everyone in the room was getting hysterical. Finally, he found the passes and handed them over to us with a big smile. We thanked him effusively and left. It took us a while to figure out how to leave the building, particularly because Jiya, now light-headed with relief, stopped to admire every single cornice in the lobby. We went to the Louvre the following day, and the passes not only saved us forty euros or so, which we could then spend in the museum shop and cafe, but we skipped the long queue and saved time. The moral of the story is that in all such situations that could either end very badly or fairly well, the key thing is to be born with a trustworthy gut and then, once the trustworthiness of your gut has been established, simply follow its guidance.

Years later, in Barmer, atop those dunes, I am reasonably sure that Ramaram Mali's invitation is perfectly in order, exactly like Anil Mehra's was. S, on the contrary, is not quite convinced. But the orange waves have now started to advance from the west. Under that flaming sky, the sand begins to glow. It is, in any case, long past the moment when one could have said no.

28

It is dark when we set out for Ramaram's house. The streets are mostly unlit, and traffic continues to be heavy and haphazard. S suggests we stop at a local chowk that is dazzling with shop lights. From a payphone, we call the parents. (In every new place, we make it a point to tell my father-in-law the name of the hotel we are in and a phone number. Just in case.) I buy chocolates for Ramaram's children.

There is a huge off-licence next to the kirana shop with the payphone, and it is almost mobbed. There are many people in trademark orange drilling suits, including two girls with severely straightened hair, the fluorescent strips of their jackets glittering in the strobe light.

We have now reached the edges of town. It is quieter.

'I will take you first to the house I have put on rent,' Ramaram says.

He parks the auto in a dark street. Sounds of prime-time television are drifting in faintly from neighbouring houses, and we follow him into a two-storey house that is so freshly painted, there are dried blotches on the floor and the hallway smells dizzyingly of paint. We take the stairs and Ramaram offers continuous commentary on every aspect of the architecture – the house has been designed almost entirely by him.

Upstairs, the main door is ajar and Ramaram walks in smartly. We hesitate by the doorway, since voices and laughter from inside indicate the residents are at home. Ramaram, however, does not think it is necessary to knock before barging in. He is the owner of the house – and apparently, he can bring people to show off anytime he likes. 'Come, sir, please come in,' he urges us. A man now comes out from a room on the right. He is a large balding man, with a massive beer belly. He is in a vest and shorts, a towel thrown over his shoulders, presumably the L&T Bengali. It is rather awkward. He is a little embarrassed – he's not dressed to receive visitors – and after Ramaram introduces us, he has no choice but to invite us in.

I try to hang back while S apologizes to the man in Bengali, but Ramaram will have none of this hesitation. He must show me the finer features of the house he has designed and I follow him inside. There is a fridge and a plastic table in this room; it's been imagined as a drawing/dining space, I guess. The Bengali takes S into the room on the right, and introduces him to the others. I can hear their voices. They are all middle-class men who have left their families behind to live like college students in Barmer. 'This place is not suitable for families,' I can hear one of them say. 'If there were townships, there could still have been a possibility. But good schools are very important – and one can't be sure about the schooling scene here.'

Meanwhile, Ramaram Mali busily switches on more lights. 'Madam, please observe the tiles,' he says. I look down. 'I chose them myself.' The tiles are rather pretty. White, with little pink flowers and elaborate vine trellises. I smile and praise his sense of aesthetics. He opens a door and takes me left, into the terrace. I catch my breath. The breeze is bracing, the dark not uncomfortable. Ramaram tries the lights here too and then clicks his tongue. Apparently, the bulb is fused. He quickly switches on the torch in his mobile and holds it close to the ground. 'Madam, I have tiled the terrace also. Later on, this can be another room. Demand for rooms is growing so fast in Barmer. I will put ACs in all these rooms before this summer.' In the narrow beam of the torch I see another set of pretty tiles – smooth ivory squares like slabs of white chocolate, dotted with ochre flowers. I admire them eloquently.

From the hall where I wait for S to join me, I can see the room the L&T men occupy, in the mirror that is stuck on the wall. It is a large characterless space. There are two steel almirahs in one corner, two single mattresses with grey pillows, and plastic chairs. Several bottles of liquor are neatly lined by size at one end. The tall vodka bottles, the squat whiskies, the small pints of rum. S takes leave of the three men, shakes their hands. We follow Ramaram downstairs – where we learn there are two rooms, each occupied by single men who work for one of the big companies – and then outside. All sounds seem to have dried up on that street now, though a couple of plastic bags are dragged along in the wind, and they leave a soft crackly imprint on the evening.

Ramaram's home is on this same five-hundred-rupee plot, but sort of back-to-back with this house. So we walk down the street, turn left, a few steps ahead, and then we enter a courtyard through a small gate at one end of the compound. It's like the second half of a revolving stage – if one part is Dushyanta's palace, the other is the forest with Kanva's hermitage. Two different worlds. It's almost as though the house for rent, with the tiles and the AC vents, is the new urban model, while the obverse is literally the village in miniature. It's an exact metaphor for the life that hundreds of thousands of Indians live.

The courtyard leads to a kitchen with a traditional chulha that is now being lit. Ramaram introduces us to his wife. She looks up from the chulha, where she has been poking the embers, a very calm-looking woman in a cotton lehenga and short kurta, both made of the same fabric, a cheery yellow sprinkled with little orange and white flowers. Her hair is covered with a matching orange dupatta. A few bangles, a simple mangalsutra, and there's a dot of red vermilion on her forehead. She is busy cooking, and asks us to sit in the other room. She promises to get dinner ready quickly though we assure her there's no hurry. Her calmness, her sense of self-containment make her an interesting foil to the hyperactive Ramaram. It seems to me that she likes humouring him, his stabs at urbanity, his obsession with the lives of his tenants. She does not mind cooking for his sudden flocks of guests. She loves him in a quiet self-contained way that fills this kitchen, the courtyard outside, with a sure stamp of happy domesticity. At this point, the children arrive – Ramaram's three, and a little boy from the neighbour's who has also trailed in to meet us. We gift them the goodies we have brought; fortunately, I have an extra bar of chocolate.

Ramaram's daughter is about ten years old. Bobbed hair and embroidered jeans. She holds my hand and takes us from the kitchen to another room. There are two boxy rooms on the other side of the courtyard, though only one is open. In the traditional rural style, the rooms too open onto the common courtyard, a style of architecture that has now gone out of fashion in cities where nobody would want to waste a single square foot on something as useless as a courtyard. Unlike the obverse house which has been lavished with attention and modern details, Ramaram's family home gives the sense of being slightly provisional. The roofing has not been completed yet – there are sheets of asbestos covering the rooms, weighed down by a large number of rocks; the walls are not plastered; the floors are not polished, let alone tiled. In one corner, where the wall has been painted yellow, there is an earthen surahi. It reminds me of my childhood holidays in Jharkhand, where we would interrupt our afternoon's play in the hot sun to drink glasses of cool water from a surahi. But other than that yellow portion, all the other walls are an indeterminate shade of grey. Ramaram seems to have left this zone alone (perhaps to approximate the dwelling they must have left behind in the village?) and concentrated his experimentations on the cash cow, the house they've put on rent, with its fancy tiles, its geyser, its concrete extravaganza. But this – this is home.

Outside, darkness has settled into a quiet night, broken by the song of crickets and the occasional strains of television wafting in. The room where we sit is dominated by a double bed with an elaborately designed headboard dotted with gilt. There is a calendar, a picture of a goddess, a wall clock and a chart illustrating yoga postures on the wall. Above these, just below the ceiling, there are two shelves that run along the room, across three walls. Many steel utensils are placed decoratively on the top shelf, at regular intervals, including the body of a mixer-grinder. Ramaram points and tells us that these had come as his dowry.

Tea comes with snacks: fried brinjals and til laddus. We invite the children to eat with us, but it seems they have already had dinner, and they prefer to watch us eat. Discreetly, Ramaram asks S if he would like some videshi. S smiles and says, 'Not today. Next time, perhaps?' Ramaram does not press. 'Sure, sure,' he says. 'Many times my friends come and we drink videshi here in this room. But we have to be careful. This neighbourhood is full of Bishnois and if they find out one is drinking or serving drinks, they will cause a massive halla. My father liked to drink. Once, these Bishnois came and smashed up all his bottles.'

Ramaram puts on a video. The small television set is in one corner of the room, next to a sewing machine, now covered carefully with a bed sheet. The children join us on the bed, and we hunker down to watch. It is an elaborately shot wedding video of Ramaram's cousin in Jaipur, the most impressive scion of the most urbane branch of their family. He works in a government bank and his salary is Rs 24,000 plus benefits. The groom sits on a white horse with a little boy in front, a ceremonial sword in hand. His face is covered with thin strings of flowers. A large party of women dance in front to Bollywood numbers, though their foreheads are dutifully covered with sheer chiffons, dupattas or ends of saris. Jewellery flashes.

We eat dinner in the kitchen. Once again, in Rajasthani style, we are served on the same plate. I remember reading that in Burmese custom, if a man and a woman eat from the same plate, they are considered to be married! S loves the bajra rotis, hot off the chulha. But there are regular rotis too, and Ramaram keeps repeating that they have become modern these days, and eat normal atta rotis like people in other parts of the country.

'Isn't bajra more nutritious?' S asks.

'That it is,' he says. 'It takes much less water to grow also. But bajra is old-fashioned.'

We talk about travel. Ramaram tells us how in these parts, travel for families is necessarily pilgrimage, and that, too, pilgrimage with a specific end in sight. But not for him, of course. At one time he used to drive a car, and he'd taken a couple across several tourist destinations. The details are very vague. One never finds out who this Sir and Madam were, or where they lived. But an album is procured, and we are shown the pictures. It's a modern couple, by all accounts, the woman in a tight red salwar set, the man in sunglasses. Ramaram has several pictures, striking poses in front of monuments. Once again, I see how loving his wife is – she shows me the pictures with a gentle pride, and I wonder if she had wanted to accompany him at all. 'Actually, I had thought of buying a car. But then, so much money went into building the house that I decided to buy an auto. It's the perfect size for my family. We can all go somewhere together. Quite easily. Doctor. Temple. Joyride. Whatever. And otherwise, I take it to town every morning after breakfast, and earn some extra cash. But basically I bought the auto to ferry my family around. Motorbike is not suitable for us.'

The subji is delicious, and we compliment her cooking. The vegetables have all been grown on their farm – and to us, city dwellers all our lives, there is great heartiness in that, an extra dash of flavour to the taste. Finally, Ramaram says that he is going to present the great delicacy of the evening. He squats next to us. He crushes a bajra roti with his hands, crumbles gur on it and then soaks it in ghee. This traditional concoction is to be shaped into little balls and eaten as afters. Politely, I try it, not expecting to like it – but it is delicious. At that moment, as the fugue of sweet and savoury flavours mix in my mouth, with the perfect oiliness of the ghee, the lights go off. Ramaram steps out of the kitchen where the glowing embers of the chulha cast strange shadows on the walls, and returns with a lantern. 'It is raining,' he reports. And sure enough, we can hear the light patter of rain in the courtyard and the roof above. The children are huddled between us, and Ramaram sits by the doorway. 'In these parts, they say, if meh and mehmaan come together – clouds and guests – it is going to bring good luck.'

Later, after the rain has stopped and we are on our way back to the hotel, in Ramaram's auto, the roads of Barmer will give off the scent of moist earth – that most stirring of Indian scents. In the hazy misted view, Barmer will grow into a dim familiarity: not the touristy high of Pushkar but the gritty tumble of the new that underpins the Indian story of the moment, and below that, like sand in shallows, a river of old certainties. It is ugly. It is beautiful. It is so far away. It is home. The night in the government room is cool and wet, and sleep comes with the soft clean weight of a clay wrap on the body, leaving us refreshed and new in the morning, smelling of leaves and twigs.

Saurav

'No, no, no, don't drop the gold. Hold on to it. Yes, I am sure. Haan bhai haan.'

Yet another bus; yet another bus depot full of jostling crowds and wandering buffaloes and dirty toilets and the sputter of oil into which samosas are being dropped two by two.

'If I'm telling you to hang on to the shares, you hang on to the shares. Who's the understudy, you or me?'

Once again, because we have come early, we get seats in the first row. This is a Gujarat State Transport bus, three seats on either side of the aisle, tickets to be purchased on board. D is by the window on the left. I am in the middle. The seat next to me is still empty.

'I am telling you, gold prices will continue to shoot up. Dump them a week later and see the munaafaa. Okay. Hmm. Hmm. Theek hai. Keep me informed. I am in a bus now. On the way to Sanchore. I'll see you day after.'

The man hangs up his phone and slips it into his pocket. A thin short guy with a sharp fox-like face, he is sitting in the first row, just across the aisle from me. He nods at me. His manner is friendly, curious. 'Sanchore?' he asks. 'Yes,' I say, 'though we are actually going to Palanpur in Gujarat.'

'Achchha, then you have to take a bus from Sanchore to Deesa, another from Deesa to Palanpur.' I nod. That is precisely the route I had worked out just a few minutes earlier in the bus stand. 'Why are you going to Palanpur anyway?' he asks. D had asked me this in the morning, though the rain in the night had softened her. She was not averse to staying on in Barmer either, but it was awful for the budget. We couldn't exactly filch dinners off people every night, I'd said. *Was so not filching*, she said, as she dried her hair with a towel after her bath.

The man and I are speaking in Hindi, though his is not the hard Hindi of Rajasthan but a rounder, softer version, with a Gujarati register. Before I begin to answer, his phone rings again.

'Bolo,' he says. 'Uhm hmm. Two khokhas? Oh-kay.'

The sun is shining brightly today. D shields her face with her palm. 'There's your enterprising Gujju taking over the world.' She nudges me softly, her eyes sparkling with mirth.

The young man is enterprising alright. His wiry frame vibrates with energy as he does some quick calculations in his head. He shuts his eyes for a second.

'Forget the gold for now and look at the silver and the chana. Arrey, baba, the chana, the soya beans.

'Sorry,' the man says, 'too many phone calls.' He slips the phone into his pocket, palpably self-conscious, and grins at me. It's a broad interested smile that extends to his eyes and makes his forehead taut. 'Myself Jignes Goradia.' He extends his hand across the aisle.

⌐

Jignes Goradia is a share broker, though neither senior enough, nor, in his own words, experienced enough to set out on his own. At least not yet. He works for a company that pays him eighteen thousand rupees a month as salary. Plus coverage for travel. Do we get paid salary while writing books? He asks this moot question, brows furrowed in genuine concern for our sanity.

Not a salary, no, D says, with that flicker of annoyance she reserves for people who ask us this question. But yes, the publishers do pay a small advance, she admits. But then, we are doing this to also see the country. 'Ah, okay.' His face is reflective for an instant. 'What is your caste?' he asks us then, as though the answer to this will help clear matters up. Apparently, it is okay for Brahmins to up and become writers, incurring such a fiscal loss.

The conductor appears and tickets are for a hundred and forty rupees each. He has a ticketing machine and smartly prints out stubs. A few more passengers get into the bus before the door is shut and a balding old man, wiping his face on a large checked handkerchief, comes and sits next to me.

'I have to travel very much for this job,' Jignes tells us, the words carrying over the new guy's head. 'Twenty or twenty-one days out of thirty, I am out on tour. I cover many parts of Rajasthan and Gujarat. Demanding job. But I enjoy it.'

'That's a lot of touring,' D says. 'Your wife does not mind?'

At the mention of wife, Jignes Goradia flushes slightly. 'She is herself busy,' he says finally. 'You see, I have twins.' At that his face becomes cocky again. Twins! Two for the price of one – that's got to be something. Love's dividend doubled. 'They keep her on her toes. It's a joint family also. Company is there. Help is there. After all, madam, travelling is the key in my job. The relation is what the customers remember finally. Profit or loss is one thing. Natural in business. But it's the relationship that counts.'

Travelling is an added feature in this old model of brokers' hard sell. I remember, long before everything went online, my father had been sold Reliance shares by a broker who did his business practically door to door.

Outside the window, there are deep leafy groves on either side of the road. A group of spotted deer frolic at the edges. When the bus passes by, they draw back and stand still.

'Our family – we are kanskaars by caste,' Jignes volunteers. 'Traditionally, we work with bronze. We have a small family shop. But nowadays it's not enough to stick to the old trades. One needs new avenues. I am slowly getting into futures trading – very exciting. Perhaps I can specialize in metal later. It's in my blood after all. Lot of money in that.' His eyes twinkle. Then he comes back to what we had been talking about. 'My wife is very intelligent,' he says, now comfortable with the subject. 'Got first class in graduation. Commerce.'

Lightly, I say, just as a talking point, 'Oh, then, perhaps you are waiting for the twins to grow up, so she can also start working?'

Jignes starts. His prominent Adam's apple bobs twice. Then he replies, lips stretched in a smile, 'If I suggest something like that, you know what my father will say? Have we men died that the daughter-in-law has to get a job outside? We are alive still and can fulfil all her requirements.'

My neighbour to the right changes the subject and begins to talk about one Bajrangdas Bapa of Bhavnagar. Have we heard of him? This is perhaps something of a colloquial habit across India, where some local guru or pir is randomly introduced into a conversation, followed immediately by a great deal of exclamation over the fact that we have not heard of this guru in the first place. ('You must have heard about Neki Mohammad-ji?' Polly's mother had asked. 'His name is known in Delhi also.')

I follow D's eyes to the front of the bus, and through the giant windshield we can see a peacock crossing the road regally, his plume trailing majestically on the road. The driver stops the bus and waits for the bird to cross.

Late afternoon, and the sun, much less potent, is now streaming in through Jignes's window with the ripeness reserved for the last daylight hour. He sits with his back to the sunshine, so his face is dark. Many people have got off on the way, and the bus, now literally lighter, is streaming along the smooth roads. We have talked in short bursts for almost the entire duration of the journey. In Jignes's opinion (he has an opinion on everything and I listen quietly, without interfering), the riots in Ahmedabad happened because the Muslims were doing well in business, so jealousy was rife. That jealousy was fatally misdirected. I do not make any comment. Jignes is not one to stick with any topic. He jumps from idea to idea, from place to place. The weather. The government. Travel. Food. Healthcare. But now that we are nearing Sanchore, he and I are both a little tired. For a quarter of an hour, we sit in silence.

'Are you carrying alcohol, sir?'

'No,' I reply.

'Of course, as a visitor in Gujarat, you are allowed to carry alcohol. But you have to register at the police station.'

'Right,' I say, 'but we're not carrying any alcohol.'

When, with a renewed roar, the bus crosses the Luni, I open my eyes. The river bed is almost dry and through the vast sandy stretches, a thin stream trickles singly. I shut my eyes again.

'Are you two married?'

I open my eyes and see D's face turned towards Jignes.

'Yes.' We both nod.

'Because the thing is, this Banaskantha district is quite dangerous for couples.' He lowers his voice theatrically. 'My friend was in a hotel in this area. It seemed like a good hotel, marble and stuff. But there were hidden cameras in the room. They had no idea obviously.' (He shifts from 'he' to 'they' without any explanation.) 'Everything was recorded. The next day the hotel people started blackmailing them. Finally, my friend had to pay one peti to get the reel back. That is why I'm telling you in advance. Do be careful.'

D immediately begins to scribble in her yellow notebook.

'Anything you need in Gujarat, any problem you have – though I'm sure there will be none – don't hesitate to call me. Because I tour so much, I have friends everywhere.' He gives me his card. The bus enters a bustling town area – and I guess the depot must be near. In any case, Jignes is going to get off in a few minutes. He has an arrangement with a hotel here – whenever he comes to Sanchore, this is where he puts up. We exchange a few final pleasantries. The man next to me has been carefully listening all the while, though he never joined the conversation, except that once, when he brought up Bajrang Bapa of Bhavnagar. He shakes my hand too though he is not going anywhere. Before disembarking, Jignes dangles his overnight bag and tells D, who's still writing, 'Madam, do think of my twins and family. Don't put me in some most wanted list or something!' Everyone laughs. He joins the queue to alight, his phone rings again, his gait becomes jaunty. 'Bolo,' he says. 'Oh Sir-ji? Hello-ji. I have just reached Sanchore. I shall come to your shop straightaway. Yes, yes, of course I've got the papers with me.'

As soon as Jignes is gone, the man next to me says urgently, 'My wife is a schoolteacher. One daughter is studying to be a CA, one daughter for the IAS, son in class twelve.' With the corner of his eye, he checks if D's scribbled that too. After that, he lapses into a genial silence once again.

I look outside. Jignes Goradia has disappeared into one of the hundreds of lanes, in one of the thousands of small towns in the country: marked by their billboards, rasping twilights, unevenly tarred streets, young men and old men standing in verandahs, with their elbows on the railings and eyes on the roads, girls walking past in twos. It has always wrenched me, these small-town dusks. At the back of my mind are two spools of photographs I know intimately but have no wish to sift through again. Dhanbad, my mother's hometown, where my grandparents lived, and where I had a few of the comforts of childhood – a jungly overgrown garden, long hot afternoons spent on a sofa, poring over colonial books filled with animals, to the sound of my mother and aunts laughing in low voices. And there was Jamshedpur, the place where we had a holiday home by the brown Kharkai. The house where my mother was happiest. After she died, we could not face going back there, so the flat was sold off. My grandfather's house in Dhanbad was anyway a government bungalow, meant to be returned to the institute – though it still stands on the ISM campus. Both places have been lost to me. But there is something about dusk in small towns, with their extenuating fear of both failure and success, which makes me feel darkly sentimental.

The bus has finally pulled into the depot. D has stood up and is already pulling our bags down from the overhead racks. Familiar noises stream in from outside. 'Looloolooloo,' she chants.

'We ought to grab a bite before taking the next bus,' I tell her, though the scent of dusk in the head is not easy to shake off. 'Those gobi parathas disappeared into the pit of my stomach long ago.'

'Flower parathas, you mean,' she corrects me.

This is Sanchore. At the border between Gujarat and Rajasthan. From here we have to go to Deesa.

'Deesa, Deesa, Deesa, Deesa,' a conductor screams on cue from a bus at the other end of the depot, but we are too tired to rush right away. That one's already too full. I stand beside one of the kirana shops, with rows and rows of Lays and Kurkure gleaming in their bright packs. The evening is pleasantly warm. Stars have already begun to appear in the mauve sky, though darkness is yet to fall. D tugs off her jacket and walks towards the toilets. I buy a bottle of water and wonder what we should eat, what we should do. Jignes suggested we stay the night in Deesa. He'd even suggested a hotel (without cameras apparently) – but I would rather go on to Palanpur, and find a hotel there.

By the time D returns from the loo, looking horrified as usual, I have one bit of trivia ready for her. 'Do you know who lived in Deesa for a while and even wrote about it?'

'Who?' she asks, lifting her bag on her shoulders, shuddering slightly at the imaginary smells she thinks she may have dragged along.

'Richard Burton,' I offer humbly.

'Really? That is, the explorer Burton?'

'Oh no. Liz Hurley's husband, Burton. Of course, yes, the explorer. There was a base of the Bombay Army of the East India Company in Deesa. Richard *Francis* Burton was posted here and conducted many of his travels in Sind and Gujarat from this base.'

'Huh,' she says, 'who would have known that?'

29

By some stroke of luck, there appears, at half past seven in Sanchore, a long-distance Volvo lookalike that is going to Ahmedabad. It will go via Deesa and Palanpur, the driver informs us gruffly, because we are badgering him at his window while other buses rev their engines threateningly around us. We rush round to the other side, and get into the bus, arguing about whether we ought to spend the night at Deesa – both Burton and Goradia add up in favour of Deesa – or go on to Palanpur, at Saurav's insistence, simply because it's in Gujarat, meaning we'll be finally done with Rajasthan. 'So you want to get there for purely psychological reasons?' I ask, dumbfounded. 'We have no idea which hotels might be available within our budget in Palanpur!'

However, the discussion remains inconclusive because once we're in the bus, we're slightly stumped. The seating arrangement is unlike any we've seen so far. On the left, there are a few regular front-facing rows with two seats each, all of them occupied, followed by one long side-facing bench. It is reminiscent of a few public buses in Calcutta that I used to take to college, before the low-floor JNNURM buses came to India. No. 240. Or 3C/2. There are luggage racks above these. To the right, however, are twin seats facing each other, and above, medium-sized bunks. It's what is called a sleeper coach (though if one were to be particular, this is only *half* a sleeper coach) and on other days, it might do an overnight journey from Ahmedabad to Junagadh. We find ourselves seats on the side-facing bench, and almost instantaneously, as the bus rumbles through the night, the people around – and above us – absorb us into their conversation. It begins with the question of exactly what we do for a living. After certain premises of that uncertain business have been established, they ask the particulars of salary one might receive from such ventures.

The men sitting around us are Gujarati petit bourgeoisie. They are immediately ready to share details themselves. One is a trader in potatoes, another supplies rice, a third is in the cloth business. They live on the outskirts of Ahmedabad and travel regularly to Barmer, even as far as Kheteshwar, on business. They are friendly and curious – and for those who do not read, what better way to pass the time travelling than conversation?

The rice trader, a small man with closely cropped hair and a butterfly moustache, remarks, 'We as a state have developed quite a lot. You know our CM? Narendra Modi-ji? He's the lion of Gujarat. One day, he will be lion of India.' He realizes that we are listening intently, and perhaps he is unsure of what the concentration writ on our features signifies. A gentle shadow flits across his face and he smiles sweetly. 'Of course,' he says, 'Rahul Gandhi is also coming up in a big way, showing a lot of promise.'

And here we encounter, perhaps, one of the most important traits that distinguishes the Indian mind from others: this tendency to be a pleaser when it does not cost anything. The rice trader votes for Modi, believes in Modi. But because he thinks that we might have a different political affiliation, he effortlessly slips in this praise of Rahul Gandhi that he does not mean, and if we choose to act on it, the conversation will proceed along other lines. It is one of the instances of the complex Indian moral compass: there is no harm, they think, in saying something if it makes the other person feel better.

So, most of the time, the Indian will tell you exactly what you want to hear, often with a pinch of Bollywood masala and jargon. A large number of foreign correspondents realize this only later (and often they do not necessarily care; the ones they want to cast as victims will exaggerate their victimhood for that particular story; for another story, they will be brave and undeterred by circumstance, as required). But westerners who come to do business certainly care – and often they are maddened by this addictive doublespeak. A British colleague in my former company, who had lived and worked in Delhi for a bit, used to say that when he approached people for something, say, a sponsorship, or to make a sale, they never said no to his face. They would always speak in birdsong: it sounds interesting; perhaps we should meet when my father/brother/CFO is present and talk in greater detail; you must come to my Diwali party. It drove him up the wall. All he wanted was for them to say no, so that he did not waste any more time with them. Eventually, he returned to Reading and an Indian was hired instead. The Indian interpreted the birdsong well, and spoke it himself.

Of course, when S says, eyes glinting wickedly, 'Ah yes, the promising yuvraj. We should have a coronation, no, for him?' the rice trader looks a bit discomfited. He changes the subject and looks at me. 'There are many decent hotels in Palanpur, madam. You will not have any problems. In fact, we will pass some hotels on this route only. You can get off at the doorstep.'

The man who has a cloth business and is sitting in one of the bunks upstairs is very interested to know about the places we have already covered, and the ones we hope to visit. 'What did you not like about Rajasthan, madam?' he asks me, and since he seems genuinely interested in an answer, I tell him the truth. 'The condition of women,' I say. 'Dowry and child marriage are very deeply entrenched evils. How will they go?'

A young man sitting behind comes and sits in front, presumably to chat. He says, 'But, madam, things have changed also. For example, my wife and my sister-in-law keep the gold they got at the wedding with themselves only, not with my mother, as it used to be in the past. You might consider the gold part of her dowry, but it is for herself only.' Back and forth, back and forth, I argue gently. They respond with sincerity. But it is too tedious to report.

Afterwards, the man who has a cloth business tells me: 'Madam, since you are writing a book, I would humbly urge you to put this in so that the public understands.' Immediately, my yellow notebook and pen come out and I listen attentively. He raises his voice as though addressing a public rally. 'Which sorts of insensitive fools have designed these iron ladders leading up to these bunks? How do they expect older people to climb up? Or ladies in saris? So tough. Or is it that they expect only young men will travel? Public awareness is required for these things, and only then will people design ladders that take senior citizens and ladies in saris into account.' He returns to his normal voice: 'Got it, madam?'

The bus stops at Deesa. We don't get off, but a very large number of locals get in, men in turbans and women in bright saris with their heads covered. Some grab the remaining seats. Others squat in the corridor between the seats, jabbering all the while. They have a very short distance to cover, they are saying. The traders, meanwhile, are busy dissecting our caste identities. 'Jha,' says the potato wholesaler, 'means Maithili Brahmin. Right? Then how come you are Bengali?'

'There is a story behind this,' S says. 'In the twelfth century, Bengal came under the rule of the Senas. The Senas were Andhra Brahmins who had become kshatriyas. Before the Sena rulers, for a long time Bengal was ruled by the Pala dynasty. The Palas were Buddhists, and though they never discriminated against their Hindu subjects, during the Pala times, the Brahmins of Bengal embraced the agamic traditions, a point where it came quite close to Vajrayana Buddhism. When Vallal Sena's mother passed away, he decided to do her last rites according to Vedic custom, thus symbolizing a reinjection of Vedic thought into the mainstream. Brahmins were brought in from two major centres of Vedic learning, Kanyakubja (or Kanauj) and Mithila. That is the time my ancestors would have migrated to Bengal.

'It is this same wave of migrations that would have brought my ancestors to Bengal from Kanauj. Kanauj by then was under the sway of the Delhi Sultanate after falling to Ghori in 1193. So the Brahmins of Kanauj migrated with a greater sense of permanence perhaps; they became the Mukhopadhyayas (mukhya "upadhyaya", upadhyaya being an old Brahmin title) and Bandyopadhyayas and so on. Later, when they flourished under the British, the "jee" that was the honorific added in north India must have got tagged to their simplified names. The Maithili Brahmins, on the other hand, kept their original surnames, and though they adopted the land and the language at the same time as the others, they remained at the margins of Bengalihood. However, they also retained ties with the Jhas of Mithila to a greater or lesser extent. The Mukherjees and Banerjees who came of age at the turn of the century fashioned themselves as original Bengalis, certainly as original Bengali Brahmins. At some point, again during British times, several people across caste lines (including some of my ancestors) became Roys or Rays – Rai Bahadur and Rai Rayan were khitaabs awarded by the British to collaborators – and this was later suitably anglicized.'

The night has suddenly become very cold. Though we are so many in the bus, the beast doesn't seem to be holding any heat in its belly. There is an elderly man sitting on the floor of the bus, in a red-and-yellow turban. 'Brahmins,' he now exhales loudly, 'are rakshasas, I tell you. Rakshasas.'

Seven

How to Find Old Friends in
New Places

I had acquired a pair of shorts from Chandni for two rupees and a quarter. In those days, for the wise Bengali, there was an extremely useful institution called the 'European Third' that traversed everywhere in Bharat.

In Howrah station, the moment I got up in that Third, a firingi hollered, 'This is for Europeans.'

I bellowed loudly, 'There are no Europeans anyway. Why don't you and I make use of this empty carriage?'

In a book on comparative linguistics, I had learnt 'if you nasalize the endings of Bengali words, you get Sanskrit; and if you emphasize the first bits of English words, you get white English.' So accenting the first syllable is like cramming chillies in awful cooking – all sins are hidden. In straight Bengali this is what is called 'bellowed loudly English'. The firingi is a native of Taltala, and so, delighted on hearing my English, he helped me put away my stuff. I delegated to him the job of reprimanding the coolie. Their entire clan works in the railways – father–uncle–this aunt–that aunt; they are very adept at chastising coolies.

But meanwhile my enthusiasm for travel was getting deflated somewhat. All these days I was busy with arrangements – clothes, passport; I had no occasion to think of anything else. But the moment the train departed, the feeling that arose in my heart was most cowardly: I am alone, I thought.

– *Deshe Bideshe* by Syed Mujtaba Ali
(Translated by Devapriya Roy)

30

The Gujarati traders had not been lying. The edge of Palanpur, where we find ourselves after alighting from the bus, boasts a row of hotels by the highway. In the dark, their names glitter above steel-and-glass frontage, and inside, dim yellow bulbs cast moony shadows on highly polished floors. Within minutes, our bus is gone and as we wear the bags, we suddenly feel cold and exposed in the consistent ebb and flow of traffic. We troop into one of these hotels. I cannot, for the life of me, remember its name. But I do remember one thing – it is manically clean. The reception is polite: if we require room service, would we, kindly, let them know soonest? The kitchen closes at eleven. Since there are hardly any options at this hour, we say we will check out the menu in the room and order something.

The room on the second floor, for 350 rupees, has an abundance of sunmica on every surface. The bed, a table opposite, the wardrobe on the right, all bear that white clapboard appearance with a brown pattern of leaves and vines round corners. There is a flat-screen TV on the wall. I fling down my bag and rush to the loo. I've been dying to go for hours.

The bathroom is tiny but clean. As I splash water on my face, I catch sight of myself in the mirror and suddenly remember something.

'Do you think Goradia was right?' I ask, emerging from the bathroom in a hurry, water dripping down my neck and wetting the rim of my t-shirt.

'About what?' S asks. He has already switched the laptop on.

'The hidden cameras?'

'He could be.'

I blunder about a bit and eventually find a fluffy white towel neatly folded inside the wardrobe. 'In that case, why are you so remarkably casual about it?'

'Look, when the duffer said if we were a couple, what he really meant was, are you planning to have sex tonight?'

'Humph,' I say, rooting through my bag for clothes. 'As though that's all couples do in hotel rooms.'

'Especially couples who have been married for years and years and are averaging 200 kilometres a day in filthy buses.' He grins.

'Quite the romantic setting,' I submit, though I do not like the allusion to years and years. It sours my mood in some ways. For I have vowed to never allow us to become an old married couple – but S is never bothered by such subtleties – it's as though he doesn't even mind being an old married couple. I shudder involuntarily. 'But then, Goradia doesn't know the exact details of the filth and exhaustion of this journey. Maybe he thought we were eloping?' That's one of my long-standing regrets; that we never eloped. Sigh. 'So you reckon, then, that as long as we crash out, give ourselves over to oblivion and not cultivate sin and base lustfulness, camera or no camera, we're fine?'

'If you start using Biblical imagery like that, though, I might get other ideas.'

'Shut up and order room service.' I settle into the bed – damn, it's cosy. 'I am starving.'

'You are starving? I could eat this motel.'

I cannot remember what side dish we ordered – but it was cheap, vegetarian, and arrived quickly – but I do know the fried rice that came in a white plastic bowl was delicious and plentiful, dotted with peas and scrambled eggs and slivers of beans and carrots. We chomp in perfect silence and after weeks, give in to the TV. I overshoot the budget by twenty rupees when I refuse to submit to S's diktats and order a coke just before the kitchen closes.

After picking out the last three grains of the delicately oily rice with his spoon, S pokes me. 'Do you think Goradia's friend was actually Goradia?'

⌐

We are so psyched we cannot sleep.

The truth about this journey is, in fact, inscribed in the peculiar grainy feel of the bare hours. We spend these hours in strange rooms where we are not supposed to get attached to bedsteads or shelves, in the silence that engulfs us when we are neither talking to each other nor to other people. Or there are the other kind of hours – hurtling along roads where the eye processes a rush of images and files them away somewhere: pigtailed girls in school uniforms, trees shedding leaves, thin dogs sleeping in the sun, clothes fluttering on flat terraces, ruins of a fort in the distance, all viewed from broken windows of long-distance buses. These bare hours are just as important as the busy ones filled with stories and trekking and photography and conversation, and far more numerous. They leak out of us at night when we sleep and swirl around our heads as we bathe.

Sometimes, bare hours suck. They leave us lean and wasted on beds, fighting each other, questioning the very vanities that propelled this project. Everything seems fraudulent, the past, the present – the elaborate narratives about our lives. Sometimes the bare hours oscillate neatly between fear number one, that authenticity is impossible to achieve, and fear number two, that we are but the reversed reflections of our friends and batchmates in office rooms and university labs, so though we claim we have left these lives behind, essentially, except for a few details, we are as insubstantial as mirror images. And then, there are finally the obscure, contented sunny hours, poised on hope. That ultimately we shall discover meaning; that the conversations we have with people and the conversations we eavesdrop on will help us understand the country, and ourselves, better; that later, buoyed by our sublime lessons on the road, we shall become better people, better citizens, better writers. That we might learn to speak of the nation, not like the studio experts we so detest, but like humble, sensitive, new post-global Indians. (Do note, that of all these, it is this last that is embarrassing to admit in print. Much cleverer to admit to the haunting pull of ennui and failure and terror of the future, than confess to the earnest optimism of national ideals. And yet, if that too is not the truth, what is?)

I am so psyched, I must go over the landscapes and conversations in my head, though I cannot calm down enough to take notes. I am buzzing. I feel I have glimpsed some truth – and have returned to tell the tale. I feel my temples throbbing with the memory, the peculiar mix of the comic and the authentic. And though my feet ache, my back hurts, my shoulders feel wooden, I wish to discuss the implications of all that we learnt just now.

Underneath the banal configurations that occupy us as we settle into the room – the comfy bed, the oily food, news on TV, the chilled drink that runs fiery down my throat – I can feel things getting unsettled. A clink, a pull, a tug, a whirr, and then a dim blue glow. I am loving it. I can feel the burgeoning of hope, and it is infectious. So now both of us feel wired and alert. It seems impossible to relax. After much fidgeting, and talking, we agree to watch a movie.

It is around one-thirty in the night, and S is finally asleep. He snores gently. I switch off the light and stand by the window. In the dark, I cannot see anything clearly. The next day, when dusk will unfold, I will memorize the view from the window. Just outside the hotel is a large dusty pavement where several cars and buses are parked; then the wide roads, heavy with traffic; and across the roads, a series of hotels with funny names and beyond, hundreds of houses. But in the dark, only two things are visible. A large sign marking a petrol pump, and far in the distance, a glittering Ferris wheel against the inky sky. It must be a mela ground. Later I realize it is to celebrate Uttarayan, the kite festival. Now, from the quiet room, I wonder lazily if the mela will be on all night – and if people are still milling about, crowding and eating, bustling in the grounds, the perfect counterpoint, a few metres away, to my quiet room. Almost in answer to my question, the Ferris wheel begins to turn – and through the darkness, the jewelled lights wink and dazzle as they splice the Gujarat sky with neat fluent swipes and I wonder if people in the top booths shriek out as zero gravity approaches.

At some point, I go to bed.

Saurav

Palanpur is a busy town, and by the time we leave the hotel for the day – late – and reach the bustling central part with busy streets and brisk businesses and girls on scooters, the sun is hot and people are scurrying in different directions with a great sense of purpose. Even shoppers who stop by the corner shops that display hundreds of varieties of kites do not dawdle. They come in many kinds – women in burqas, women in saris with scarves around their heads, young men in garish trousers and sweater vests, children in jackets accompanied by old people – but they all choose kites quickly and have them packed up in swathes of newsprint. We walk through a narrow lane where bougainvilleas have built a pink arch and enter a restaurant with a high pink ceiling, fans hanging from long rods and plenty of old-world charm. We stuff ourselves with ice cream and jalebis. (Gujarat is, of course, famous for ice cream.) And after the sugar high has been achieved, we begin to wander through the streets again.

'Remind me why we're in Palanpur?' D asks.

'Why,' I say, attempting to be opaque, 'I thought any town would do?'

'Do not be opaque,' she instructs. 'Something must have triggered the choice of this town in your head. What is that?'

'Some of the most famous diamond merchants of India come from Palanpur. Bharat Shah, for example. Now, Surat is the hub of the diamond industry. But I thought we might as well visit Palanpur.'

'Then let us pursue a diamond story,' D tells me. And as though diamond stories grow on trees, she begins to march smartly towards the end of the street.

'Business has been bad,' Babubhai Patel says, dispensing with the initial caginess that has characterized our unannounced visit till now.

A couple of streets from the restaurant, we had chanced upon a discreet signboard above the closed shutters of a shop, and though the signboard was entirely in Gujarati, there was a diamond sketched on either side. We took the narrow flight of stairs next to the shutter and reached a nondescript corridor overlooking the road. Down the corridor was a door, and when we entered (read: barged in), we suddenly came upon a workshop floor where many men were sitting on low tables lit by tube lights and working away on diamonds. We introduced ourselves, said we were travellers, and in minutes we were sitting in front of the proprietor of Moolchand Bhai Patel & Co. Ltd. Come to think of it, the caginess was perfectly in order. They did not know us from Adam.

'The industry has been in recession for most of last year. We were actually shut between February and November in 2009. Our job is to process diamonds that come from Bombay and Surat, and only 10 per cent of that is sold to jewellers locally. The rest of it goes back to the source. So obviously our business is quite dependent on the state of demand outside. And I mean demand outside of India, specifically the United States and Japan.'

'So how are you coping with the recession in America?'

'Like I told you. We were shut for ten months last year. And now we have only about a hundred workers. Down from 750 in 2008.'

'That is considerable downsizing?'

'What to do? There are ten such big processing units left in Palanpur and all of them are in the same state. The situation was so bad till recently that many workers left the diamond-cutting business altogether. There is now a shortage of skilled workers even for the reduced demand we face. And this is a highly skill-intensive business.'

Both D and I nod our heads in near unison at the last line.

'There are some fifty-six separate steps involved in cutting a rough diamond to something that can be set. And some 50–75 per cent of the initial stone gets wasted.'

'Is Palanpur a major centre for diamond cutting?'

'Well, not any more. Almost 90 per cent of the diamond-cutting business is in Surat itself. Of course, it is another matter that Palanpur has produced most of the big diamond merchants of Surat and Bombay. Like, you know, Bharat Shah. But nowadays small factories like the ones you can set up in Palanpur, given the level of outsourcing from Surat, are not that profitable. Most of the profit is in retail. It is true that you can set up a mill with much less capital than it would take to make a big showroom. But the rate of return is much lower.'

'So how long have you been in this business?'

'I started when I was seventeen and it has been twenty-two years. I learnt the trade in Bombay.'

'This isn't a hereditary business, then?'

'It is, but we tend to spend time in other people's factories to cut our teeth.'

There is a pause.

Babubhai adds, 'I am not going to let my son get into this, however.'
'Why?'
'It is just too tension prone. I have high BP and blood sugar.'
'Because of the cyclical nature of the business?'
'That and other things. You have to be alert all the time. Every day we tally records to ensure there is no theft. Workers often have to be hospitalized as they ingest highly dangerous diamond dust. We keep vehicles ready at all times for this. Safes have to be updated.'
A large imposing Godrej safe stands behind Babubhai's seat.
'I was wondering how the diamonds come here from Surat?'
'Via courier. It is the safest means with insurance cover.'
'And this is a proven method?'
'Totally. But again, this trade is a little too strenuous. Also, the merchants dominate this business and control mill owners. The marble business, which has steady demand, is more worthwhile.'
'Have you diversified into that?'
'Yes. It is running side by side.'

31

The sky is lavender when we check out of the hotel. On the horizon, there are four distinct stripes: a thick purple band, made jagged by roofs of houses that interrupt the skyline, above which is a luminous orange band, and straddling that, a weary yellow-gold strip. Finally, between the lavender and the yellow-gold, a slight pink funnel. There is a little breeze and occasionally one can spot a fine spray of dust lifted from the ground, along with old newspaper sheets that flutter and get crushed underfoot. We walk to the stand from where jeeps leave for Ahmedabad. It is on the same side of the road as the hotel. Across the road, one by one, tube lights begin to gleam in people's windows, their white fluorescence contrasting with the deep yellow of the street lamps.
'Do you think this is a good idea?' S asks.

'For the final time, yes!' I say. 'You've been blathering on about the budget continuously but now, when we have a chance to save money on a hotel, you begin to have second thoughts?'

'But I don't like staying in people's houses,' he mutters.

'But this is Diego for crying out loud,' I say, so loudly that two or three people, clutching kites, turn to look at us. S glowers at me. His jaw hardens. There is nothing he hates more than a public scene. I lower my voice and widen my eyes but do not compromise on the tone. 'We know him forever. Plus, Jiya wants us to stay at his place. It's important for her.' (Jiya, as you know, is my best friend from college. And Diego is a decent Bengali boy with a flowery Tagorific name. His father, like many other Bongs of his generation, was crazy about Maradona – and though he had no control over the matter of the 'bhaalo naam', he had put his foot down on choosing his only son's pet name. And somehow, the name stuck. Through school and college, Diego was always Diego.)

'Don't get me wrong. I have always been fond of Diego. But we might be imposing on him; he may not have a place large enough for guests.'

'Jiya says his flat is not that small. Also, I don't really understand your attitude. He is a close buddy from college. Someday, he'll marry one of my closest friends. We're Indians – *jodi hao sujon, tentul paatay no'jon* (If your heart's in the right place/ Nine people can be accommodated on a tamarind leaf). There is absolutely no reason why we should not stay over at his place. Especially when we're doing a budget journey.'

'Years have passed since college,' he says finally, and lapses into a prickly silence.

I'm suddenly cranky. I want to go to the loo but we are not even sitting in the bloody jeep yet. Do I want to walk back to the hotel and explain to the reception I want to use their bathroom? By then the jeep may have come and gone. 'Not that many years,' I counter, irretrievably contrarian now.

Roughly around the same time I met S, Jiya met Diego. In fact, come to think of it, those days S used to go around calling Diego his 'protégé'. Ours was that kind of a college. Seniors were always mentoring juniors. Jiya read English with me, Diego studied in the physics department. It was our first year in college. Whether we did Bengali honours or botany honours, we had all come to Presidency with a similar sense of entitlement – the entrance examination was tough and fair – and similar opinionated views on the arts, two things that were quickly sharpened into similar-looking spear tips. We wore them on our heads like horns. The college, one of the oldest colonial institutions in the country, had a great tradition of exclusivity our seniors introduced to us with one single pompous word: meritocracy. And in this meritocracy, there would never be any ragging. It was all about mentoring; and these cynical-as-hell seniors helped us imbibe the clubby vibe.

We imagined very mixed friends' circles for ourselves – and for the more political ones among us, that was to some extent true – but the rest of us mostly associated with batchmates from similar class backgrounds in smug interdepartmental galaxies. Everybody knew everybody else would go places and everybody was competitive. Our group included a large number of people from the economics department – S's juniors – a few from English, physics (this included Diego), sociology and political science. At one point, all of us marched to the American consulate to protest the attack on Iraq, and on the way back, munched peanuts and made plans for the weekend. Perhaps it was on that march that Jiya and Diego really became friends, and then, quickly, that friendship deepened into love, tempered by the possibility of some family drama. Jiya was an heiress (her dad and the American consul were often at the same parties) while Diego was middle-class like the rest of us.

Diego and Jiya's is one love story that I have been tracking since long before it even became a love story – so yes, I have my reasons for wanting to look him up in Ahmedabad. They seem to have run into some sort of a rough patch now, though Jiya, ever loyal, is evasive about it in the phone calls she occasionally makes to me from Kent. Ever since she went to England to study, our daily phone conversations have stopped.

Finally our jeep arrives. It seems all the people around us, clutching their precious kites, are also going to Ahmedabad. We jostle with them and eventually get our tickets. Seventy rupees each. Our backpacks, along with other assorted baggage and the kites, are tied securely on top of the jeep. When everyone has been crammed in, in sheer disbelief I begin a headcount, and finally whisper to S, who is sitting opposite me so our legs are tangled together, the number. Twenty-one people. In addition to the driver and two children (fortunately, not whiney in the least) on parental laps. 'Greed, sheer greed,' S tells me, an acerbic twist to his lips. 'Sheer, sheer greed on the part of a driver who expects impossible profits,' I write in my yellow notebook. Later on, after travelling with twenty-one people in a vikram in Mathura, I'd look back fondly on this journey.

We cruise through the darkness, and thankfully, the roads are smooth. The moment the jeep begins to move and I lean back, I realize that I am doomed. The horrible window clasp is going to cut into my flesh if I rest even a little. For the rest of the journey, I must hold my back ramrod straight. It is particularly difficult on a full bladder. S is half-asleep, an expression of pain writ on his face, I notice his lips are chapped. His legs have been tamed to fit into the jeep in such a way that they appear dead – and definitely separate from him. I resolutely discourage conversation and entertain myself by imagining what reviewers will say when my novel finally appears. It always works.

A couple of hours later, the view outside begins to change from the highway mode – the warehouse-like structures, tyre shops, dhabas and darkness gives way to brisk city lights. In fact, I realize with a sudden unleashing of happy butterflies in my stomach that I have, in fact, been missing the stomach-crunching, cheek-by-jowling big-city madness I am used to, a great deal. All the touristy small-town wonders are great for the soul, no doubt – but the anticipation of sharing the air with at least a few million others drives an electric spark through my cells. The sort of anticipation my body reserves for a meal at my mother's, after months of staying away: it goes to the heart of what human cells recognize as home.

People start to get off in the suburbs and the jeep slows down in the thickening traffic. I dial Diego's number, once, twice. But there's no response.

32

'Do you have the address?' S asks me.
'Yes, it's in my inbox. But he's going to meet us somewhere central, he said, and take us home with him.'

By now the back of the jeep is relatively empty. Three or four people are still in the middle, and two are sitting next to the driver. But behind, we can stretch our feet and breathe and talk like human beings.

'Where exactly are we supposed to meet him?'

'He told me to call him once we near the city.'

'Hmmm, okay. Just remember – at some point we also need to buy tickets for tomorrow night.'

'What tickets?'

'To Junagadh. We'll take the train. Don't make a face. Hurtling pace, remember? I have a feeling you'll love Girnar.'

'But how far is it from Ahmedabad?'

'Quite far. We'll take an overnight train.'

'Damn. I am exhausted. I was hoping to rest a day or two. Drink a cappuccino maybe. Go to a beauty parlour.'

'I am sure there are beauty parlours in Junagadh. But I doubt if the budget can afford these frivolities.'

'First, a beauty parlour is not a frivolity but a necessity. I definitely need to get my eyebrows done. Do you know how much more it hurts if I let it go for weeks and weeks? And the budget is exactly why I thought I should do it in Ahmedabad where there's no hotel bill to be paid. But apparently we have to rush through to Junagadh in five minutes.'

'You know what you signed up for.'

I glower. He glowers. The phone rings. It's Diego.

'Hey,' he says, and his voice, I swear, has not aged a day from when S introduced him to us as his 'protégé'. It makes me smile. 'Sorry, I missed your call,' he says. 'I've come to buy our dinner. At this local restaurant. Usually they deliver but today the delivery guy's not turned up.'

'Hi,' I say, finally getting a word in. 'No problem. Hey, it's been a while, right? Hmm. So we've entered Ahmedabad. Where do we see you?'

'Right. How about the GPO?'

'Sure. We'll get there. Oh, and Diego, about dinner...'

'Ya?'

''S doesn't eat meat any more, only fish. So vegetarian is fine for us if that's alright?'

'Oh?' he says, surprise flickering in his voice. We have shared many, many meals in the past. Lots of chicken biriyani and chicken chowmein. The canteen used to make these incredible chicken rolls and chicken samosas. 'Sure, sure,' he tells me, 'I'll get some paneer.'

'Great, thanks.'

'So we'll see you then. GPO in forty-five minutes.'

'Hey, Diego, wait. Who's *we*?'

'Remember Rohan? Rohan Saraf from economics, our batch, Saurav's junior? He's in Ahmedabad too. On work. Since you guys were coming, I thought it would be good to have a reunion. He'll be here any minute now, so we'll see you guys in forty-five.'

'Sure. I mean that's great.'

33

Diego's flat is large and airy, and when we hear the rent, we shut up and sit back for a bit. For 5,500 rupees, he has what would be called a 2BHK, in a decent homey neighbourhood with nice if slightly clean-freakish neighbours and ample parking space, though he does not yet have a car. Rohan tells us, settling into one of the chairs in the drawing room, 'I love this city, yaar. Every time I come here I find myself saying, I could easily live here. It's getting cooler too. There are discos and stuff now. Good restaurants.' Rohan studied at the IIM here and is intimately familiar with the city. 'I mean, I like Bombay a lot, sure, but it's such a battle every single day. Think about it. I pay 22,000 for a smaller place; I spend hours on the commute;

the girls are impossible to please. I tell you, I'd move to Ahmedabad in a heartbeat.'

'I don't mind Ahmedabad actually. At least, I didn't while I had a bootlegger,' Diego says. Affecting a grown-up manner that sits slightly heavy on his youthful frame, he brings out a squat bottle of whisky and glasses. He has also, thoughtfully, got coke for me since he couldn't find any vodka, my usual poison. Not that I particularly want a drink. I go into the kitchen and help with the food. It's still hot. There's a spicy chicken curry and kadhai paneer with rotis. I find four plates. Diego bustles around, handing me ladles and bowls, and his household avatar unleashes a new flood of nostalgia in me. I was a third in so many of Diego and Jiya's big moments. The first day Jiya visited him at his house, I'd been dragged along too. As some sort of a chaperone to placate Jiya's drivers. Diego lived in a wonderfully well-maintained small two-storey house, with his parents and aunt. He was an only son.

'We are meeting after, what, five years?' Diego stops for a second. 'Well, we haven't met since you came from JNU in your first year. Ya, about five years.' He flashes his snaggle-toothed smile and takes off his jacket. I notice that Diego, who was always reed-thin, now has a small beer belly. He goes off to the drawing room carrying two plates and I follow with the other two.

'So what happened to your bootlegger?' S asks, taking a gigantic bite of the tandoori roti. He's sprawled on the divan – and I curl up next to him. The food is oily and very comforting.

'Oh that. It's a tragic story.' Diego folds his legs under him on the other cane chair, next to Rohan. 'So one of my colleagues gave me this guy's details. And I kid you not, it was very cloak and dagger. I'd call him – but he wouldn't talk business then. It would be a hi-hello sort of conversation. Then, later, he'd call back from a different number. I'd tell him what I needed. He had the Gujarati work ethic. Very prompt.'

Rohan gets up. 'I need some more chicken. Do you guys need something?'

'Roti?' S gestures.

'Carry on with the story. I've heard it once.'

'You eat non-veg now?' I ask Rohan's retreating back, finally putting a finger on the thing that had seemed odd to me. Odd because back in the days we hung out – Rohan was not a close friend, we didn't, for example, invite each other home – he was a vegetarian. Or eggetarian.

'Like most good Marwari boys, I am a vegetarian at home. Outside, I eat everything. Now. After IIM.'

In a fraction of a second I remember something, with the peculiar clarity our brain reserves for the stories of our youth: when you remember what you wore or ate, when you can recall exact conversations. It is 2002. A large party of Presidencians is gathered around two tables joined together at Coffee House, perched atop Bankim Chandra Chatterjee Street with its booksellers, just off College Street, breathing in the smoke – all around us there are smokers – and talking nineteen to the dozen. Jiya and I have come along, ostensibly to research an article we will write for the college newspaper we have just started. S is there too, along with two of his friends who are always called by their last names: Rao and Bhotika. We are not yet lovers – but there is a certain tension between us, and I watch him as he eats his mughlai paratha with immense rapidity, demolishing it with a knife and a fork in a few minutes flat. 'This is my lunch every day,' he tells us, and this girl from political science, Piya, asks, 'You come to Coffee House every day?' 'Yup,' he says, and spears the last piece of potato with his fork. Rohan Saraf, who we later learn lives with his uncle's family since he'd lost both his parents in an accident, promptly orders a mughlai paratha too. When it comes, crisp and smelling delicious, he abandons the knife and fork in two minutes. The rest of us pretend not to notice this – and I am pretty sure some of us don't notice it at all – and carry on talking, but Piya from political science, whose father is a bureaucrat, giggles sweetly and pokes Rohan with her elbow. 'Aahaa, after all, the good Marwari needs to eat his paratha with his hands, no, for full satisfaction?' The rest of us are quiet for just an instant, but when Rohan laughs along gamely, we may have joined in.

'What news of Piya?' I ask, interrupting Diego's story. 'Sorry, sorry,' I mouth immediately.

'No, no, that's fine. She's gone off to Italy – and in fact she's in love with an Italian guy. In fact, some of her stuff is in my house. In *this* house. When she left Bombay, she left a bunch of things in my hostel room, in two bags, and I've had to bring them here with me to Ahmedabad. And there's no sign of Piya. I think I'll have to take them to Calcutta and dump it at her parents'.'

'That's very Piya,' I say. 'I'm pretty sure she'll settle down in Italy. I always felt she'd be an NRI.'

Rohan has returned and we can now focus on the tragic tale of the bootlegger.

'So with his Gujarati work ethic, supply chain and business instincts, he was running a good dhanda. We were his regulars. And once he promised to deliver something, he never failed. Then I went to Calcutta for a couple of weeks.'

'The time Jiya came from Kent?' I ask.

'Yes, right,' he says vaguely. 'And after that I called him. Usually he called back within the hour. But a whole day went by and no response. I called him again and again. Same thing. I phoned around – tried some of his other regulars. But no one had any news. For a while I worried about him. Had he lost his phone and with that all our contacts? Or had he died suddenly?'

'Did he die?' S asks. He collects our plates – only Rohan is still eating – and goes to the kitchen. Diego refills all the glasses.

'I thought he had, really I did. Then one day I was shopping for grocery and I ran into him on the road. "Where have you been?" I asked him, genuinely affected. "We were so worried, man." He looked weather-beaten. Then, over a cup of coffee in Barista, he told me the whole story. You see, he would bring the bottles of liquor in water tankers. In the middle of the tanker, there would be barrels filled with sealed bottles. He had perfected the chain – worked on the contacts. It was a good business. Great returns. Then one day, his water tanker had an accident. Nothing major, but in the impact the bottles broke. Soon the scent of whisky began to waft around. Policemen who had come to inspect the minor accident were suddenly alerted to the strong smell of liquor. He had to pay six lakh as fine. That's the standard. Now he's changed trades – he's thinking of opening a shop.'

'Listen to this,' Rohan says. 'I heard this at work. Why can't a Gujju or Maru play hockey?'

I remember. Rohan's talent was PJs.

'Why?' we chorus dutifully.

'Because the moment they're in a corner, they open a shop!'

⟶

That we would get to the dreaded part sooner or later was a given. And after we'd put away the plates and decided on the sleeping arrangements – Rohan and Diego would share the bedroom while we slept on the divan – it begins. Who's doing what these days? Rohan is in corporate high-flier mode. (And he's never going to leave Bombay, unless he's going to Hong Kong or Singapore. I mean, obviously. Who does that?) Diego enjoys his job – it's responsible and grown up – but the government stodginess of it, and the fact that none of the others is in Ahmedabad, makes him hold on to the college gang tighter. He's in touch with *everyone*. Add to that everyone else he was pals with in the master's programme. And I begin to sense what makes Jiya uncertain. He recites the exact coordinates of people – most of the science guys and several of the economics ones are doing research in America, the rest have fancy jobs. And then there's us – we got married and now we've quit our jobs to travel and to write these books? It's a bit surprising.

Books are okay, Rohan says. It's not that he doesn't read. He does. The idea of the journey is interesting, sort of, but why aren't we simply blogging about it? And we've moved back to Calcutta? That's brave, both of them say. Rare. Very rare. Everyone leaves Calcutta after Presidency – that's the rule. Soon I begin to get a headache. My nose begins to itch. The last dregs of *pure and authentic feelings* that had flooded through me yesterday now vaporize, leaving me open to doubt or despair – both to be honest. It's like a Sunday, when you've had a glorious brunch, browsed in a bookstore, walked in the park, and then, come dusk, your parents drag you to the nursing home to meet an old grand-uncle who's very ill. Suddenly, in the famed cancer hospital with its marbled doorways and tasteful art, you see the lobby full of people with wilting faces and dishevelled clothes, people who have learnt to rearrange their lives around their loved ones dying over a reasonable time frame. It sounds self-involved but you cannot help wonder what you would do in case of illness, given your financial circumstances. My last two bank statements dance on my eyeballs, and largely to distract myself I start an eyebrow exercise I'd learnt online to quell my throbbing forehead.

I'd begged S to *be nice* – a general code in our public interaction, since he displays an alarming tendency to shock people the moment they begin to tot up their pretty successes and trot out their certainties – whether revolution or consumption. S will take up the challenge pronto: be all-annoying and against the grain. Things can get ugly.

My stomach feels queasy.

Five years are a little bit too soon, I begin to think, for reunions. Ten years are better. In ten years, there are other things that blur self-definition – spouse, kids, parents getting old, parents getting sick, the ease with which one puts on weight, even lay-offs, perhaps, since in ten years, economies can shift tectonically. My eyes glaze over and I begin to get that slightly breathless feeling I recognize from Monday evenings in our garret apartment when though there's food at home we would go out to eat just in order to blur the general sense of uneasiness, and then, while waiting, worry about the money we are spending unnecessarily eating out.

I excuse myself and get up to go to the bathroom. I lock the bedroom door. I shower and douse myself in talcum powder. I root through our bags, then, finally, I unpack stuff on the bed. I find fresh clean clothes for both of us for the night and then pack everything in the bags again. When I return to the drawing room, feeling chirpier, I find the atmosphere convivial again and they are talking about other things. Diego has been joking about a colleague, a scientist, who has recently got married. He got 15 lakh in dowry. Rohan pipes up with far more salacious details. It is possible for an IIM grad to get dowry up to 1.5 crore. More, maybe, if he's both IIT and IIM.

For a few seconds, I am numbed. My chirpiness vanishes in an instant. 'Are you going to take dowry?' I demand of Rohan Saraf. 'I am not going to,' he tells me, enunciating each word coldly. 'But do you know what my aunt said when I told her this?' He looks at the boys – from this point onward, he only addresses them. 'She's beginning to look for girls for me,' he reports. 'I told her, you figure it out. I will come for a week, meet the final girls once and pick one of them. Anyway, when I told her this dowry thing she said, "If our boy is from IIM and we are not asking for dowry, do you know what the ladkiwaalein will think? They will think there is something wrong with you and we are trying to palm off damaged goods."'

Diego titters. S gets up and goes to the bedroom to change. I throw my weight flat on the divan. The blinding success of frenemies was an infinitely better subject in comparison.

Then, Jiya calls. Diego shushes me, speaks to her for a bit, and tells her right at the end that there is a surprise for her. He then hands the phone over to me. I squeal. Jiya squeals. For the first few minutes we end up speaking over each other, then waiting for each other, and finally, when we interrupt those silences, our conversations overlap again. Jiya, I say finally, you speak. Go. She laughs. Through Diego's phone her breathy laughter, always slightly anxious, always slightly unsure, makes me the bossy friend all over again, discussing questions for the next day's paper. 'Hurry up, Jiya. It's a trunk call, for crying out loud. You're not that much of an heiress in pounds.' She laughs again. In Kent, it is evening and her classes are over for the day. She is walking back to the flat she shares with two Korean girls after picking up one or two things from the store. She has a paper due tomorrow and she's not written a word yet. It is dark and cold and miserable. She's been living on cheese and milk and smoked chicken. 'And how are you, Dippy?' she asks me. 'What's Diego's house like?'

I settle down on the floor to chat.

Saurav

It is Uttarayan morning and a holiday in Ahmedabad. Diego goes back to bed after seeing us off. Rohan has not stirred. We find an auto to take us close to the old city. Johnny Mawan, the friendly autowallah, informs us at the outset that he is a Christian, and then points to the back of the auto where there is a rack full of magazines. We both find something we like to read, though every few seconds we look up to observe the kites that are flying over the city and the few that are tangled in the trees. Lunch is cheap and filling in a small restaurant near the station, but as we wait for the food, last night's conversation hangs heavy between us. Our exit from the predominant dharma of our peers is still new enough to plunge us into anxiety from time to time.

We walk down the roads of the old city, entering from Delhi Darwaza, and it is the similarity to buzzing parts of old Calcutta, the commercial belt, filled with shops and tradesmen and narrow old streets – Bada Bazaar, for example – that soothes us. D suddenly takes it into her head to buy some apples. These are got from a fruit seller on a cart. Then she demands a knife. 'Why on earth?' I say. 'Just use your teeth.' She does not listen to me and marches into one of those dingy cast-iron shops and emerges with a fairly large knife. I take it from her – lest there be an accident – and it's still in my hand when I hail an auto. The autowallah agrees to take us to Sabarmati Ashram but first, he says, I must put the knife into the bag straightaway. 'This is the old city, sir. After the riots, a new law was instituted. The police can arrest anyone wielding a weapon. Knives are included.'

As the auto crosses over Subhash Bridge, I see a Sabarmati which is flowing, albeit at low ebb, with a part of its rocky bed visible. I remember something I had heard from my father. In the late 1970s, when he worked in industry here in Gujarat and often visited Ahmedabad, the river was a dried-up mess. In any case, the Sabarmati is a non-perennial river which had water only for a few months in the year.

'Modi has done wonders for the Sabarmati,' the autowallah says. 'There used to be markets and slums on the river. Modi relocated all that. He is building that waterfront you can see from here and has brought water for the Sabarmati from the Narmada canal. Now there is water most of the time.'

The bridge culminates in a large circle, where the autowallah takes a gentle left to enter a tree-lined avenue with empty pavements, except for a solitary paanwallah sitting under a parasol and conversing with what is probably his second or third customer of the day. The auto stops right opposite the duo and the gate of Sabarmati Ashram comes into view. But once we enter, I realize I was perhaps premature in judging the day's prospects for the paanwallah. Quite a few people are milling about inside the leafy settlement that was once Gandhi's experiment in sustainability and simplicity.

It wasn't always Gandhi's though. Sabarmati Ashram has been a site of pilgrimage through antiquity. It is believed to be the site of one of Rishi Dadhichi's ashrams; Dadhichi set up several such abodes across India, the chief one being in Naimisharanya, near Lucknow. Rishi Dadhichi is immortal in Indian memory for the sacrifice of his mortal self to help Indra fashion a weapon out of his bones. This was used to defeat the nearly unassailable Vritrasur.

Vritrasur was a gifted asura who had strayed from the path of dharma and had blocked the flow of rivers on earth through the creation of some ninety-nine fortresses. Rising to be head of the asuras, Vritrasur exposed the impotence of the devas when they challenged his might. Despondent, the devas finally turned to Vishnu, who revealed to them that Vritrasur could only be killed by a weapon fashioned out of the bones of a rishi since he had acquired numerous boons through austere penance in the past. This precluded the possibility of him being slain by any conventional weapon. Dadhichi willingly gave up his body to restore balance in the world.

It is hard to imagine that the symbolism of this story would have been lost on Gandhi. By settling down on this bank of the Sabarmati, Gandhi may have sought to internalize Dadhichi's message as he fashioned the greatest weapon of sacrifice – satyagraha – against an enemy that was no less complex than Vritrasur, a colonial edifice on a 'civilizing' mission, apparently standing for modernist development, but actually standing on the damaged psyche of a civilization much older than theirs.

We walk along the pathways that are a playground for squirrels, following signs that point to the Mahatma's cabin. As I approach the house, I begin to notice a heaviness that has been welling up inside me. Having been raised in Bengal, I have always been acutely affected by Gandhi's decision to favour Nehru over Bose to succeed him as the dominant voice within the Indian National Congress in the late 1930s. And like other people from the state, I too grew up to be aggrieved with this choice, even so many decades after it was made. Once, when historian Ramachandra Guha had come to JNU to deliver a mess talk, I remember vehemently opposing his support for Nehru by raising not just the 'Bose question' but also the way in which Nehru had dispensed with other rivals such as Shyama Prasad Mookerjee. 'This man must be a Bengali!' Guha had retorted, after which a spirited discussion had ensued.

The small forecourt of 'Hridaykunj', the quarters of Mohandas and Kasturba, is lined by a little wooden fence with a door between two mini stone pillars. As I enter, a goosebumpy sensation rises from the base of my spine, culminating in tears that begin to wet my cheeks. I am overwhelmed. As I peer inside the Gandhian quarters (spartan doesn't begin to describe it) with its mat, munim desk, a pillow and charkha, I can no longer harbour doubts about the strength of the man's sadhana for India, if I ever did.

Outside, I sense that D too has been moved. We begin to meld into the crowd that has suddenly congealed. There are many parents here accompanying dewy-eyed children, dutifully asking them to take off their slippers and escorting them inside for a darshan of the sanctum. It is as if they are going to meet a clan elder who is still around. A very Indian pilgrimage this.

'My life is my message' written in Gandhi's hand is kept as one of the displays in the 'New Museum' that holds all sorts of memorabilia. That message, as is obvious from Sabarmati Ashram, is not limited to seeking total independence from British rule in India. It is a call to a mode of living where self-sufficiency is blended with inter-generational equity.

Thus, Gandhi, in his book, *Village Re-development for the 21st Century*, emphasized the need to keep the fertility of the topsoil intact and not subject it to industrialized chemical farming for higher yields that wouldn't last much longer than a couple of generations.

His simple words have been completely ignored by several generations since independence, so that we are at a point where topsoil, along with water, is one of the two most valuable commodities in the world today. Large corporates are grabbing relatively virgin (in terms of chemical fertilizer and pesticide use) farmland wherever they can get it, whether in Ethiopia or Argentina. In many parts of the world, subsistence farmers are suddenly becoming cash rich by allowing topsoil brokers to cleave 4 inches of their existing fields to be deposited several thousand kilometres away. The *good earth* is no longer a punch line.

We walk out of the museum area into a garden at the back which is almost entirely deserted but for a flock of parrots on a tree and two children – a brother-and-sister duo – sitting in the middle of kite-flying paraphernalia and several kites. The stillness is redolent with a sense of peace.

It is broken when the phone rings.

I squint at the number and hand the phone over to D. It is her supervisor.

34

We sit morosely outside Sabarmati Ashram on a bench. Buses and cars go past. In between the passing vehicles, in soft nano-snatches of silence, I can sense twilight advancing. I exhale noisily.

'What did he say?' S finally asks.

I bite my lower lip and unconsciously strike a suitable pose: body tightly rolled up, legs drawn closer to the trunk but still dangling, and move back and forth in acute agitation. 'Remember how I'd given the money and documents to that classmate of mine? Angela Savitri?'

'Yes. She was supposed to pay your fees at the school office and do the registration for you.'

'Apparently it wasn't done.'

'You mean, she didn't do it?'

The speed at which I rock on the bench increases.

'So,' I continue, 'if I want to remain registered as a student, I have to get there in person. By Tuesday or Wednesday, latest.'

'Back in Delhi?' S sounds incredulous.

'Yes,' I reply, quickly allowing myself to become very angry. Everyone knows whose idea this project is. Naturally, the last thing I would have wanted is an interruption. But the fault is in my stars – there are always such fatal mistakes I make. 'Look. I was a fool. I knew Angela was not reliable. I should have done it myself before coming.' I feel so stupid that I want to lie flat on the pavement and smack my head against the kerb. God, I am foolish. I could have easily done it myself before we went to Jaipur. It is, in any case, a semester of waiting. Until the viva voce for my MPhil dissertation is scheduled, I am, in a manner of speaking, free from any academic compulsions. Just the registration. A mere formality. But I hadn't gone in person – Paharganj was too far away from the campus, I was packing for the trip, I'd seen others do it for friends all the time, and Angela had, in a moment of utter reliability, said she would do it. Easy-peasy, she'd said, her posh accent underscoring the 'pea'. But now my supervisor had spelt it out. If I wanted to retain my place, I'd have to go and do it myself.

'What do you want to do?'

I have no answer.

We keep sitting on the bench by the road. The buses and cars go past. The twilight has now crept up the trees and swarmed to the tips of branches. Any moment now there will be a giant leap and dusk will cast a gargantuan net on the sky, and the clouds will thicken into evening.

'Are you saying we have to return? Go back to Delhi?'

I still don't say anything. Shadows lengthen. Across the road a kite floats down lazily on the back of an evening wind that rises from somewhere. It lies like a red gash on the pavement.

Eight

How (Not) to Get Late for Girnar

I've always believed that when you do a thing you should forget everything else and do that one thing with heart and soul. When I was interested in mundane pursuits, I was a perfect materialist. You would never in your life have imagined that I could be interested in spiritual subjects. And when I was doing Sadhana, I forgot everything else and I did it. For example, for ten months in Girnar I lived in an Arka (*Calotropis Gigantea*) tree in an old cemetery, eating only Arka leaves, doing a ritual to please Anjaneya. Arka leaves cause violent purging and vomiting. Do you know how 'hot' Arka is? Arka means Sun and after two or three days of eating those leaves my mouth and tongue had swollen to twice their normal size. But that didn't stop me, I continued with the ritual. Aghoris always overdo a thing.

– Robert E. Svoboda quotes Aghori Vimalananda in
Aghora, Chapter 10, Girnar.

35

Saurav

14 January 2010, 8:30 p.m.

'Haven't you brought blankets?' the lady says incredulously. It reminds me of a smug classmate in the fifth standard saying, 'Haven't you done your homework?' Indeed, the cold Saurashtra night is proving to be a veritable class teacher hell-bent on teaching D and me a lesson for taking it lightly.

'Your wife should have thought of it,' she adds, casting a glance at D. 'My wife is the bookish type,' I tell her, affecting despair.

Our impression of winter in Gujarat had been largely shaped by the past few days – a warmish Palanpur and a nice, cool Ahmedabad, with road travel in packed buses and jeeps in between. Now, as the train snakes its way to Junagadh through a mostly barren landscape, ghostly in the moonlit night, the near-empty sleeper compartment and its ill-fitting windows conspire to spread an eerie chill.

D finds warmth in her book. She strains her eyes to read in the dark. It is an Agatha Christie she nicked from Diego's house. I find no comfort. I wander from this bunk to that, hoping to sleep for at least an hour or two. Nada. The cold is uniformly bitter everywhere.

At four in the morning, several grave-looking men get into the train. They are wearing formal office wear, and carrying office bags. They take off their highly polished shoes and place them neatly by the window. They take out sheets and blankets from their office bags, blow up air pillows and go to sleep. Apparently, they are railway employees commuting to Veraval where they work, and they do this every day.

15 January 2010, 4:30 a.m.

The scene at Junagadh station as dawn breaks: a throng of people all wrapped up and bustling around trains, the smell of milky tea being boiled over and over in the same utensil, dull oblongs of white light on the grey platform, cast by tube lights fixed on the corrugated ceiling. This could be an early morning shot of Jamshedpur and I could be eight, accompanying my parents aboard the Steel City Express for Howrah, the Jharkhand winter as bone-juddering as the Kathiawari one.

The brain discerns some patterns of more recent vintage as well: an eager autowallah immediately agreeing to take us to our destination – Sabri Shopping Centre, Kehra Chowk – asking a fare which we suspect is higher than par but one which we acquiesce to after yet another weary journey. And then rocketing out of the station area in what seems to be the world's fastest manned three-wheeler.

Whether it is because it has risen out of a sparse countryside at the foot of a range or whether by municipal design, Junagadh does not seem to have many trees. The streets are clean enough, by Indian standards anyway, and like Palanpur, this place too has decent pavements and covered drainage. The buildings near the station are typical of most growing Indian towns – three or four storeys, built with complete indifference to aesthetics of any kind, comprising shops on the ground floor and a cyber cafe or two in the first.

Our auto comes to a halt near a large but somewhat shabby shopping complex. It has an exaggeratedly small entrance with shops (now shuttered) lining the corridor that leads to the staircase. Ascending the stairs, we notice the sign for Hotel Madhuvanti on the first floor, pointing to the left. Apparently, there is another hotel on the second floor too.

On the first floor, we find Hotel Madhuvanti. But there is no door. Instead, from the other side of a locked grille, we can see a reception desk, shadowy in the half-light. A man is slumped on it. The desk is in a channel that opens into a wide courtyard. The boundary of the courtyard, we are to see later, is a double-storeyed wall made up of rooms. I remember how surprised we were later, with the scope of the building. One would have never imagined from the exterior of the building or the staircase area that within its walls would be a big courtyard lined by rooms stacked on one another.

A suspicious voice issues from the man at the desk, who seems to be stirring. 'Yes?' It sounds more like, *What the hell are you doing here, you morons with backpacks?*

'Oh, we have a booking. We called...' says D in English.

'No rooms,' the man says abruptly, cutting her off. It's not what one wants to hear at the crack of dawn, having landed in a strange town. But like a true veteran of such endeavours, D now proceeds to give him the precise time and content of our call, wherein we had confirmed a booking and room charges (negotiable), interspersed with information about our project, all in Hindi. 'And we have arrived well within the approximate hour we had told you over the phone,' I added, also in Hindi, pointing to the wall clock which read 5.15 a.m. We had promised we would be in by six in the morning.

The weight of our arguments and our heavy rucksacks seem to have the desired effect. The man shuffles towards us unhappily and unlocks the doors. As he opens the guest ledger and advances it towards us, he says: 'I thought you were a couple of those foreigners, you see. Last week two ran away without paying me.'

As it turns out, Junagadh isn't on the backpacking circuit and establishments here don't particularly fancy hippyish travellers like, say, in some circuits in Rajasthan. Our petition in Hindi convinces them that we aren't like 'those foreigners' – the ganja and dreadlocks variety – and a room is quickly made available.

It is on the second storey, to be accessed by a spiral stairway from the courtyard, and worth all the trouble. It has marble floors that give an instant clean, light feel though on close inspection, D finds the curtains are dirty and the plaster is peeling. It has three mattresses in all, one double and two singles, with the one by the window giving a view of the Girnar range. The mattresses are laid on concrete plinths rather than on wooden beds. Predictably, we crash out on them and go to sleep.

15 January 2010, 11:45 a.m.

After we wake up and drink tea (it takes a very long time to come), we have occasion to investigate the premises. If the black-and-white courtyard outside is promising now, one can imagine how it must be in the evening when stars appear in the sky. The windows of the room open on to a bustling street. There is a tea shop and a snack shop, both doing brisk business through the day. The pop of frying travels upwards, along with the aroma of chickpeas, that most favoured ingredient in Gujarat. But what delights D most is the gentle fragrance that wafts in from somewhere. 'See, can you smell that?' she asks me, repeatedly, until I admit to a fine, sweet, slightly fruity note in the air. 'It must mean there are good spirits in the vicinity,' she announces, launching into a story about a saintly ghost who lived in a tree in the corner of the courtyard in her grandfather's house in Jharkhand and filled the place with a scent of wild flowers and sweet incense on certain nights. Later on in the evening, we would, however, ascertain a more earthly source for the fragrance. There is a small shop selling ice-cream soda, with multicoloured bottles lined up on the counter.

15 January 2010, 1:30 p.m.

Our necks feel the sun as we walk through Junagadh, familiarizing ourselves with the landmarks near our hotel. We walk down Jayshree Road, wondering aloud who this Jayshree might have been, and then up and down Police Lines. The winter sun in Saurashtra – Kathiawar – is just as deceptively bright as its night is cold. The name Kathiawar comes from two communities that in Indian census-speak have 'dominated' this region for centuries – the Kathis and the Ahirs. Interestingly, both the Kathis and the Ahirs of the Kathiawar region are claimed by some British historians to be of Scythian origin. The Kathis, who are Suryavanshi Rajputs, however, maintain that they are descended from Kush and are originally from Rajasthan, whereas the Kathiawari Ahirs, like those in Haryana, consider themselves Yadavs. The Kathis, therefore, are closely linked to the Kachhwahas of Dhundhar who also consider themselves descendants of Kush. One often hears in TV studio discussions, especially in the context of elections, a passing reference to 'Ahir' as a term by which the Yadavs of Haryana and western UP are known. But while this is not incorrect, the fact is, across India, Ahirs consider themselves Yadavs and trace their ancestry to the ancient Abhira tribe, Ahir being a prakritization of the Sanskrit word Abhira.

So the Abhiras or Ahirs are not limited to the regions surrounding Delhi, but are spread throughout India, including the Deccan, where they are known as Gavlis (the notorious gangster Arun Gavli belongs to this denomination), derived from the term Gvala or cowherd. And though their customs reflect a great degree of localization, marriages between Ahirs from different regions of India are not at all uncommon. A point often missed by region-centric analysis of India's polity is the deep intra-caste linkages that exist, reinforced through caste endogamy but regional exogamy. For instance, the pan-Indian network of chamars has allowed the Bahujan Samaj Party (BSP) to create a presence in states like Maharashtra and Karnataka which are not even contiguous with Uttar Pradesh.

'Do you have a headache? I have a headache,' D says, looking to see if a cake shop is around. 'I think you are hungry,' I say, trying to shift the conversation from the specific to the general. 'It's time we got some lunch.' The Barmer incident is still quite fresh in our minds and there is unlikely to be any German (or fancy) bakery in Junagadh either.

Instead, what we have is a place that describes itself as a Thali Palace. D relents. 'Alright, might as well. Have it your way, fine. Lunch.' The restaurant has a one-page menu listing various thalis mostly priced at Rs 50. Since this is to be one of our two meals for the day, we agree to order one each. I settle for a Gujarati one whereas D opts for the Punjabi. (Usually, I'm the one who makes a big song and dance about trying out new stuff but D turns out vindicated at the end, having made her usual effective choices. Today, however, my Gujarati thali is quite good. Errs on the side of too sweet, but good enough. And plentiful. Unlimited jeera rice and parathas.)

'Can you finish my paratha? I'll just have the sweet now,' says D, pushing her thali towards me. I have already availed myself fully of the unlimited clause, but I barely lift my face while acquiescing.

'Anyway,' I say, after all the food has been attended to, 'the walk to Uparkot should burn some of that.'

15 January 2010, 4 p.m.

Uparkot rises out of the end of a street lined with ornately carved houses in the Kathiawari style, at the edge of the old quarter of Junagadh. It is to Uparkot that Junagadh, which means 'old fort', literally owes its name: the former has been around for over 2,000 years now. First built in 319 BC by Chandragupta Maurya to mark one of the western outposts of his dynasty's pan-Indian empire, Uparkot hill is only 2 kilometres away from his grandson Ashoka's famous rock edict of Girnar, which is considered the first of his rock edicts stretching from Kandahar to Guwahati. The title of 'major' is appended because the group of edicts one is dealing with here touches upon diverse subjects related to statecraft, including, as it happens, sustainable irrigation systems.

Perhaps taking their cue from the Mauryans, subsequent rulers of Uparkot laid a lot of emphasis on water management – the key to Uparkot's two millennia of inhabitation, broken only once for a period of 300 years between the sixth and tenth centuries.

The signature water preservation structures in the fort complex are a couple of giant step wells, baolis as they are known in many parts of India. The younger of the two, Adi Kadi Vav, draws its name from two servant girls of the then Chalukya (or Solanki) royal palace who had agreed to be sacrificed so that groundwater could fill the well, as per the advice of royal priests who deemed the sacrifice of two virgins mandatory for this to take place. Apparently their belief wasn't unfounded and water did indeed burst forth from the sated earth, and locals to this day celebrate the sacrifice of Adi and Kadi by hanging bangles and saris at the entrance of this massive structure hewn out of rock.

Much older than the Adi Kadi Vav and born in less unfortunate circumstances is probably the oldest step well in India, Navghan Kuvo, built by Raja Navghan of the Chudasama royal family almost a thousand years ago (although some historians believe work on it may have been started even earlier, by an ancestor to the king who built Adi Kadi Vav). The Chudasamas of Junagadh consider themselves to be Ahirs, and descendants of the Abhira tribe.

These two step wells perhaps represent the highest architectural achievements of Chudasama rule. During this time, Uparkot was attacked many times (sixteen incursions have been recorded), with one siege lasting over a decade. And it is Navghan Kuvo that often hid defending armies, who would then creep out at night to reduce any unsuspecting ingressing forces.

Standing at the fore courtyard of Navghan Kuvo, we look at numerous pigeonholes hewn into the rock face, perpendicular to the stepped archway entrance of the baoli, almost as if a book written in braille has been made to stand on its spire. To the right of this entrance is a gallery hewn from rock, which allows one to peer down into the well shaft of the baoli. 'Go in, go in,' a man in traditional Kathiawari headgear, sitting with his daughter, says to me cheerfully. It is an odd moment. It is as if he knows that I will find something I have been looking for. Something that I may even deserve to.

I ask D to remain upstairs and clamber down the stairs alone. There are some young men standing outside the Kuvo. They look at me expectantly, perhaps hoping that I might find something that is report-worthy. As I head straight down at an acute angle, it is clear that the staircase begins to curve round the shaft of the baoli, greying and weathered. I descend the stairs and feel the warmth of the sun fade away. I reach the landing at the bottom of the first flight of stairs and round the bend to see the well shaft through a gallery opening and find the young men still peering down at me, although now with the sun on their backs, their faces obscured.

Navghan Kuvo has a rather unique design among step wells in India, in that it has a single stairway that bends round a squarish well shaft, all the way to the bottom. The landing after each flight of stairs is just that, and not a full-fledged storey that in more ornate step wells provides pillared ledges which serve as balconies around the shaft. This step well is hewn from soft rock and is given constructed support only in very few places, with just one gallery opening on each storey and the well shaft's wall on three sides. Navghan Kuvo was clearly not designed to double up as a place for social hang-outs besides being a water conservation structure, as many other intricately designed baolis were.

At the third storey, I hear a flopping sound behind me, amplified in this old vertical cavern, but I don't see anything when I glance over my shoulder. Maybe Navghan Kuvo is a hang-out after all. For the ghosts of Chudasama soldiers who must have hidden here during countless sieges, waiting to chop off the heads of unsuspecting enemy scouts.

I hear the sound again and turn abruptly, only to find a pigeon hopping down the stairs right behind me. It halts momentarily on a step above me. It looks up with its head tilted ever so slightly, but then resumes its descent and goes past me. After a few steps, it reaches the landing and disappears round the bend. Well, it's at least a hang-out for pigeons. They don't seem to mind the lack of carvings and engravings that characterize other baolis.

According to the *Silpa Sutras*, a baoli is supposed to be like an underground sanctum sanctorum, or garbha griha, with the storeys embellished with sculptures of devis and devatas, replicating the ambience of a shrine in an ecologically sensitive structure of civic utility. And make no mistake, Navghan Kuvo is also a shrine. It is a shrine to its deity: water. There are no delicate niches, no balconies, and no carvings to pause and mull over. It is a primeval pilgrimage that puts beyond belief the civilizational article of faith that is water.

As I walk down the last few steps to reach the bottom landing, where the pool of the baoli resides, there is very little light to discern anything on the walls. This low illumination is, of course, by design since the central idea of a baoli is to retain as much water as possible by minimizing evaporation on account of the sun.

I ponder over the durability of Indian civilization on account of its water-conserving habits and find the pool strewn with plastic garbage dropped from above. Milling around the pool are a group of pigeons walking on their own poo. I try to locate the imperious step-hopping pigeon among them, but it is an exercise in futility. Dejected by the state of the pool, I begin my climb back to the surface. By the time I reach the third-last flight of stairs from the top, I find D descending, her determined hand movements cutting through the sudden glare.

'You were down there for a while. I decided to find out what was happening since nobody else was going down.' She stretches her hand to grasp mine. 'This pigeon shit smell is pretty strong,' she says.

I smile and am glad that she is here.

She turns and we start walking back up, together, when we suddenly hear this huge noise reverberating through the well. It's the pigeons taking flight down below, all at once. I take her hand and start running, not knowing if they will fly round the stairs. The sound keeps growing all the time. At the exact moment we both make it out into the light, a large group of pigeons launches out through the well shaft into the air.

⌐

After the momentary unnerving by a bunch of subterranean birds, we gather our wits and proceed to one of Uparkot's other subterranean structures – a Buddhist monastery dating from the second or third centuries AD. This monastery has also been hewn from the same kind of soft rock as Navghan Kuvo next door, but it has carved pillars supporting the ceilings of its underground rooms. Abandoned for years, weather has taken a toll on its walls. It is perhaps still possible to conjure up scenes from the time of the Sangha when you look at the fire pits in the middle of the rooms, used, perhaps, for both homa as well as cooking. The monastery is currently under the supervision of the Archaeological Survey of India (ASI) and is being renovated.

A Buddhist bhikshu is supposed to eat only as much rice as his joined palms can hold. Outside the monastery a weighing machine conclusively proves that I haven't followed that idiom in years, if ever. The machine is owned by an old woman who charges two rupees for this service, telling us she has no earning members left at home.

Not too disconcerted by my weight (since I have actually lost a few kilos since Pushkar), I drag D towards Uparkot's next attraction – a Juma

Masjid that is also undergoing ASI renovation. Just outside the mosque lie many, many pirs, resting under the shade of trees, swathed in green silk.

Inside the masjid, shafts of light pour in through the windows, doors and three octagonal openings on the roof. The entire masjid seems to reverberate with a warm serenity that is difficult to describe but easy to imbibe. Carved pillars support this unique structure, unusual among masjids in India, which are known for greater austerity in the interior. This has something to do with the fact that the Juma Masjid was originally the palace of Rani Ranak Devi, the queen of Chudasama king Ra Khengar, who was a descendant of Ra Navghan, before it was converted into a place of worship by Mahmud Begada in the fourteenth century.

Begada or Begadha, which literally means the conqueror of two forts, was the name taken by Abu'l Fath Nasir-ud-Din Mahmud Shah I, a sultan of Gujarat's erstwhile Muzzaffarid dynasty, after he subdued the 'gadhs', or forts, of Pavagadh and Junagadh. The imprint of his dynasty is visible in three Turkish cannons lying around in Uparkot, which were abandoned by the Ottoman fleet during the Battle of Diu. This battle saw a pretty interesting coalition, comprising ships from the Sultanate of Gujarat, the Ottoman Caliphate, the Mamlûk Burji Sultanate of Egypt, the Zamorin of Calicut, the Republic of Venice and the Republic of Ragusa being defeated by a Portuguese expeditionary flotilla in 1509.

There is a flight of stairs that takes us to the roof of the masjid revealing spectacular views of the entire Girnar range on the southern spur of which rests Uparkot. Powerful as ever is the presence of Girnar Mountain, the highest peak of the range and the focal point of Ranak Devi's worship, when the masjid was still her palace some 300 years before Begada found it.

Ranak Devi was famed for her beauty. The Solanki ruler Siddhraj Jaisinh, based in Anhilwad Patan, who had desired her from a time that preceded her marriage, eventually decided to acquire her irrespective of the fact that she was now married to the Chudasama king. The twelve-year siege that Navghan Kuvo withstood was precisely on account of Jaisinh's efforts to win Ranak Devi and it ended with the demise of Ra Khengar and the sati of Ranak Devi that Jaisinh ultimately agreed to. Kathiawari lore maintains that Mt Girnar was taller than it is now but during her time in the captivity of Jaisinh, Ranak Devi is said to have chided it for holding its head high while she had been doomed thus. At this, an avalanche had set off at the crest of Mt Girnar which stopped only when Ranak Devi beseeched the peak to not destroy itself.

Mt Girnar is the real reason I have brought D to Junagadh. When I was struggling with my first book and needed something – a book, an idea, *something* – to settle my mind, D's supervisor, the noted Kannada poet and playwright, Prof. H.S. Shivaprakash had recommended Robert B. Svoboda's *Aghora* series of books which document the life and views of his guru, the aghori Vimalananda. It is through Vimalananda that I learnt the significance of Mt Girnar as a mystical site for seekers of different religions, whether Hindu, Jain, Buddhist or Muslim. For instance, the orderly graves of Muslim pirs outside the Juma Masjid probably belong to those who chose to be buried in the shadow of Mt Girnar.

Since almost the early days of Islam's entry into the subcontinent, there has been a mystic trail stretching from Mansura in Sindh to Uparkot in Girnar for Sufis. Sufis believe in undertaking sadhana which will keep them at the 'Chautha Aasman' that corresponds to the Anahata or Heart Chakra, fourth in order from the base of the kundalini. Through their meditative practices, they seek to fill themselves with ishq (a complex Sufi term that cannot be translated as divine love or even simply love) by maintaining their kundalini at the Chautha Aasman. They often choose this with deep deliberation, rather than pushing the kundalini all the way to the Saatvan Aasman or the Sahasra, which is the thousand-petalled lotus at the crest of the head, said to lead to moksha.

16 January 2010, 11:30 a.m.

The day after. We are late for Girnar. Very late.

The sun is now nearly overhead. And here we are, still motoring in an auto on Bhavnath Road towards Bhavnath Mahadev temple, close to the foot of Mt Girnar. This ancient temple is dedicated to Lord Shiva and marks the beginning of the Girnar Parikrama undertaken by Hindus on Shivratri, each year, and essentially involves a circumambulation of the base of the mountain.

Incidentally, Jains also join this parikrama and the temples on Mt Girnar, whether dedicated to Hindu deities or Jain Tirthankaras, are considered sacred by both. For Jains, the temple of the twenty-second

Tirthankara, Neminath, built in the twelfth century AD, is of particular significance since it holds an idol of Neminath that dates much further back into antiquity than the temple itself. Neminath is believed to have attained self-realization while practising sadhana on Mt Girnar. His temple is located – along with other important Jain pilgrim sites, like the Rishabhadeva Temple which is dedicated to all twenty-four Tirthankaras – at a height of 3,000 feet.

Some distance from the Bhavnath Mahadev temple is Girnar Taleti, the base of the mountain where the steps begin. Since time immemorial, numerous akhadas of sadhus and Naga babas have located their campuses here. We begin to climb the steps furiously: one, two, and then on and on, to fifty-six, they are all numbered. There are 9,999 steps in all till you reach the crest. The sun is now positively glaring down on us. We realize that we should have come here much earlier in the day as we had been advised. Before daybreak.

As we slow down, we see some pilgrims being carried in cloth harnesses by two-man teams. Such an 'ascent' would require you to go through the indignity of getting yourself weighed at the foot of the mountain.

By the 800th stair, our lungs are gasping for air. Others can sense it apparently, since some of them come up with words of encouragement. 'Don't worry. You'll make it. Ambaji Mata's temple is at 5,000 steps. It's good for couples.' The Ambaji temple on Girnar is famous for guaranteeing happy marriages. Incidentally, not too far away on Mt Girnar is a mosque that is visited by couples looking to be blessed with progeny.

The climb, while strenuous, is breathtaking (it is, unfortunately, literally so in our case). The forested mountain lit up by the sun affords spectacular views of the rest of the range and the countryside. The stone stairway is steep but dry, and is lined with spontaneous lingams and the silk cloth of offerings to pirs tied around trees. The five peaks of Girnar with their various temples come into view from time to time. You can feel the stairs rise and fall along the mountain. Cold comfort, given that we are struggling on the thousandth stair, some 3,500 steps away from the Jain temples and 8,999 away from Lord Dattatreya's shrine that marks the end of the stairway.

Lord Dattatreya is considered a combined avatar of Brahma, Vishnu and Shiva and was born to Rishi Atri and his consort Anasuya, who gave shelter and advice to Ram and Sita during their exile. It is believed that Lord Dattatreya had no teacher other than nature; he learnt the secrets of nature from observing flora and fauna around him. He is, in that sense, both the ultimate student and the primordial teacher, and is revered as the adi guru of the Nath sect of yogis. The Nath yogis have given the world, among other things, the *Hatha Yoga Pradipika*, the defining text of what is understood as yoga today, put together by Yogi Swatmarama, who considered himself a disciple of Gorakhnath, one of the key gurus of the Nath Sampradaya.

But we are clearly not yet ready to receive. We fight over whose idea it was to sleep so late (the fight has not been resolved to date, but let me confess to you that we were detained watching episodes of *How I Met Your Mother* which Diego had forced into our laptop). We sit by the steps and glower at the good devotees skipping down with their children, we perspire and hope the fiery thumping in our chests will subside. The heat and thirst make it impossible for us to trudge along any further, and despite our pride, we decide to call it a day. Some langurs sitting a few feet away stare at us peacefully. Their look suggests that they are neither surprised nor disappointed. They know we will return.

Someday.

On the way back, we see a tank by which Narsinh Mehta, Vaishnava saint, first poet of the Gujarati language and composer of Gandhi's favourite hymn 'Vaishnava jana toh' used to spend a considerable amount of time – the waterbody now bears his name. It is tempting to see Girnar as a meeting point given the way in which it removes dichotomies. Digambar and Swetambar, Hindu and Muslim, all blend here. But it is probably more of a starting point. A place where souls have found themselves, irrespective of the temporary name ascribed to them by the inherited body.

Girnar has been a holy site for people of different faiths who have carved niches for themselves in the region. And these niches have been defended and supported by all of India's great empires. With the Ashokan edicts are those of Saka Kshatrap Rudradaman I and Gupta Emperor

Skandagupta. Uparkot was built by Chandragupta Maurya, who was Jain and needed this bastion to watch over the pilgrim trails to Girnar. Chudasamas and Solankis were ultimately feudatories of the Gurjara Pratihara empire which ruled most of north India for a period of nearly four centuries. The Mughals made it a point to consolidate their hold over Junagadh once they defeated the Muzzaffarids. During the reign of the nawabs of Junagadh, Girnar was under British watch and they, in their turn, have left their imprint on Uparkot in the form of pumping stations for a tank commissioned by the nawab and modifications to the ramparts of the fort. All Indian empires seem to have sought the spiritual blessing of Girnar for their temporal prowess.

16 January 2010, 2:20 p.m.

'Bhaisahab, which is the bus to Somnath?' I ask in Hindi.

The man looks over his shoulder in the direction of the bus bays and replies in Gujarati. 'It isn't here yet. You can take the bus to Veraval instead,' he says, pointing to a bus that has just started up. 'From Veraval you can take an auto to Somnath,' he adds.

This seems reasonable since I have already checked on Google Earth that the two places are quite close to each other.

'Get on board. It'll leave soon,' he warns.

'Tickets on the bus itself?' D asks, in Hindi.

'Yes,' he replies in English.

The bus to Veraval doesn't take long to weave out of Junagadh to enter a state highway that is a little bumpy but flanked by trees that serve as frames to a countryside redolent of a coastal plain. I draw this inference because the ride to the Saurashtra coast is remarkably reminiscent of our bus journeys through Puri where we go often, to visit the temple of Jagannath close to the sea.

As I point out the cooling tower of a power plant to D, a voice from behind us says in Hindi, 'Where are you from?'

'Delhi,' D says.

'Okay.' The man looks reassured as if he had suspected something more sinister.

After that, the man comes and sits across the aisle from us and a muddled monologue follows for close to an hour during which he curses

and praises, by turns, politicians at both the local and state level, as also
the state of Gujarat State Transport buses in the region.

'Your stop is almost here,' the conductor informs him gruffly. At
which point he reluctantly gets up, waves at us and goes to the front of
the bus to disembark.

'Do you know he is a Brahmin by caste?' the conductor tells us. 'But
he doesn't behave like one. People have high regard for Brahmins who
maintain their respect in society, no? This fellow drinks all the time. He
is also a Gujarat State Transport employee, a driver as it happens. So he
can get onto all the buses you know, off duty. He has four daughters, very
decent girls, but he squanders his salary on bad habits. Drivers get good
salary. Eight to ten thousand rupees. But no. He often gets into fights
during these bus rides, when he's going home after duty. That is why I
came over here.'

We listen without blinking.

16 January 2010, 5:17 p.m.

From Veraval we take an auto that rushes along a coastal road towards
Somnath. The smell of fish fills the auto as we go past several boat-
building enterprises and fishing hamlets.

At the cusp of evening, we reach Somnath, basically a few streets
hemmed in by the large compound of the temple. Perhaps because we
has heard stories of the repeated destruction of Somnath, we are a little
taken aback at its form now. The courtyard is fully tiled and the running
of the temple seems to have been completely modernized, with security
grilles, shoe bays, sitting shelters. Only the wandering cows remain from
a less corporate past. The temple itself sits in front of the sea and is now
fully restored, all plastered and painted like a modern Indian temple.

Inside is one of the twelve jyotirlingas of India, placed in a sanctum
that seems to have been on the bucket list of many Islamic warlords of
the Indian subcontinent, including but not restricted to Ghazni, Khilji,
Begada and Aurangzeb. A mass of devotees sways inside, the temple
scents – incense, smoke and camphor – mingling with the assurances
and vulnerabilities that seem to reek from their bodies. The temple
bells sound; the sea breeze mixes with the chants that resound from the
priests.

We retreat to the back of the temple where there is a sea protection wall with a 'Baan Stambh' or arrow pillar symbolizing that there is no land between the temple and Antarctica. Gulls fly past us and D says, 'Do you realize this is the first time we are seeing the sea on this journey?' The sun hovers on the horizon, ready to drop. The sea, reflecting the colours of dusk, undulates towards us.

The Arabian Sea.

The sea, this sea, was part of the nawab of Junagadh's argument in favour of acceding to Pakistan at the time of Partition, since his domain would have 'direct' connectivity with Karachi by boat. He acceded on 15 September 1947. This argument, however, proved hollow in the face of the Indian blockade that allowed neither men nor material to reach Junagadh, despite the nawab apparently having access to the sea. The result was severe shortages in Junagadh and deep civil unrest, providing an opening for resident Indian nationalists, led by Samaldas Gandhi, to set up a rebel government called 'Arzee Hukumat'. Once the nawab had vacated the palace, having handed over the power of attorney to his dewan, Shahnawaz Bhutto, father of Zulfikar Ali Bhutto, Arzee Hukumat captured the nawab's palace and Uparkot.

Shahnawaz Bhutto requested the Indian government to intervene and take over the reins of the erstwhile princely state to protect the lives of its citizens. Samaldas Gandhi's Arzee Hukumat was invited by the Government of India to administer the state in the interim, an offer he declined. Nehru, meanwhile, wanted to orchestrate the incorporation of Junagadh in a democratic fashion and conducted a plebiscite in February 1948 which found over 90 per cent voting in favour of integration with India. How could the Republic of India, which is the greatest of pan-Indian empires, not follow in the footsteps of all its predecessors, whether the Mauryas, the Guptas, the Gurjara Pratiharas, the Mughals and, of course, the Raj, in retaining Junagadh?

Nine

How (Not) to Tell a City What You Feel for It: Delhi

It took me quite a while to become an experienced vacationer, because travelling was not something you did much in Russia, at least not by *your* choice. Because we were not allowed to move freely, we used to approach our vacation time with a different attitude. We used to brag about places we *couldn't* go. A typical vacation discussion sounded something like this:

ALEXEI: I can't go to Miami this year!

NIKOLAI: Miami? You call that a vacation? I can't go to *Paris*!

– Comedian Yakov Smirnoff, *America on Six Rubles a Day*

36

It is a conjecture not unfounded that I am overcompensating with this punishing travel routine now because of not having travelled very much – or very far – as a child. I do remember rollicking summer vacations in Jharkhand where my parents grew up. Proper summers, replete with picnics by luscious waterfalls, skits put up by cousins, and mutton curry and rice at night on a dining table that stood rather apologetically on the traditional red verandah (where you were meant to sit on the floor and eat). The verandah ran along the house at the back and gave way to a courtyard. Behind the courtyard was a messy overgrown garden with a well in the middle and the tree of the saintly ghost by the furthest wall – but I am getting distracted here. My dad did want to take us for more vactioney stuff (the sort of things my Bengali classmates always boasted of: Rajasthan total package or Kanyakumari via Apollo Hospital in Chennai) but the fact is that his filial responsibilities were many and those were not times when people's disposable incomes had reached the proportions they now have. At least for us, family getaways were not that common. Once, after my boards, my parents and I went to Nepal; one time in class six we zigzagged across Orissa (now Odisha) in our little second-hand red Maruti; and the most memorable holiday for me was the week in a gorgeous little villa perched atop a hill in Darjeeling, from which we could see the Kanchenjunga every morning, reflecting the moods of the sun. I was in class eight.

The first time I came to Delhi, it was for an entrance exam, and I was twenty, in the final year of BA. We were a group of four. My friend Chumki was accompanied by her dad, and my uncle, who came as my chaperone. Chumki's dad was a very resourceful gentleman, full of bounce and enthusiasm, and he booked us rooms at Banga Bhavan, the West Bengal government's guest house, which can only be got by pulling strings at several levels. Thus, my first view of Delhi was of wide tree-lined avenues with bungalows and government buildings in large shady compounds on either side. This leafy old-world stretch was interrupted only by the pocket of tall buildings that comprised the central business district at Barakhamba Road. The day after the exam in DU, we went, first to Janpath to shop (my friend Chumki bought a flowing white skirt) and then to raucous Karol Bagh, a mind-bending maze of traffic and noise, signs and people. I loved it. The glimpse of that original Delhi has stayed with me over the years. I can't remember what Chumki bought at Karol Bagh but I do know that the arches of several houses had caught my eye.

The second time, in 2005, I came with my mother to gain admission in JNU; we stayed with relatives in Dwarka, and it was the third place I saw in Delhi. A suburbia with multi-storey houses, obsessively numbered buildings and blocks, and many, many schools. It was late July and the concrete was baking under an intense sun. On most days, the streets were deserted after eleven. I could not wait to shift to the campus. After all, the truth was that I had followed S to Delhi, and I could not wait to throw myself into university life, with its politics and the tremendous

sense of radical freedom its enlightened students breathed (that was the
JNU hard sell). I moved to one of the girls' hostels, to stay as a 'guest'
with one of S's classmates, that is, as a legal illegal. After a month or so,
I was allotted a room of my own.

Soon our world in Delhi was pretty much the campus. Built on
the foothills of the Aravallis, with large forested stretches still extant
and the red-brick buildings as non-intrusive as one could possibly
imagine, the campus was beautiful. The neem trees shed in spring,
the bougainvillea flamed at fall. There was little need to venture out
– except to libraries and plays. In any case, it was still a Delhi where
Ansal Plaza in South Extension was the only mall. We went for
occasional movies and desserts to PVR Priya, close to campus. It was
only after we got married, left JNU's protective bubble and began to
look for a place for ourselves, that we bought furniture, piece by piece,
that we got our first gas connection, and received our first salaries. It
was only then that we really got to know the city. I remember every
individual excursion vividly. The price we paid for each thing. Yet,
I have no general impressions of Delhi from that time. I was too
absorbed in humdrum householding, at which I was woefully inept (I
still am), and the fact of my love for the city became known to me only
after we took the decision of moving our stuff back home.

Afterwards, we continued to come to Delhi regularly. We stayed
with friends or at guest houses in the Bengali neighbourhood of C.R.
Park in south Delhi, packing each day with meetings and errands.
Every single time, we were assailed by an intriguing play of twin
sentiments: unease that what was once our home was now merely
another hostile city, and intense anxiety that we might never come
back to live here again. Once you leave Delhi, the entry barriers seem
to get higher and higher every year, the incumbents more and more
smug. So we observe the rising prices with increasing horror and fall
back with relief on the grapes-are-sour presentiment, that it was all
for the better. But much like an unattainable lover becomes unsuitable
in the mind yet induces a certain delirium, when the train goes past
the suburbs of Delhi, and I begin to see the rows of unpainted brick-
wall houses standing against the dusty blue of the sky, my blood starts
pounding. When the train draws into NDLS and we pull our bags

from under the seats and I collect the bottles of water, one part of my mind rushes towards the wall of noise that vibrates in the station – and I cling to it. Half a feeling bubbles in my mind. And for about half a second, I recognize it, and then, embarrassed to let it gain body, I quickly turn to look at the line of bossy old coolies in red who have begun to file past us in the corridor.

Today, while writing, I can see the half-body of that disconnected feeling, and I have learnt to be more forgiving of my own disloyalties. As long as I have Delhi, I think, it doesn't matter if I do not travel any more again.

Saurav

Twenty minutes after the train draws into the platform, we step out of the railway station, and though we are walking briskly and our bags are heavy, the chill hits us immediately. A sock in the stomach. It is the quiescent cold of Delhi, steady and intense, and the grey sky makes it seem more acute. There is the usual melee of passengers jostling outside, arguing with coolies; a few dogs; several touts. It all seems muted though, because of the weather. People lining up outside the ATM, the snaking queues of autos and taxis, even the guys advertising their vehicles, seem a bit dazed. Fortunately we have no need for transport. This time in Delhi, we shall do exactly what hundreds of thousands of travellers coming to India do: live in budget rooms in Paharganj.

This is not our first time in Paharganj, though where we stayed the last time, Arakashan Road, is not exactly a backpacker hub. There are many mid-range hotels there, all marble and ACs – but low on sunlight or character – which advertise their names in giant lettering that glows in the night. Many foreigners in their late thirties, and several travel groups, favour this street. Indeed, at night, the general squalor or seediness of the place gets completely masked by the fluorescent haze cast by the rows of hotels, with their hoarding-like titles. A friend of ours, Neel Mojumdar (my batchmate in Presidency, D's professor's son), is now living in a hostel on Arakashan Road, attending one of those expensive tutorial homes that prepare students for the civil services (basically, hanging out and watching movies and getting drunk when he can afford it). It was Neel who suggested we stay on Arakashan Road. Apparently, the family which owns the hostel where the tutorial home boards its students also owns a hotel, and he got us one of the sunless marble rooms for seven hundred rupees a night. It was from there that we set out on the journey.

But this time we'll be staying where the Israelis do – and hopefully we can get the sort of bargains they manage. I'd called Hotel Namaste India yesterday and booked a room.

While I am studying the map of the area in *Lonely Planet* to figure out the location of the hotel, D has hailed a cycle rickshaw. Apparently the guy – wearing a jaunty cap and matching jacket – knows where Namaste India is, though he says, 'Why do you want to go there? I will take you to a much better hotel. For decent people like you. I can tell.'

'No need, no need,' I tell him, annoyed. But D is already perched on the red seat.

'We need to see Hotel Namaste India only,' she explains. 'Take us there.'

'Why?' asks the man, mystified.

I am now sitting next to D, feeling extremely foolish as any grown man in a cycle rickshaw might. Apologetic too. 'Shooting purpose,' she tells him, flashing him a charming smile. 'Doordarshan. Budgets are very small.'

'Oh,' says the man. 'But Doordarshan programmes show good values.' He starts pedalling fast. But then, of course, in Paharganj, even if one pedals fast, one is not going anywhere. There are hundreds of people, cars, autos, other rickshaws and cows clogging the road. Later we see, 20 feet down the road, past shops bursting with bags and clothes and semi-precious stones, a bullock cart hemmed on either side by a black Honda City, going in opposite directions. Both the black Honda Cities are driven by young sardars in turquoise turbans. Deeper, far deeper into Paharganj, there is a park. And beyond the park, the backpackers are sighted. Sleepily they emerge out of tiny lanes that wriggle out like arteries from the main road, and rubbing their eyes and shaking their afros, they enter cafes with dingy fronts.

'Look, look.' D pokes me with her elbow. 'That's a German Bakery right there! My Jaisalmer grief is finally over. Can we come and have breakfast here?'

There are shops selling kaftans and ponchos and beaded bags – and one or two selling books. I realize I am going to have a tough time with the budget here. Finally, the rickshaw-wallah says. 'We're here.'

'Where is Namaste India?' D asks.

'In that gali.' He points to a tiny lane on the right that is barely even visible. 'Go past the urinal, the shops, the cyber cafe and you'll find it. Nice old building. That much is true. Of course, nowadays nobody likes these buildings. When you said shooting, I immediately understood. Otherwise, what would decent Indian youths from khatay-pitay homes like you two be doing here?'

⌐

The man at the counter has an imposing moustache. However, the pink walls in the exact shade that Barbie might favour take away slightly from the severity of his countenance.

'Hello,' I say. 'We have booked a room here. I called…'

'Who are you?' the man interrupts sternly. 'We don't give our rooms just like that.'

I bristle at the rudeness but try to keep my voice even. 'My name is Saurav Jha and this is my wife Devapriya. I called from Ahmedabad, and you said that rooms are available and we just need to show up. When I asked the tariffs, you said room rates begin from three hundred.'

'I don't remember any such phone call.'

There is an impasse. I hesitate, unsure whether to turn and leave or blow my top or look up call history in my phone. 'Wait,' says the man finally, looking away from the computer screen he's fixated on, his moustache quivering, 'Did you say three p.m.? There is a possibility that you may have spoken to my brother.'

That explains it. The man I had spoken to on the phone had a similar voice but a mild engaging manner.

'Do you have I-cards?'

'Yes,' I reply patiently, producing my driver's licence.

'And Madam?'

D scrabbles around in her purse and produces her PAN card.

He takes a cursory look and purses his lips. 'There is, unfortunately, only one room available. It is a large four-bedded room. For 600 rupees.

A couple of German couples came in last night and took away the two regular doubles.'

I shake my head. D groans. 'Look, let's just take whatever is available. I have to go to JNU immediately afterwards.'

'The budget?'

'We spent two whole nights on the road. On the way to and from Junagadh. I bet you can adjust!'

Meanwhile, the man thrusts his nose in our direction again.

'What is this about JNU?'

'I am enrolled there,' D explains.

'You are a student at JNU? Then why on earth do you want a room here? Oh, that is very fishy.'

'It's because we are writing a book,' she says. 'It's for research.'

'Madam, to me it is fishy why you will come all the way from JNU here. Wrong reasons, I am sure.'

'Wait,' I say, though now I realize that we could have just picked up our bags and left. There are plenty of rooms in Paharganj. But somehow both D and I are bending over backwards trying to explain the legitimacy of our room requirements to this guy. I bet he doesn't ask firangs all these questions. It's because we're Indians! 'You have Internet, right? Why don't you google my name? Saurav Jha. My articles on *World Politics Review* will show up. They have a photograph too. You can check. It'll tell you about the book I have written and this one that we're writing now.'

The man narrows his eyes and peers suspiciously at the computer.

D hisses at me. 'Why are we allowing ourselves to be humiliated like this?'

Now I get angry. 'You said we should take that expensive room just to hurry matters up! Instead of traipsing out again. It's all so that you can take a quick bath and go to the campus.'

'Fine,' she sniffs.

'This does seem bona fide,' the man says unhappily. 'But we have to be careful. There are problems of all kinds in this area. Do you have any document that *says* she is your wife?'

'We're not carrying our marriage registration certificate around for crying out loud!'

'Wait,' D says. 'My passport. It gives Saurav Jha as spouse.'

Both the man and I look at her. 'But it's not on me. I've stowed it safely with a friend. I shall give it to you in the evening.'

'For sure?'

'Yes, absolutely.'

'Fine. Please fill your details in the register.'

While I write, D wanders over to the bookshelves. After I finish, the owner begins to scribble his notes in the register. Two Israeli girls in hippie gear – bright flannel ponchos and harem pants – drift down the stairs behind us and go out through the main doorway. A lackey appears from somewhere and tells the man urgently, 'Sir, *bahut der se darwaza nahin khol rahin hain. Aaiyegaa?*'

The man jumps up. In a trice he's out of the counter area. With stiff military carriage, he marches up the stairs. Midway, he looks back and asks us to follow him. The lackey twinkles at us genially. Apparently, our room has been cleaned and is ready for occupation.

The corridor upstairs is gloomy but it has just been swept. The lackey unlocks our room and switches on the lights. The first thing that arrests me is the use of arches. It's a fine touch, and the room is large and satisfying in a nostalgic sort of way. The walls are bubble-gum pink, the floor is traditional terrazzo in mossy green and the four separate single four-poster beds are covered with starched white sheets. D has already located the bathroom. The man disappears to add weight to his boss's opinions a couple of rooms away. He leaves our door open.

I keep the bags on chairs and with my thigh begin to push one of the beds towards another. Suddenly, rising well above the scraping sound this generates, a dull screech of wood against the floor, there is a loud banging on a door. The owner is heard shouting, 'Madam, madam, please open the door.' Banging. 'Madam, can you hear me?' More banging. 'Hello, hello, please, can you open the door?' Still more banging. This goes on for ten minutes. D appears. She immediately collects the pillows from the other two beds and lines them up on ours. The plenitude of extra pillows! She says she's feeling blessed. 'Hmph,' I snort. 'Three hundred rupees extra for your pillows and blessedness.'

The banging comes in a last flourish of rat-tat-rat-tat-rat-a-tat-rat-tat. 'Madam. One final time. If you don't open the door, I will have to call the police.'

There is a pregnant pause.

'Maybe someone's OD'd inside,' D tells me.

There is a click.

'Yez?' a languid female voice is heard, her accent uncertain. 'Can we 'elp you?' There is another voice, this one, clearly French.

'Madams,' the owner says. 'I was knocking so hard. You did not hear?'

'No, we were zleeping,' one of them offers. The r is rolled perfectly.

'Wiz earmuffs. Eet eez so cold.'

'Your friends left a while ago. They told us to check on you. That they had also tried to wake you up and failed.'

'What friendz?' one of the girls asks.

'We have no friendz. You are making miztake. We must sleep now. Merci.'

We hear the door shut.

'What friendz?' the owner mimics. '*Arre wahi doh Angrez ladke. Ek saath hi toh aaye thay? Hum kya jaane* friends *ya* enemies? *Humlog ko bataaya ki nahi bataaya, ki ladkiyan behosh bhi ho sakti hain?*'

'*Bilkul bataayaa,* sir-ji,' the lackey agrees strongly.

They pass our door and the owner pops his head in. 'One thing. Guests are not allowed in the rooms. Got it?'

D spends the day at JNU, getting her work done, running from counter to counter in the red-brick buildings, while I finish a pending article. We meet at Chittaranjan Park at her friend Gee's for dinner. We collect the passport, regale the charming Chatterjees with our tall travellers' tales, and get a photocopy of the passport on the way back. When we return to Paharganj, it is half past ten and we are exhausted. We present the photocopy to the man at the counter, but it is the brother. 'Oh, that's fine,' he says through his moustache, glancing casually at the passport and pushing it away. One ID proof is enough. We have a copy of your driving licence, I think.'

'Actually, your brother insisted,' D tells him. 'This proves we are married.'

'Oh, my brother?' The man shakes his head apologetically. 'Don't mind him. Also, if you like, you can take a book or two from the shelves.'

37

'Hi, Neel,' I say. 'Come on in.'

It is evening. Our second day at Hotel Namaste India.

'How did you manage to get past the gorgon at the counter?' S asks, his eyes still on the laptop. The second article should have been sent off by afternoon. But he's busy catching up on news from around the world – and it's still not done. I am in a pretty vicious mood. Waiting for hours to check my email. The computer will be handed over to me only *after* the revenue-earning work has been accomplished. 'Apparently, guests are not allowed in rooms. This hotel is worse than many hostels.'

Neel waltzes around the room vaguely for a couple of minutes and then begins to take off the various layers that provide buffer to his Bong frame from the audacious cold outside. First the jacket. He keeps it lovingly on one of the spare beds. I can see one sweater, one woollen turtle-neck skivvy below. 'I bet you're wearing thermals too, Neel?' I ask innocently. 'Yes. Of course. Woollycot.' He uncurls the grey muffler which was wound first around his neck and then around his head. I realize this is going to be an interesting performance and sit down on the opposite bed and nibble a cookie. After the muffler is unwound, a grey monkey cap is revealed. It goes well with the sweater. 'You can take off the monkey cap, Neel, it's not *that* cold inside.' Below the monkey cap, he is wearing a pair of leopard print earmuffs that are being sold in Paharganj by the hundreds. He changes his mind – it's too cold – and wears the monkey cap again. He plants himself on the bed, next to his jacket. 'Neel,' I say seriously, handing him a cookie, 'it is not safe.'

'What?' he asks, loudly.

'It's not safe to walk around in this state.'

'What state?' He looks a bit shifty. 'I had only one gulp. The others were drinking. But I was leaving to meet you guys. Okay, two gulps.'

S bursts out laughing. 'Not *that*,' I say. 'Your ears are under so many layers, I am scared you won't be able to hear the honking. The traffic in Paharganj is dangerous.'

'What?' Neel asks, looking up from the box of cookies. 'I can't hear you.'

'How did you get past the gorgon at the counter?' S shouts.

'Don't know about dragons. The gentleman at the counter was very nice. He didn't say anything about no visitors. Of course, I also told him I am a lawyer.'

'Ah, nice, the shift must have changed,' S said. 'It's the brother. The other one is very khadoos.'

Neel Mojumdar is the sort of boy whose looks, in Bengal, would be compared to goddess Durga's elder son, Kartik's. He is fair, even-featured, has a thin moustache, and a genial, slightly goody-goody expression. His mum was my professor, and he was in S's batch in college. Studied history. He used to write poetry in those days under the pseudonym 'Red Rose' and once or twice waylaid S in the corridors of the economics department to read him some of his latest work. He can be a delightful person to hang out with. (Mostly.)

After the third cookie, Neel feels warm enough to take off the monkey cap and loosen the earmuff somewhat. The conversation finally progresses.

'So, this girl I am in love with?' he says.

'Yes. Norkim,' I supply, eating the last biscuit. He had told us details of his unrequited love story the last time we met. She studies with him in the same tutorial on Barakhamba Road, and does not return his longing looks.

'She has *finally* agreed to a date.'

'That's nice, Neel. That's progress.'

'She was standing with her friend Gurmeet. So I asked them both.'

'Are you sure you can call it a date?' I ask carefully.

'Sort of. Gurmeet may not come. Any ideas where I should take her?'

'Wimpy's,' I say immediately. 'You should have a spicy chicken fillet burger with extra cheese.' My mouth begins to water. Sometimes we used to go to Wimpy's from our office on Tolstoy Road.

S finally shuts off the laptop and says, 'Shall we go then?'

'Can we go to Wimpy's?' I ask immediately.

'No,' he replies shortly. 'Our room has pushed us over-budget already.'

We'd planned to go for dinner together. Neel is not familiar with this part of Paharganj so we thought we'd show him around and point out the cheap eateries. I've already fallen in love with the place. (Not the hotel, though. The gorgon/kind man blow-hot/blow-cold thing has got too much. The gorgon demanded to see the passport the minute he spotted us this morning.)

'Not so soon,' Neel says. 'Wait, I have some stuff for you guys. I just returned from home.'

He takes out a battered box from his bag. There are sandeshes, slightly misshapen from the train journey, but delicious.

'You know what happened on the train? So these three Bangladeshi gentlemen got in. I began chatting with them. We got along famously. When the TC came, I got my ticket checked. Then the gentlemen offered theirs. After studying them carefully, the TC said. "Sir, where are you going?" "Delhi," they replied immediately. "By what train?" The men looked at me as though the TC was daft. I rolled my eyes. "Rajdhani. Obviously." "Which Rajdhani?" the TC asked. Now the Bangladeshis were stumped. "Delhi Rajdhani?" One of them offered. The TC sighed. "There are two Rajdhanis from Calcutta to Delhi. One from Sealdah station, one from Howrah station." "We got in from Howrah," the men replied. "But your ticket is from Sealdah!"'

He waits a moment.

'Then?' I ask.

'"I am a lawyer," I said, entering the conversation.'

'And then?'

'Then what? We are an atithidevo bhava country. Seats were found for the three gentlemen on the Howrah Rajdhani after I established that the ticket should underline the bit about the station.'

'Good.'

In this manner, Neel Mojumdar keeps us entertained for the better part of an hour, and then we decide to get dinner. It takes Neel about ten minutes to gear up, and then all three of us troop out. We walk through the pissy lane rapidly and emerge onto the main road, with the dazzling shops and crowds. We sit in one of the tiny restaurants where one gets a limited thali for forty rupees. We order three thalis.

'Hey,' Neel says loudly (he's wearing all his ear guards), 'you guys want to come with me and see Norkim from a distance at the bus stop tomorrow?'

'Much as we like to stalk unsuspecting future civil servants, I am afraid not,' S says. And then adds, apropos of nothing, 'We are going to Mathura tomorrow.'

'We *are*?' I ask, flabbergasted. This is the first I am hearing of Mathura.

'We can't hang around and haemorrhage money here. *Hurtling pace.*' He snaps his fingers.

'Oh nice,' Neel says. 'If it weren't for the date-type thing with Norkim, I could have come.'

'Neel,' I tell him meanly, 'how much did the tutorial charge for these classes?'

'Don't be such a killjoy.' He scowls. 'Seventy-six thousand. I am not going *anywhere*. I will attend classes on the Constitution of India. Happy?'

38

It is possible that we have finally morphed into travellers. Our constant bickering from last evening eases as soon as we sit in the bus to Mathura. I feel a little flicker of good cheer inside; S relaxes perceptibly. We begin to find each other tolerable again. We can even bear to laugh at each other's jokes. People crowd in, bringing the distinctive smells from their worlds: Paan Parag, travel, ittar, besan batter for pakoras. The conductor jabbers away with the driver. Salesmen get in from the front door and after showcasing their wares – peanuts, amla digestives, Chinese toys and pirated Hindi books – exit from the rear. The familiarity soothes us both. Paharganj had dulled us into an uneasy stupor; we are glad to be on our way.

The moment the bus leaves the depot (the noisy, smelly, insanely crowded Sarai Kale Khan), my phone begins to ring. It's an unknown number, and initially, the reception is scratchy. Finally I realize it's Zvika.

'Hey guys,' I say, '*so* great to hear from you. Where are you? Still in Rishikesh?'

'Just reached Delhi,' he says. 'Paharganj. We've checked into Hotel "Yes Please" (snicker, snicker). You?'

I groan. 'We were in Paharganj till this morning! We've just left for Mathura in a bus. It's near Agra. You guys have already done Agra, no? Damn. We'd have loved to see you.'

Zvika conveys this to Motty in Hebrew and we hear twin groans.

'So much bad luck! Anyway, we thought we'll check with you guys once in case you were here.'

'How long will you be in Paharganj?'

'Not sure,' Zvika says. 'There is so much to see. Your country is just too big. We have to go to the south also. I want to start travelling tomorrow itself. But Motty wants to wait a little. Rest. Like an old man. Rishikesh was really great. How were your journeys?'

'Lovely, very lovely. So SJ will email you our coordinates then. Is this your new number?'

'Yes, we've finally got a SIM card. So, happy journey then.'

'Have a good time in Paharganj. Try the German Bakery, okay. Give my love to Motty.'

⌐

Our initial euphoria wanes a little when we find how very slowly this particular bus moves on the highway, stopping again and again. And then some more. It seems to be waiting for passengers who have not even left their homes yet. I try reading a book I nicked from the Paharganj hotel – a novel with the intriguing title *London Is the Best Place in America*, but soon it begins to get shadowy outside. There is no real light inside the bus. In any case, I cannot remember too many details of this journey. The notes are cryptic. Make what you will of this scrawl:

Haryana:
1. 'Hell or Helmet – Your choice.'
2. Vandalized stadium.

Our co-passengers are also quite the traveller's delight. They spit incessantly from the windows. Sometimes they clear their throats in elaborate fugues before spitting. In between the spitting and the chatting, they find time to shell groundnuts briskly and pop them into their mouths. At dusk, we stop at a local dhaba. When we get up to disembark, in the grey light spooling in from a couple of tube lights outside, we find the floor of the bus strewn with groundnut shells. There is constant crunching underfoot.

The dhaba is in the middle of a depressing clearing by the road. Eatery, corner shop, perhaps even animal shelter of sorts (several large pigs sleep contentedly in a muddy patch). Men line up against the back wall to pee. We stretch our legs and look elsewhere. Giant billboards on either side of the road proclaim the leadership of certain Yadav strongmen who, they would have us believe, are deeply involved in the development of their constituency. I am irresistibly drawn by the aroma of frying – a powerful smell of old oil that masks the stench of urine – and we share a giant double-fried alu paratha. It is greasy and satisfying in a primal way. I can't find a ladies toilet, and in sheer annoyance, buy a large bar of Cadbury's to distract myself.

Our co-passengers have congregated by the bus, and now that they have eaten their fill, they are burping happily and wiping greasy hands on flimsy serviettes a young boy is handing out along with the parathas. One woman hitches up her sari to clean her kid's ass, having secured a tumbler of water from the dhaba (she's thrifty, does not believe in spending fifteen rupees to *buy* a bottle of water). The boy looks impassively at the crowd around, many of whom smile at him and make small talk. The mother finally throws the dirty diaper under the bus, soaps her hands, adjusts her sari coyly and then clambers up with the little boy.

By the time the driver and conductor finish their meals, it is pitch-dark. Bats hover above our heads in the inky air. I look at S, who is sporting a long face. 'Who died?' I ask him, but he just shakes his head.

'I am beginning to worry now. Check the time. Given the bloody speed of this bus, it doesn't seem likely we'll get to Mathura before nine.'

Ten

How to Row Your Boat Ashore

'Goodbye, Professor Godbole,' she continued, suddenly agitated. It's a shame we never heard you sing.

'I may sing now,' he replied, and did.

His thin voice rose, and gave out one sound after another. At times there seemed rhythm, at times there was the illusion of a Western melody. But the ear, baffled repeatedly, soon lost any clue, and wandered in a maze of noises, none harsh or unpleasant, none intelligible. It was the song of an unknown bird. Only the servants understood it. They began to whisper to one another. The man who was gathering water chestnut came naked out of the tank, his lips parted with delight, disclosing his scarlet tongue. The sounds continued and ceased after a few moments as casually as they had begun – apparently halfway through a bar, and upon the subdominant.

'Thanks so much; what was that?' asked Fielding.

'I will explain in detail. It was a religious song. I placed myself in the position of a milkmaiden. I say to Shri Krishna: "Come! Come to me only." The God refuses to come. I grow humble and say: "Do not come to me only. Multiply yourself into a hundred Krishnas, and let one go to each of my hundred companions, but one, O Lord of the Universe, come to me." He refuses to come. This is repeated several times. The song is composed in a raga appropriate to the present hour, which is the evening.

'But He comes in some other song, I hope?' said Mrs Moore, gently.

'Oh no, He refuses to come,' repeated Godbole, perhaps not understanding her question. 'I say to Him, Come, come, come, come, come, come. He neglects to come.'

Ronny's steps had died away, and there was a moment of absolute silence. No ripple disturbed the water, no leaf stirred.

– E.M. Foster, *A Passage to India*

39

It is long past nine and apparently past bedtime in this strange new town.

And yet, though this is the impulse of the hour, it is only a half-truth. It is neither strange – since I was a child, Mathura featured heavily in the Krishna lore one heard and so it is familiar in a profoundly non-literal way – nor new. In fact, Mathura is one of the oldest continuously inhabited places in India. If in the age of the Buddha, it is recorded that Mathura suffered from bad roads, dust storms and an infestation of wild dogs, between the second century BC and third century AD, it was a leading metropolis on the trade route, renowned for its magnificence, prosperity and the generosity of its populace.

We sway on a rickshaw, squashed together, bags and all. The buildings are silent in the dark. A few windows gleam yellow or white behind thin curtains, but the cold seems to have lowered a net on the neighbourhood. Though the bazaar where we found the rickshaw was full of people, here, in the old part of Mathura, near the ghats, there seems to be no one about. The houses and dharmashalas, imposing structures with traditional facades, are impassive in the night. Shops are shuttered. Kiosks are locked up. Street lamps are few and far between, and where one finds them, the copper light they pour on the uneven littered streets invariably throws into relief one or two thin men, all muffled up, walking briskly or cycling. At one point I look up to the sky and, on the tangle of wires running past a derelict building, at least a hundred grey pigeons are asleep. I point them out to S. But he remains grim, disinterested in anything but the destination. I strain my ears. Is that the lapping of water?

The bus had dropped us off at the highway and after walking nearly half a kilometre, we came to a bazaar where we found our rickshaw-wallah. He knew the place we'd booked in the old town and agreed to go, but he did warn us it would take a while. We had no option but to agree.

When we finally arrive, I realize that we have struck a good bargain. The hotel, a Bengali-run establishment, is on the Bengali Ghat and looks on to the hauntingly beautiful black river. The raja of Burdwan had this ghat built on the Yamuna, and the hotel, across the road which runs along the ghats, is built on a plot of land that was granted by the raja. Ever since Gaudiya Vaishnavism was established in eastern India by Chaitanya hundreds of years ago, devotees from Bengal have been flocking to Mathura. It is a simple but substantial building, redolent of Bengali architecture from north Calcutta, pale yellow with red stripes marking its shuttered windows, now shabby with age. The durwan has been waiting for us, and greets us in Bengali. A middle-aged man quickly emerges from inside, the quintessential dada of Calcutta neighbourhoods, wearing a woollen cap and brown sweater, speaking a faintly accented Bengali. We get done with formalities in a trice. He takes us upstairs to our room which is ready.

The house has been designed in the traditional way, a central courtyard ringed by a corridor with trabeate arches and rooms that open on both sides to ensure cross-ventilation. There is substantial jaali work on the whitewashed walls. The corridor is dusty. Coolers and unused furniture clutter the corners. Since we've been given discounted rates (I'd spoken to the owner's wife in Bengali), we don't get a room with a view of the river, but if we walk down the corridor, there is an open space at the end commanding fine views. The room is cosy. The mosaic work – a pattern in green, yellow, white and brown – is reminiscent of old Calcutta too, but the wood panelling on two of the walls is more like in hill stations than in pilgrim towns. I immediately ask for a cup of tea. I've not had any tea in the evening, and it's given me a headache. There is a little carved wooden desk in the corner with a matching mirror angled on it, and that is where I write my notes as I sip the very milky tea. S freshens up in the bathroom. In anticipation of our arrival, the staff have kept two veg thalis for us.

We eat in the dining room downstairs, and the food is hot and evocative of home. Masur dal with nigella seeds – that underrated spice not used too often in north India but a mainstay of Bengali cuisine. Alu bhaja. Begun bhaja. Fine-grained rice. Afterwards, we walk to the river. There are marble benches and a cupola-like structure on the ghat that gleams in the dark. A boat is moored just off the steps and it bobs about. The breeze bears a suggestion of spirits and other creatures in the distance, but neither of us speaks out their names. We investigate the lane at either end, though the dark imposing houses are silent and reveal nothing. We return to sit on the benches. Far away, the water and the night sky meet. On the back of the breeze comes a soft slow rhythmic hum, but we can't be sure of its source. Suddenly there is a flash of white which recalls me to the present.

A swan?

With a graceful gait, it glides on the black waters, slowly coming into focus.

And then we see it. It is not a swan, but a pelican. And far more majestic.

'Is it a good omen?' I ask S, who seems delighted at its appearance.

'Perhaps.' He smiles.

It is half past eleven, and in the stillness of the night we hold hands for a while. A fine mist begins to cloud the surface of the river and then, as it sometimes happens, the mood dims perceptibly. A certain reserve descends on us. A sense that we will never be able to paraphrase what we feel here, now, enters our throats and holds us back, even as we feel the thing. But what is the *thing*?

Neither of us voices are doubts aloud, perhaps for fear of disappointing the other – though the other has already disappointed and been disappointed. I stare at the undulating river until my thoughts are lost. The pelican is gone.

'Can we come back here again – and live for a month?'

'But we've just arrived,' he says, surprise registering in his voice.

'Still,' I say. 'We will come back once more – and *that* time I shall know.' Know what to do with these sensations.

Abruptly, I get up and turn to go in.

Something has soured in me and I am not sure what it is. Perhaps it is just exhaustion.

40

The next morning we wake up late and have breakfast, if not in bed, then near enough. S eats at the table in the corner while I recline against the bedpost and chew. Alu parathas served with tomato sauce, yet another Bengali quirk. The strange sourness in me last night has now been transmitted to S. He checks his mail in silence, addresses some of his correspondence. I walk down to the common verandah. The sun has climbed high. The river is bright. People are walking past the river but the steps of the ghat are deserted. The boat we saw last night is no longer there. I come back to the room and see S lying down, palms crossed on his chest.

'Is there a problem?' I ask him.

'Do you think I should sign a contract with that power magazine and do a couple of articles for them every month?'

I know which power magazine he's talking about. Somebody we know has just joined as the editor. (The guy is a bit psychotic – he'd killed seven cats in his childhood. Told us so himself quite casually. He used to be a colleague of S's at one time – and to all appearances is a clever, suave chap. Hopefully reformed.)

'Will they pay well?'

'Decent, I guess, but before that I will have to meet them in Delhi.'

'When?'

'They haven't said yet. The day the promoters of the magazine come from Bombay. I am still not sure I should say yes though.'

'If it's a regular gig, it's not such a bad thing, is it?' I remark, sitting down on the bed next to him. Fact is, I am a bit stretched by the constant worry about money that itches just below the skin and shoots nervous tics up and down. It's exhausting. I lie down next to him and say, 'I know it's soul-killing. But still. Worrying constantly about money is soul-killing too.'

He grunts something in reply.

We lie still, my right foot lightly touching his left. Outside our window, a pair of mynahs nip and trot on the sill and their shadows do the same on the opposite wall, the one that faces us. A pale yellow wall with paint peeling where the door hinges.

Finally, S gets up.

'So I'll write to them then and say I am interested. If I can get a connection, that is. The Internet is patchy. Not sure if the photon will connect. Do you want to get ready for the day?'

I begin to root for clothes in the backpacks. If there is a laundry service here, we should get a few of our clothes cleaned and be prepared for the onward journey. I have no idea where we will go next. Every time I think about it, a window slams shut in my head. It's peculiar. The mynahs fly away, and their place is immediately taken by a pair of pigeons who coo dramatically. Their shadows seem fatter, now that the sun is higher still.

⌐

Lunch is served in the dining room at one. It's a Bengali veg thali again, though with items different from last night's dinner. The paneer is made in the traditional style, with cumin and ginger paste; the grains of rice are fluffy and separate. We lick our fingers clean. Dada gets the plates cleared and tells us the Chaubey-jis want to meet us now, if we are free. They are in the next room. 'The Chaubey-jis?' S asks. What dada tells us in Bengali, casting dark glances at the next room, translates into roughly this: the hotel is owned and run by a Bengali family but the Chaubey-jis have some sort of stake in it too. Sweat equity or whatever, going back many years. They are locals – priests perhaps, I gather from the name – who have been *sort of* associated with this hotel for many years as guardians and liaison men. It is all a bit vague. But dada's loyalty is to the Bengali owners and he considers these people outsiders who merely stir up trouble and muddy the waters.

When we enter the next room, the elder of the two men welcomes us. He is in a white dhoti and cream kurta, holding on to a stately lathi even as he sits. I have a feeling he likes to bang it on the ground to emphasize a point. The younger man, whom he introduces as his nephew, is busy organizing chairs for us. The nephew wears grey trousers and chappals, a brown sleeveless sweater over a cream half-shirt. A navy-blue muffler is folded on his shoulder like a gamchha might be in summer.

'I have heard that the Chaubey-jis of Mathura are great gourmands,' S says.

It is clearly a good opener. The old man laughs happily and tells us that it is *one hundred per cent true*. And which other place can boast of butter, ghee and cream as authentic as those of Braj? The land where the lord himself was a cowherd!

It is, however, quickly established by S that we have not come here on a religious tour. Implicit in this is the conviction that we are not going to need their services after all, and we don't want to waste their time. But the two men, though their earlier shine is dimmed, remain seated. They seem eager to chat even though business is not likely. The old man begins a discussion on UP politics. The politicians are corrupt and thuggish. They appear only at election time, and their philosophy is *jiski lathi uski bhains*. The public is sheep-like. There is unbelievable inflation. Sugar is at forty-four rupees a kilo now! *That* Sharad Pawar, sugar baron, single-handedly responsible for this. And how much more money laundering, how much more? All the money raised in the name of cleaning the Yamuna has been siphoned off. Good DMs come occasionally but they are not allowed to work by the politicians. The rest are corrupt to the core. There was one Dr Harikrishna Paliwal – a legend among DMs. His children used to go to school in a rickshaw, his wife never wore a sari worth more than three hundred rupees. But how many like him are there?

Chaubey-ji says *public, inflation* and *legend* in English, also, *corrupt to the core*. The rest of his rant is in a Hindi strongly inflected with Braj. It is funny for me to see Braj employed in this context because to students of early Bengali poetics, Braj bhasha is the most poetic of all the Ardha-Magadhan prakrits. It is the language of poetry, not politics. Tagore wrote a number of songs in Braj bhasha – including a set called *Bhanusingher Padavali* (The Verses of Bhanusingha) – in the tradition of Vaishnava love poetry, and these highly melodious songs would be intelligible to speakers of Bengali, Hindi, Maithili, Oriya, Bhojpuri and Assamese too.

I rein in my mind and pay attention to what he is saying. There are several demands for separate statehood from within UP now: Braj Pradesh, Rohilkhand Pradesh, Harit Pradesh and Bundelkhand Pradesh. And he, for one, hopes to see a Braj Pradesh, together with parts of Rajasthan, created before he dies.

The courtyard is now in shade; the room is thrown into shadow. The sun must have gone behind a cloud. When we crossed the courtyard, on our way to lunch, sunlight had flickered in little pools on the mosaic – pink alternating with yellow – but now it is uniformly even. This room where we sit is pleasant too. Green arches, pale green mosaic, antique chairs with some sort of a furry throw on them. I tell the Chaubeys how beautiful I find the old town to be. 'Funny you should say so,' he remarks. 'Young brides these days don't want to live in these old houses any more. They want to live in those new flats coming up beyond Govardhan Chauraha. New kitchens, marble, AC vents on windows. To the youngsters, the old town is a litany of complaints: waterlogging in the rains, narrow lanes, crowds of pilgrims, old-fashioned people.' He says this without malice, however, as though understanding of such fancies. The nephew looks a bit shifty and gazes at the ground. 'But one thing is there about the old city: great warmth, great bonhomie. *That* these children will not get in the new townships.'

The conversation goes on. I see dada walking about in the courtyard. I hear children playing outside. Chickens clucking. Songs on the radio. I half-hear S taking their leave: we have to go into town for a few errands. Lovely talking. Is there a courier shop nearby? The nephew answers in detail. The old gentleman says enigmatically, after we get up, 'I'll tell you two things before you leave. The first is a couplet we firmly believe in: *Mathura ki beti/ Mathura ki gai/ Bhaag phute/ Toh baahar jai.*' (A daughter of Mathura/ Its milch cow too/ Only if her luck runs out/ Will she look for a city new.) He gets up and walks to the door with us. 'The second is this: the gopis are never going to leave Braj.'

Outside, though the sky is suffused with light, I cannot feel the sun on my face. The river is still. There are clouds gathering in the sky. But by evening they'll have blown over.

41

It is one of those days. We feel overburdened and yet light as air. We want to meld into the strange town as though we belong. Not have to look for more than an instant or a half-glance at that face or this sign painted on a blue door or the little girl in pigtails: the twisted skein of clues – the lanes, the dharmashalas, the samosas, the kirana shops – is entirely familiar. Not take any photographs. Not wonder why it is so dirty (it *is* very dirty) or extend the conversation to a philosophical position on why India is so dirty (colonialism made people give up on the macro-world over which they had no control and in which they had no stake, to withdraw inside micro-worlds, homes, which are, to the contrary, scrupulously clean) or even exclaim at the perfect adorableness of the menagerie that peacefully inhabits the most distinguished pile of rubbish (it is a giant mound of trash by the walls of a white house where cows, pigs, ducks, dogs, cats and monkeys cloister). We do not look curiously at passers-by in the hope that they will reveal something meaningful. We don't wear the friendly traveller smile.

We sit in the rickshaw and talk about the possibilities of money, and our plans, not noticing the giant poster stuck on an unplastered wall: 'Meet Tina, Super-successful animator. Like her, you can be, part of the booming animation industry.' We speak intensely, about our own troubles, as though we care nothing for the *Salmon Institute of Technology and Management*, or sheep nodding rhythmically in a street clogged with thousands of motorbikes and bicycles, or even at the bank of black clouds that roll in.

We simply rush ahead in our need to get to the kotwali and courier the little present – a green flannel hippie cloak – for our nephew in Calcutta. Mathura has reminded me that winter is waning rapidly in the plains and the gift, bought in cold Paharganj, has been lying in my bag for days. If we are in time and it goes out tonight, maybe it'll reach in two days and he can wear it to school before Calcutta gives over to summer. We might have to find an Internet cafe and check our mail (the hotel is in an unfortunate blank zone). We might have chai and samosas somewhere. That is all.

It is one of those days when the book could not matter less.

Ironically, I realize while writing, it is also one of those days when we have relinquished our lives to the reality of books: that *real* living is experienced only in the pages of books. Otherwise, it is the mere marking of time.

42

'Two tickets to Govardhan,' the conductor repeats, handing us stubs. He takes off his sunglasses and slips them into his pocket, he flashes a bright smile, exhibiting a fine pair of teeth. His khaki shirt is unbuttoned at the collar. He wears a bright red vest underneath.

'Can we get a bus to Barsana?' S asks him.

'You're going to Barsana?' the conductor repeats, as though he's not quite sure why we might want to do that.

We nod.

'There is no bus route to Barsana,' he says. 'The road is very bad. You will have to take a vikram on share.' Vikrams are three-wheelers, larger than regular autos, and sturdier. 'They leave every half an hour from Govardhan for Barsana.'

Outside the window, we can already see the eponymous Govardhan hill, brown with green patches, sharp against the azure sky. According to the *Bhagavata Purana*, at Govardhan, the villagers of Braj would gather for an autumnal festival in honour of Indra. This was a ceremony that was in practice from the days of yore. Krishna, however, told them that instead of worshipping far-off gods, they ought to give thanks for gifts that were closer home. Under his guidance, the villagers performed a giri yajna for the first time. Their cows were decorated, fed heartily, and sent off to do a circumambulation of the hill. After all, most of these villagers were cowherds, and the fertility of their charges is what would ensure their general well-being (go-vardhan literally means an increase in the number of cows). They prepared great mounds of food for the benevolent hill deity, and Krishna, appearing as Govardhan, accepted their ritual offerings. Naturally, Indra was most annoyed at this turn of events – at his devotees suddenly taking refuge in a mere mortal and neglecting the proper gods their ancestors had worshipped! As he unleashed his fury, dark rain clouds gathered above the hill, and day turned dark like night. Rain and hailstones began to pound the lands and forests of Braj and lightning zigzagged across the sky. Krishna retaliated with an impossibly elegant solution. He simply lifted the mountain with his little finger and held it aloft like a giant umbrella that would protect the villagers and their livestock. The storm continued for a week but since Krishna would not budge, it was Indra who had to finally give up and withdraw his arsenal.

Govardhan is widely regarded as a central trope within the landscape of Krishna. The day after Diwali, the great Annakut festival is held in its honour, when fifty-six types of delicacies– chhappan bhog – are prepared by the women, and thousands of locals, pilgrims and cows make the ritual circumambulation, led, not by a priest but by a local Yadava. Since our time is limited, we have decided to defer the popular Krishna-lila tour for the next time. It is supposed to be a promising if slightly meandering journey through the Braj landscape, stopping at every site linked to Krishna lore (here he stole the gopis' clothes; here he sported with the gopis in the moonlit grove; here he showed Yashoda the cosmos revolving in his mouth) culminating in the ritual circumambulation of Govardhan. Instead, we shall visit Barsana, the birthplace of Radha.

It is some sort of a personal pilgrimage for me. More than any other heroine ever, it is Radhika who was my lodestar for the longest time. In my growing years, peculiar hormonal configurations had induced a great hunger in me for the tragic. I did not rate any love story highly in which a couple were granted a happy ending. After all the lovemaking in forests and secret bowers, dancing to his flute and playing in the rain, Krishna left Vrindavan for Mathura, after which he became the ruler of Dwarka, never returning to his childhood home or sweetheart. What happened to Radha after he left is not recorded, though various poetic opinions are hazarded. Madness, self-imposed exile or death – some say she walked into the dark waters of the Yamuna one evening – are general theories. (Thus, if we were to follow Virginia Woolf's theorization on the matter, Radhika was also a lost writer.)

Radha, whose beauty and pride are unequalled in legend, has remained in literature as the youthful heroine whose lover has gone away, leaving her to walk their old haunts alone, shuddering at the memories each place evokes. The poster child of vipralambha shringara, as it were, matched perhaps only by Kalidasa's yaksha as he grieves for his yakshini and employs the clouds to send a message to her. Every mundane thing is redolent of the Dark One: rain clouds, the neck of a peacock which is also the colour 'shyam', her own reflection in a clear pool, the reeds by the river where they lay together.

The final statement on Radha's viraha might be said to have come from Tagore in an astoundingly powerful song where Radha likens Death to her Shyam:

Marana re tuhu mama Shyama saman
Megha barana tujha megha jata juta
Rakta kamala kara, rakta adhara puta,
Taapa bimochana, karuna kora tava,
Mrityu amrita kare daan
Tuhu mama Shyama samaan

(Death, you are to me, my Shyama;
Your rain-cloud complexion, your dreadlocks rain-cloud too
Blood-red your lotus limbs, your lips a blood-red hue;
There is compassion in your lap; it soothes my heat,
Grants to me the nectar of death,
You equal Shyama to me.)

Though Radha was known for a long time in Indic texts, the centrality accorded to her in Vaishnava myth and cult is a comparatively recent phenomenon. She became popular in Sanskrit poetry only in the eleventh and twelfth centuries. Though Krishna's dalliance with the gopis is an important theme in *Bhagavata Purana* (composed around AD 900), Radha does not appear in it. Her acceptance by the Vaishnavas seems to have happened sometime between the composition of the *Bhagavata Purana* and Jayadeva's *Gitagovinda*, which was written in the twelfth century in Bengal or Odisha.

I first encountered *Gitagovinda* in a historical romance by the Bengali writer Saradindu Banerjee, *Tungabhadrar Teere* (By the Tungabhadra), set in Vijayanagar. Though it was not a tragedy, it quickly became one of my favourite love stories. In it, the hero Arjunavarma uses the most profound line from *Gitagovinda* to woo the heroine Vidyutmala: '*Dehi pada pallavamudaram*'. (Place your foot on my head, says Krishna, seeking forgiveness from Radha.) Later on, when I studied the text in a course on Bhakti literature in my MA days, I learnt the context for these lines that I'd only half-understood then, though the suppressed erotics had made me all tingly. In *Gitagovinda*, when Radha sees Krishna dancing with hundreds of other gopis, she is furious and refuses to see him. Finally, he comes to her to beg forgiveness and says the 'apocryphal' lines – *Dehi pada pallavamudaram*.

Jayadeva, the poet, wanted to ascribe these words to Krishna, as he begs forgiveness of his beloved, but Jayadeva, the devotee, demurred. When he presented this problem to his wife, dancer Padmavati, she suggested he take a bath, eat lunch and then they would think about it together. Jayadeva left absent-mindedly. When he finally returned home, still undecided, Padmavati was shocked. But hadn't he just returned, eaten lunch and retired into his study to write? Of course she was sure of it – didn't she talk to him as they ate? There was something strange in this affair. The couple rushed wordlessly to the study. It was as bare as Jayadeva had left it. But, as he came close to the manuscript, he found that the verse had been completed:

Place your foot on my head –
A sublime flower-destroying poison of love!
Let your foot quell the harsh sun
Burning its fiery form in me to torment Love.

(Translation by Barbara Stoler Miller 113)

It is no exaggeration to say that Radha is the central character of *Gitagovinda*, even though Krishna is portrayed as both the lover and 'lord of the universe'. It is also a text that feminists love to refer to. In a triumph of the female-centred Tantric traditions of yore, it is Radha who comes out on top in the love play; it is she who decides the post-coital rituals. The feminism is a crucial Shakta intervention in the Vaishnavite Charyapada tradition and reverses the purusha-prakriti relationship to privilege Shakti, the unchanging principle. Unlike in Bhakti poetics where the bhakta is the seeker and the divinity the centre, in *Gitagovinda*, it is Radha who is the still point at the heart of the text, and Krishna the seeker.

⌒

Govardhan is hectic, noisy, and absolutely bustling with pilgrims. Little groups of men, women and children of different ages rush to do a parikrama of Govardhan hill, then rush to the small restaurants to eat ghee-laden food to their fill. I am not going to lie, the aroma of desi ghee being browned in massive cast-iron pans fills our hearts with hope. We decide to eat there on the way back from Barsana. For now, we cross the road and start walking in the direction of the vikram stand. It is a busy square; cackling rickshaws, honking cars and giant yellow tankers fill the narrow roads; hawkers gawk; a camel pulls a cart. Several highly committed pilgrims have decided that on the way to the Krishna temple, they will not only walk barefoot – everyone does that – but via a series of sashtanga pranams. Which translates into the following jumpy formula: they will lie flat on the ground, mark the spot where their head reaches, stand there, lie down again. It is a tortuous process, but not the most difficult of mannats. Elsewhere, we have seen Shiv kanwariyas carrying water and walking barefoot to Haridwar from Delhi and back, the old and toothless climbing 9,999 steps to Girnar, chatting and sipping juice, thin men travelling to Nizamuddin Dargah in weather-beaten buses over weeks and cooking humble meals on the road. This is stuff we Indians routinely do.

The vikram is a curious vehicle. There are seats on both sides, which quickly get filled. Six people each. We occupy the minimum number of inches possible, and look outside. Our assistant driver stands beside the vehicle and calls out for passengers. Another four people are fitted in front. 'Can we go now?' I ask. But the guy waves my question away. He quickly rounds up a woman holding a baby, accompanied by her husband and two older kids. They are found seats at the back, in what would be the dicky in a regular auto, where a wooden plank serves as a bench. The woman sits coolly, facing the traffic behind us, and after ensuring her kids are alright (one is on the father's lap, the other between them) she begins to breastfeed the baby. Her head is neatly covered, but her bosom is bare. All very nonchalantly executed. Another man sits next to the husband. The assistant and another guy then stand on the floor of the vehicle, their bodies almost entirely outside. They chat from the top and even play with their mobiles while the vikram negotiates, first, horrendous traffic, and then, after we leave the main streets of Govardhan and lush green fields open up on either side, horrendous potholed roads. Though Barsana is only about 25 miles north of Mathura, it takes us upwards of an hour to get there.

What happens to me in Barsana is peculiar. Perhaps because of the personal significance of the journey, and how charged the moment is for me, my memory presents me with a bag of tricks. There are certain images I retain vividly. There are certain things that have gone blank – and for the life of me, I cannot summon up any details. To top that, there are no notes for Barsana. I was so sure that the details were indelible in my head I took no notes (a callous decision undoubtedly).

So I shall tell you in the order I remember. There is a cloistered little town area; a busy mixed lot of Hindus and Muslims; shops on carts that sell fruits and jalebis; a green mosque in the corner; massive garbage dumps. From there, we go uphill to the prettier part of the town, where a beautiful haveli stands, though it is deserted and unkempt. The Radharani temple is at the top of the hill. The way up has steps hewn into the rock face, on either side of which are small traditionally designed houses that are intended to go uphill as well. These are painted in bright colours: pinks, greens, creams and blues. On the stairway, people coming down greet others with 'Radhe-Radhe'.

And then, truth be told, I have nothing. No recollection of the temple, the idol, the others who must have been present.

I remember that I bought a little donga made of saal leaves and filled with offerings for ten or fifteen rupees, a little red veil, a few items of puja. And I remember, even though the solemnity of the atmosphere was a bit marred by popular Bollywood tunes set to dharmic lyrics, I shed a few tears under a tree.

I remember walking. Uphill, around a grand old palace, surrounded by trees. There were posh cars that came via an alternative route and deposited some slick Radhaswamy sect members, who adjusted their saris and brushed their starched kurtas and then went off somewhere. There were views of the little cluttered town from upstairs – and the houses, between giant cell phone towers, appeared blue and happy. There were lush green fields on the other side. I remember walking through a grove with brown leaves and green grassy beds and haunting vistas of the old fort. We came upon monkeys. Hundreds of monkeys, suddenly, spread out over the forest – on trees, chattering, looking after babies; on the ground, under the tall trees, fucking, delousing, eating – sometimes all three simultaneously.

We sit on the cool steps of a temple.

'It is said that here Radha was once entertained by a huge flock of dancing peacocks. Seeing her rapt in that performance, Krishna too danced as a peacock. That is why he wears a peacock feather in his crown. It was gifted to him by the peacock who was the chief of that flock.'

S laughs. The light has started to weaken. The warm orange of the afternoon is now a paler shade; it is the hour when Radha would have begun to prepare for her nightly rendezvous. *Abhisaar*. Paint her feet. Anoint herself with sandalwood paste.

S asks me, 'What was that story you were telling me about the gopis begging Krishna to return?'

I tell him what I've read. 'According to an account in the *Bhagavata Puraṇa*, Krishna, it is said, on a certain moonlit night, conceives of a desire to dance. As he begins to play his flute in the groves of Braj, all the gopis forget their work at home, and rush towards him in frenzy. One rushes with her hair only half-braided. One rushes leaving a child half-fed. They gather and dance beneath the moon. It is always spring in these stories. In order that every gopi has him to herself alone, holding his undivided attention, he divides himself into a hundred Krishnas, and they sport by the river. Then, suddenly, without a word or a hint, he disappears, having danced with the gopis for several hours at a stretch even as the moon shines wanly. Some versions add that he disappears to break their pride because they'd begun to take him for granted. Other versions go deeper into philosophy. They say this is part of his lila. Whether he comes – in this song or any other – or not, is entirely beside the point. Lila is the irrational, illogical exuberance of a young child's play.

'Disconsolately, the girls look for him everywhere – amid the trees enveloped in the silvery darkness and on the banks of the Yamuna – but he remains elusive. Now he was there, now he is gone. "I say to him, come, come, come, come, come," the gopi sings in Foster's account in *A Passage to India*. But "he neglects to come". That is where Godbole's song ends. So Mrs Moore responds to its tragic overtone – "But he comes in some other song I hope?"

'This episode is a favourite act with raas lila performers. But they usually take the story one step further. Having looked for him everywhere, the gopis are first deeply distraught. Then, in consolation, they trade remembrances with each other, acting out the things Krishna did when he was among them – they mimic his walk, how he played his flute, what mischief he was up to all the time, and the manner in which he worked his miracles. And seeing the intensity of their devotion expressed in their remarkable pageantry and playacting, he returns.'

Saurav

It is night and we are by the black river on Bengali Ghat. We had supper in Govardhan – double-fried paneer parathas – and now we sit on the bench. Tomorrow, we are returning to Delhi. For one, I have to meet the power magazine people, though I am still not sure if it's a good idea to work with them. For another, I've realized that before we do our continuous yatra, I must wait for the money from my big article to come in. Oh, I haven't told you about the night of the big article, have I?

When one is terribly broke, one often wakes up in a sweat in the middle of the night. If perchance one's prospects depend on uncertainties like books and ideas, one can add a fair amount of panic to the mix – a constriction in the throat, a sound of the roaring sea from one's gullet, a general numbness. Add to this the presence of extended family, and it is inevitable that a blame game between spouses will ensue at midnight. In fact, it is mandatory.

In the course of our life as born-again free spirits, many, many such fights have ensued. The night of the big article is not, however, one of them.

We have moved to Calcutta. Several months have elapsed. The books are not out. A few of my articles have been published in *World Politics Review*, but nobody in the family reads *WPR* anyway. One evening, there is some conversation, about fruit juice or something equally ridiculous, wherein D perceives a slight that, in her defensive crouch, hearkens to our financial situation. I still cannot decide whether a slight was intended, but it rattles her. Back home, she and I inhabit a gloomy subdued mould. I sit to work. She doesn't even read, just lies face down on a pillow, muffling tears, and eventually goes off to sleep.

It's two in the morning when she wakes up with a crick in her neck. She gets up, finds a Tiger balm, and then goes to the bathroom. She comes out, gets a bottle of water from the fridge. She looks awful.

'There's some news,' I say.

'It better be good.'

'I'd asked J (the editor of *WPR*) if he wanted a larger piece on India's strategic posture for the upcoming year. He's agreed. They have a special edition planned for February.'

'Okay,' she says, coming to look over my shoulder at the computer screen.

'It's not a regular piece,' I tell her. 'It'll be a 5,000-word thing, and he'll pay 800 dollars.'

'Eight hundred dollars? Is that like 35,000 rupees?'

Outside, our neighbourhood is asleep, though sometimes dogs growl and very occasionally cars speed past. In the pause between her question and my slight nod, there is suspended the possibility of exhaling, of the sweet flood of relief, perhaps even more than relief, of vindication.

I nod, a broad smile on my face, though the money is pitiful in comparison to what we used to earn together. In the superb silence of the night, she raises her hands and begins to dance around the room, adroitly stepping past furniture, even though the promise of one article is but slender.

Now it is end-January and my editor has written to me with a deadline. I need to find a quiet place where the Internet works properly – and finish the piece. That place can only be Paharganj, though we've agreed that this time, we have to find a better room. And since we leave for Delhi tomorrow, we are waiting for the boatman to return and see if he's willing to take us for a spin. The idea seems to have pleased D inordinately. The lacrimal excess that Barsana induced in her has worn off.

43

Gingerly, I follow S into the boat. It rocks under our cumulative weight, but once we sit down and the boat begins to cleave into the tide, and the moist breeze cools my cheeks, I am not afraid any more. Our boatman is Gopal Nishadh and, in the manner of archetypal boatmen, he has a lovely turn of phrase.

His Bengal connection is strong, he opens. Not only does he work here at the Bengali Ghat but – his voice dips pleasantly – his wife is from Bengal. Twenty years ago, she had come to Mathura with her family, on a pilgrimage. One of her brothers lived in Mathura with his wife. They were staying at his place. Gopal had taken the family on a boat ride. It was love at first sight. She had long hair and was only seventeen or eighteen years old. Early next morning, she came to these ghats. When he came to get his boat, half an hour after sunrise, he found her waiting, a ten-rupee note clutched in her palm. She said she wanted to see the river at dawn – would he take her?

Bas, he said.

One after another the ghats glide before our eyes, a moving scene. It is like witnessing, for a few minutes each, different rooms in a long house from a slow-moving night train. A few of the rooms are lit up and filled with laughing children; a few are dark caves with mosquito nets and mashed food where the old are waiting to die.

For Gopal Nishadh and his missus, love was not enough. Her family was far more prosperous that his; they owned land in Bengal. She knew her father would not agree. When the family went away, she stayed back with her brother and sister-in-law, in whom she confided. One month later, after Gopal's mother agreed to the match, they ran away and got married. Her father was furious and threatened to come to Mathura and do something drastic. But it was harvest time. No farmer in his right mind would leave his fields. After their first child was born, the two of them travelled to Bengal, and all was well. Now, of course, four children later, neither of them is as youthful – like the two of us, he says – as they used to be, and his wife has no time for boat rides. But one thing Gopal Nishadh considers his duty: the facilitation of romance. Often, there are young couples, including married ones, who have no privacy at home, no place where they can just sit and nibble chips and share an ice-cream cone on summer evenings and chat about nothing. He provides them this open-air room.

We are now passing Swami Ghat, where devotees are milling about and several boats are moored at a makeshift quay. There is a temple lit by an overhead halogen lamp, and the resultant glow is a bright reddish-gold globe that is mashed up in the water. There is a Bhagavad Katha happening this evening, and the narration, interspersed with music, comes to us scrambled in the wind. We pause and observe the busy shapes through the mist. To the left of the temple is another fine building, old, and lit up by a tube light. Its flat white is somehow flatter in the river, more wavy, and it bounces off the opposite wall. Near the

Sati Burj (a four-storey tower built in 1570 by the son of Behari Mal of Jaipur to commemorate his mother's sati), girls are floating diyas in the water – little bursts of flame prick the surface of the dark river, but they don't float towards us. Instead, marigolds and crushed petals of other flowers surround our boat, and when I reach for a beautiful pink petal shaped like a shell, my fingers tingle in the water.

Gopal Nishadh belongs to the kevat caste. His six brothers are also boatmen, though with the next generation, things are likely to change. The family occupations of many people in Gopal's generation will not necessarily be passed on. And yet, this passing is lamented by Gopal himself. For one, the community of Nishadhs had been blessed by Shri Rama himself, when a Nishadh ferried him across the Mandakini. When Rama had asked the good boatman what he would like in return, the man had not been tempted by wealth or afterlife. He had simply said that his descendants should always be able to do their work safely, and make their living from the river. So, one of the offshoots of this is that if a Nishadh ever sits down to fish, he will *always* find something at the end of his line. (This story was later independently related to us by our friend Prem Paramlal, a carpenter employed at JNU, who was also from the Nishadh community. His father came from Bundelkand but Prem grew up in Delhi. At one point, he had a gig by the Yamuna and his friends would insist that he sit down to fish, since he would invariably manage to catch stuff. His friends might sit perfectly still and dangle the juiciest bits for hours without any luck – but Prem would never return empty-handed.)

We are now deep into the river, and the bright, colourful ghats have given way to a dark neighbourhood, which is designed like a ghat, but the houses beyond are bare and unlit. From the boat, mid-river, the perspective changes. The ghats, so solid when one stands there looking at the waves or flickering lamps or floating flowers – its steps so white, its benches so orderly – seem insubstantial from the water. Unreal. As though the darkness around us, the sky, the river, these are the only real things. All other construction is mere child's play, to fill up time in a world where simple things have got complicated. These buildings here, ghostly under a single strobe light, seem to be deserted. Or worse, forgotten.

'What is that hum?' S asks Gopal.

He strains his ears and replies, 'Oh, that is from the shallows. You see, through winter, some particularly faithful pilgrims erect tents on a shallow flat some distance away, in the middle of the river. All through the night, they stay awake and sing and talk. Some sadhus are there. They tell stories. It is called *kalpabas*.'

'In the middle of the river? That could be scary,' I say, looking at the vast blackness in front of me and trying to imagine pilgrims and their tents.

'True,' Gopal says reflectively. 'Fear lurks about the waters. Let me tell you, boatmen witness some really spooky stuff. I don't want to boast, but I have saved a hundred people from drowning. One hundred. You can write that down – no problem, everyone knows. So I am always alert. Whenever I see someone flailing about, I immediately jump into the river, though with one hand I keep my boat chain in my grip, and I try to drag the person into my boat. Then I row them ashore. But sometimes, you see someone struggling and you rush the boat there. You jump into the water, you are trying your best to save them, but somehow, you can't seem to get them to safety. They slip through your grasp. You go close to them and they elude you. It seems they want to be saved but yet they want to drown. At that time, you must *immediately* get back into your boat and row away, chanting the name of God. It is someone who has already passed on, but his unhappy soul keeps enacting the drama until it is able to move on. But one thing is there: once I am in my boat, nothing can touch me.'

Eleven

How to Perfect the Paharganj Posture

Not only is it a rich and ancient civilization but you wouldn't BELIEVE what you can get in the chemists without a prescription.

– Dexter Mayhew in a letter to Emma Morley, while on his gap year in India, David Nicholls, *One Day*

44

A small restaurant in Paharganj. Two Chinese girls and two young Indian thugs with friendly faces sit at a small table in the corner. Eventually, it emerges, one guy is a tourist guide and the other is his friend. All four are first-generation English speakers and are in search of what good time is to be had.

Thug 1: I am off to China next week to develop a resort. This is the latest thing. Big American company sells shares of resorts. My good friend from America and I will work this deal. I don't like this travelling by bus that we had to do. You girls suffered. Next time, I will personally get tickets for plane. We will *fly* to Jaipur.

Girl 1: But *why* are you going to China? Stay, no. We are having fun.

Thug 2: No, no, don't worry, he will be back by the time we go to the Yoga Festival in Rishikesh in March. In your company he is finally forgetting his old girlfriend with whom he broke up five years ago!

Girl 1: What happened?

Thug 1: Did not work out.

Girl 2: Bursts into peals of laughter.

Thug 1: What?

Girl 2: You've been single for five years, hee.

Thug 1 (self-consciously): No. Only one year. Other girls came into my life. But nothing serious.

Girl 1: But I want to go to the sex temples!

Thug 1 looks to Thug 2: *Kahaan hai*?

Thug 2: There are two options for sex temples. Khajuraho and Hampi. No, wait, one more. Konark also.

45

'Will you *please* hurry up?' I say, talking through blue walls to S in the bathroom.

'Yes, yes,' comes his muffled reply. 'I'll be out in a minute.'

My stomach clamps open and shut in response. He takes *such* a long time in the bathroom. Even after years and years, some things remain prickly territory. I exhale loudly. 'It's nearly half past twelve.' I raise my voice again. 'The boys will be waiting. We were supposed to meet for *brunch*, not lunch.'

He doesn't reply. Or, at least, I don't hear what he says. The water hits the bucket in a steady stream, and he begins to hum cheerfully above the din.

Already dressed up for the day, I flop back on the bed, exhausted from fanning my flame of annoyance. I decide to let go. If we're late, we're late. I let the small of my back dig into the mattress and my feet, sticking out over the edges, are motionless. I stare at the blue walls of the square room, and allow the thoughts, vague and illogical, to flow right through me, mounting no resistance to their content.

It is the Paharganj posture. I think I have mastered it.

A functional room with utilitarian furniture. A bed with side tables on either side; a writing table with stains etched into the surface from teacups left for too long; a couple of chairs. On the left wall, a laughing Ganesha has been painted by a tourist who lived here for many months, about eight or ten years ago. It's a lucky Ganesha, the manager told us, and even when the rooms were being renovated, they always painted around it to keep the picture intact. If one stares at the wall long enough or hard enough, one can notice minor differences in the many variants of blues that have, at different times, been used around it: a soft sky colour, a watered-down cobalt, and beneath these, the bottom layer, a shade that ink bottles from my childhood called 'Sulekha Turquoise'.

Should I text the boys?

I only have to stretch my hand and there, on the night table, is the phone – perhaps I shall text them *we'll be late* if S does not get out of the wretched loo in another five minutes. If I scrabble around a bit more, there is the book, which I do not want now, and then, a tiny jar of Vaseline, which I realize I do want. I apply a tiny pearly smear on my lips and rub it in. Delhi: a city where you have to use lip balm round the year. That had been my view in the beginning. In moist Calcutta, lip balms were more cosmetic than essential; in the dry Delhi air, one has to use them all the time.

It is surprising how quickly we settled into Paharganj, once we found a decent guest house (though it is not *as* cheap as we would have liked it to be). Major's Den is run by a genial octogenarian army man. We've been assimilated into the subculture that is constantly, spontaneously, simmering here: the art of drifting. Like the soft bubbles of thickening full-fat milk, boiling for hours on low heat, the skein on the surface broken every few minutes by the noise and extravagance in the streets. Every stranger contributes to this slow process of reduction; every integer counts, however alone in that large disparate group of travellers from across the world, a community of sorts.

They're all people who begin in Paharganj, after arriving in New Delhi, and in the initial intoxicated days rush about the country, doing touristy things, taking photographs, calling home with stories of high drama and great views. Then comes a time when the forts and mountains begin to get mixed up, hearts are broken once or twice, love is found and lost. Or none of this, but simply the uncertainty that was kept at bay by the novelty of it. All the fears of failure and success come back to haunt. And then, they regroup in Paharganj, take stock, plan a future course of travel. A certain lassitude descends on the soul – not a soul sickness at all, for that is what many have come to India to overcome in the first place, but a sort of soul curiosity that goes best with hash and dim rooms and few words. They end up spending long days over long weeks in Paharganj, with the few friends they have made along the way, as winter flares before the end of January and a grey pall descends on the capital. Sometimes it rains.

The grey streak is occasionally broken by irregular afternoons of brilliant sunshine at Connaught Place or old Delhi, when they (we) allow their (our) weary souls to give in to sudden effusions of energy and good cheer. New friends are made, new archaeological masterpieces photographed, great optimism about the future felt, classified and recorded in new diaries bought from any of the hazaar touristy shops. All in the course of a single day. And then, poof! The next day, they (we) wonder where all that action evaporated, wonder at the possibility of that enquiring mind, that sanguine spirit, with its meaningful thoughts and questions even existing in this context. Outside, it is still winter. Grey. Miserable. The streets are dirty in the way of Indian streets, casual litter being pushed around by busy feet. New hotels are coming up everywhere, and there is brisk construction work. Sand. Cement. Purposeful men hauling tools. Beyond the disrepair and chaos of the Main Bazaar, the tangle of electricity lines and the bumper-to-bumper traffic, signs of beauty in the architecture are tough to find. In a way, that helps. They (we) cannot absorb the outlandish beauty of tombs and mausoleums and rich intricacies of havelis just yet. Inside sun-starved rooms in hotels with bizarre names, there is only the certainty of drifting. It is enough.

And then, when hunger begins to gnaw, it is imperative that they (we), who have whittled things down to the most basic of impulses, step out and walk through the crooked alleys, emerge onto the familiar roads, and choose between the several budget options available in thalis. It is usually the most exhausting decision of the day.

46

When we finally get to Madan Café, we find Zvika sitting alone at a table for four. 'Hey guys,' he says at the same moment I say, 'Sorry, sorry, sorry!'

'Where's Motty?' S asks.

'He's coming in five minutes he said. That was twenty minutes ago.' Zvika makes a face. 'I've already ordered. In fact, I've already *had* one banana lassi. You go ahead.'

We must manage our budget and stay in line. So we order plain thalis (at forty rupees each, they're frightfully cheap).

'Motty,' Zvika begins in a tone of annoyance, 'is *always* late. He takes so much time to take his bath, get ready, choose his clothes, wear his shoes.'

'Tell me about it.' I nod in commiseration. 'I was ready half an hour before your SJ even stirred out of the bathroom.'

S doesn't respond.

Madan Café is a tiny rectangular space with a narrow front where barely five tables fit. Outside, there are a few tables on the pavement. It is very crowded at lunch hour. Fortunately for us, Zvika had come in time to claim a table. There is a now quite a mob at the doorway, peering in to see if there is any place available. A few of the faces are already familiar to us. A party of African American women we have spotted on other days too, fifty-somethings with rich smoky laughs that leap out of the cafes and restaurants where they sit. One Israeli girl with three guys. Several lean Europeans.

Once the crowd clears up a bit, we can see him. 'Finished combing your hair?' Zvika asks as Motty walks to our table after greeting the owner of the cafe – he's always doing these thoughtful things – and pulls up a chair. He ignores Zvika and shakes our hands with genuine pleasure. He begins to study the menu. I notice his hair has been brushed beautifully and pulled back in a gleaming ponytail. Self-consciously I run my hand through my hair, bundled up in a scrunchie and roughed up in that lazy last half-hour in bed.

Zvika has immediately begun chattering about his favourite

subject: the latest developments at the Chabad House in Paharganj, where the twins have now become regulars. The rabbi's kids, who remind them of their nephews and niece; the atmosphere of tranquil calm around the kiddush and sabbath rituals; the regular dinners to which the rabbi's wife graciously invites the boys. Since they have done the whole important-monuments-and-old-Delhi-and-shopping gig already, their Paharganj days have been freed up from touristy anxieties. It is the Chabad House that keeps them involved now.

We listen, smiling, commenting, sipping water, wishing our bloody budget extended to fresh pineapple juice, which the people at the next table are consuming in gallons. The sounds in Madan Cafe – the strange languages mingling, plates clattering, the owner shouting to the boys who work there – are familiar background music to us, a foil to our conversations.

When we returned from Mathura and met them for dinner, the twins were already full of stories about the Chabad House. It happened in a circuitous fashion though, this sudden intrusion of religiosity in their lives. On their second trip to Rishikesh, at the Kumbha Mela, the boys hung out with lots of people curious about religion. These chaps were always asking deep questions, half-seriously, half-stoned: What is man's position in the world? What does religion do in society? What should one meditate upon? What does karma exactly mean? What is freedom? What is the true meaning of sex? There were these words that everyone used all the time, consistently disagreeing with each other's interpretations; there were these confusing discussions that never got very far. But on the other side was something simple: the faith they witnessed. At the crack of dawn, when the mist hovered like fine cotton wisps inches above the water and the cold sent shivery fingers up people's spines, they'd see old people taking dips in the Ganga. *That* article of faith. Did we see?

We'd nodded, and Zvika's eyes had shone. 'It got me thinking. Then when we came to Paharganj, a few mates took us to the Chabad House. And you know, it is nice to talk to the rabbi. There is another rabbi visiting from the Andamans, you know? His wife is going to have a baby. They have come to Delhi for the baby to be born. I've been chatting with him, you know, young guy, and think about it – there is a tiny Chabad House in the Andamans. Just the rabbi and his wife. So lonely. Life is so hard for them. Yet, there they are. Something to learn from this.'

Motty had nodded along, but not said much. He was still processing things, finding out for himself.

The food arrives. The boys are having brunch stuff – French toast, yogurt and cereals, lassi, fruits. S pounces on his thali. I look mournfully at mine and say that tomorrow, nothing doing, I will eat a pancake. Motty says, 'Don't worry, Dippy. Afterwards, we can go to the German Bakery. Their coffee is nice. I'm not ordering any here.'

'What are you guys doing this evening?' Zvika asks.

'I'll start working on my article,' S says. 'I've finished reading up for it.'

'I think I'll read a book,' I demur.

'You mean, you'll *buy* a book,' S says, unpleasantly.

'Yes, I shall,' I tell him heatedly. 'I have some independent means.'

'We'll be going to the Chabad House to help with some preparations for a party they are throwing next week.'

'Oh, that's nice.'

'So, after the party,' Zvika says, 'shall we plan our day out?'

'Absolutely!'

We plan to take the boys on a journey through the Delhi we know, though we've not fixed a date yet. In Paharganj, one leaves things like date and time fluid till the very last moment. In any case, it'll have to be on one of those happier, sunnier days.

Zvika insists on paying at Madan Cafe. 'We owe you guys one,' he says. 'From Jodhpur.'

'In that case, cake's on us,' I say happily.

We leave Madan Cafe and begin to walk, in twos, through the heavy traffic on the main road. Cars honk, cows react to the honking and bumble into carts selling CDs and DVDs, Motty gets nearly knocked down by a car and I scream at the driver in colourful Hindi, the sun pops out suddenly and my memories scramble. I do not know which day this is. It is funny how conversations can be spun forever between people who have become comfortable enough to share silences. Some days, one of us is annoyed in general, or at another. Private fights are transposed on to innocent conversations in the group. Other days, we work towards our group energy in such harmony that we could be a case study for a management class. Every day is rich in detail.

The beaded bags and fancy lampshades that are mounted on storefronts dazzle in the slanted sunbeams that have softened the gritty face of Paharganj, make even the rubbish look nice. Hawkers sell earmuffs and sunglasses. A beggar zones in on us, looks at the twins, and says something in Hebrew. 'He's asking for money.' Motty turns to us. S slips him a five-rupee coin. He shakes hands with the twins in turn while they compliment him on his Hebrew, and we start walking again. 'We've been told to not give to beggars, SJ,' Zvika says. 'Is that wrong?'

'Hmmm,' S sighs. 'Look, it's true there are rackets, and it's also true there are addicts who beg to facilitate a drug habit. But you know what? It's like every other complex moral conundrum. If you feel like giving, just give. Don't follow these guidebook rules.'

'There is a mystical angle to this,' I pipe up. 'There's a poem by a famous Hindi poet that I remember every time I turn away a beggar. The poet looks into the eyes of a man asking for alms, and wonders whether it is perhaps the Buddha himself in disguise. If he refuses, the guy will turn the Buddha himself away. In any case, gods in India pay visits either as beggars or as animals. So there. You can't be cruel to either.'

'There's your Buddha,' S says, pointing at the beggar who had just made five bucks from us. The guy is now badgering a mild-looking Korean couple who stand under the red awning of a shop, feverishly turning the pages of their guidebook, hoping for some advice. The beggar amps up his Korean a notch or two and the couple practically sprint. He waves at us cheerfully and squats outside the shop, chatting in Hindi with a hawker who sells maps of Delhi.

⌐

'Can we go to a cyber cafe for a moment?' Zvika asks.

'Sure,' we reply, and follow him as he darts into one of the innumerable galis. The Main Bazaar Street is a long stretch and, like the veins of a leaf, there are thin, bent alleys that branch out from the main road, and then, sometimes divide into even narrower by-lanes. The sun has driven people out of their rooms onto the streets, and the restaurants are thick with the sudden profusion of good cheer and sanguine energy moving in its viscous way, from one end of the street to the other. We enter the cyber cafe, and Zvika, who is a regular, begins to check his mail. 'I might have some work stuff too,' says S and after presenting an I-card to a young boy – barely fifteen – who is manning the desk, finds a machine. I roll my eyes at Motty, and the two of us hang around by the door, talking about this and that.

A short bald man wearing round glasses and sporting a butterfly moustache enters, looking surreptitious.

He comes and stands close to the boy at the counter.

'I am from Bengal,' he announces.

He looks at Motty and me and, out of a sense of deference perhaps for my ladylike sensibilities, lowers his voice and asks in English, 'Is there a urinal anywhere close by?'

The boy at the counter, in a tomato-red sweater, returns a blank face.

The bhadralok holds up the little finger of his right hand and whispers, 'Where can I do small work?'

The boy remains blank. I suppress my giggles and wonder if there is a way I can delicately tell him to go to one of the restaurants. In any case, why is *this* gentleman in this part of Paharganj? Maybe he stepped out from the station and got a little lost.

In sheer desperation, the bhadralok rephrases his question with one pan-Indian word.

'Peshaab?'

'*Yaahaan nahin ho sakta*,' the boy in the tomato-red sweater growls. Can't be done here.

The bhadralok is embarrassed at being shouted at. He shuffles out of the cyber cafe in penguin gait.

47

It is night and, one by one, the shops are closing their shutters and winding down for the day. We are waiting outside the ATM for S, who is in the queue. We are horsing around as usual, making fun of Zvika. A rickshaw-wallah asks Zvika something. He's on the road while Motty and I are on the pavement. 'No,' Zvika says. The rickshaw-wallah sidles closer to him. 'No, no,' Zvika says. The man scuttles off. Zvika mutters rude things under his breath. 'Oof, these guys,' he tells me, 'always saying ganja-coke-charas-women, you want? Anything you want? So annoying.'

'No one ever asks me anything,' I say morosely. 'You guys are so lucky. Your hair. Your noses. Your clothes. You fit right into Paharganj. Whereas they just consider me an aunty, a day tripper sort.'

S emerges from the ATM and, as is his manner, begins to rush us. 'Let's start moving. C'mon. You guys are slower than some very sick monkeys.'

'Shut up. *We* are boring. Nobody is trying to sell us drugs or anything,' I inform him.

'Don't worry, Dippy.' Motty pats my hand comfortingly. 'One of these days a man will come and take you to a corner and say in this secretive style, *books-books-books-books-80 per cent off. Any book you want!*'

'Haha, very funny,' I say, not smiling in the least. Zvika and Saurav have begun enacting this tableau on the pavement. How I go into a shady corner with a shady guy and return with two Marian Keyes for the price of one, once-read, no ink marks. Huh!

Eventually, even our never-ending bye byes end, and we call it a night. We turn left from the ATM and walk down through the dark streets to our hotel. There are groups of thuggish chaps lurking in corners but by now we are used to them. There are other regulars one spots: the Japanese couple in colour-coordinated clothes who live in the hotel next to us; the Indian businessmen in safari suits and shiny shoes who come regularly to the bars and then walk to their cars parked near Major's Den; the British chap who buys dinner for these two urchins in one of the restaurants (I hope he is just a well-meaning gora assuaging some vague guilt and not a paedophile, but one can never be sure. He always makes me a bit uneasy. Then I feel guilty for being cynical. Then, again, I re-revise my opinion and wonder if I should speak to the kids once or look for their parents. In the end, I do nothing.)

We get back to our cold blue room. We change and get into bed. I read for a few hours while S works on his article. It is peaceful at night, and by now, almost like home.

48

The German Bakery in Paharganj is owned by Alam from Dhanbad district, and since it was established at the outset that S's mother and my grandmother were both from Dhanbad, the bond that results is, by Indian norms, extremely strong.

We spend hours in the bakery, although, bound as we are by the budget, we can never order magnanimously. (The boys too are on a budget.) Sometimes it's just the two of us; often, all four. The room is an inverted L. There are several tables in front and, by the wall, a large glass counter which showcases the cakes of the day. The chocolate cake is my favourite, replete with home-made buttercream icing, exactly like the one my mother made when I was a girl. The baker is a Nepali guy who plays fantastic chess. If he is not busy, he might play a round with guests. Next to the glass case is a window to the frenetic kitchen from where food arrives, accompanied by regular shouts. At a right angle to the kitchen window are a desk and a chair where Alam sits, poring over accounts. And behind Alam, you climb two steps to a plinth-type place with a low coffee table surrounded by cushions. We like it best if we get the coffee table.

It is raining. It was drizzling gently when we idled on the streets, enjoying the wet breeze, watching a few hippies get into a big fight with each other, but soon after we step into the German Bakery, a cold curtain of rain begins to sluice down. It's afternoon, but so dark outside that it seems nigh evening. We woke up late today – and then

S took his own sweet time – so the coffee and cake I order are literally my first meal of the day. S gets a chowmein; Motty orders sandwiches; Zvika opts for a cheese paratha.

'Are you going to tell us that story today, Zvika Hillel? *Finally*? The weather is perfect.'

'Which story?' Zvika asks innocently, though his eyes twinkle and I know he knows which one.

'Let's see, *not* the one about how you got into trouble in the army barracks,' S says.

'Not the one about the pineapple,' I add.

'What's the pineapple?' Zvika interjects, utterly confused. (There is no pineapple story.)

'But the one about the girl,' says Motty. 'We've given you enough time to mope. Enough space. Now tell us.'

'Fine,' he says. '*Fine*. So this was a girl in the first group I was travelling with. Before Motty came down from Nepal. She was beautiful.'

'Jewish? I mean, Israeli?'

'Yes,' he says, his expression clearly saying, *does it matter*?

'But not Baghdadi?'

'No, Dippy. Why are you asking these mom questions?'

'Just asking. Go on.'

'Anyway, she was very beautiful and sweet and kind. I think everyone was in love with her a little. At least, I fell in love with her from the first day. But I didn't want to do anything silly, so we became good friends. I would try to make her laugh. That was the main thing. The days went on. We travelled in a large group, and I thought we were becoming close. You know? Every morning, I would feel restless and sick in my stomach until I saw her. There would be one perfect moment. Peace. My stomach would relax. I would feel hungry suddenly. And immediately after that, I'd feel restless again. As she moved around, ate breakfast, my stomach would flutter at the smallest thing. It was intense, whatever it was I felt. Like pins and needles. I thought it was love.'

He pauses. I sigh and eat the last mouthful of my cake.

S and Motty exchange a glance.

'You could try to tell this story a little quickly,' S states.

'No,' I order. 'Tell it at this exact pace. You two shut up and listen.'

'I discussed it with this one mate. He said I *should* do something about it. So this is what I did. I wrote a note...' At this the boys begin to snicker. I shush them, listening intently. Zvika smiles goofily and continues, 'I put it in an envelope and slipped it under her door.' The boys begin to guffaw. 'Ignore them, ignore them,' I instruct Zvika.

'So I slip the letter under her door, and wait for morning. In fact, I can't sleep all night. Then, morning comes. We go for breakfast. She comes in, smiles at me, smiles at the other mates, sits next to her friend Shosh, *exactly* like on other days. I can hardly eat in tension. But she doesn't say anything at all. Nothing. One day, two days, three days, a week goes by. I don't understand what happened. Meanwhile, we've moved on to another place. I think maybe she didn't get my letter at all. Maybe there was a doormat or something and the letter remained under it. I said this only to console myself. There were no doormats in the other rooms, so what was the chance of a doormat in hers? Then one day there was a bonfire and stuff. All of us were sitting around it. One guy was singing with a guitar. A few people even danced. After a few drinks everyone was relaxed and very open. People were confessing stuff. Then this girl told a story. She said her *best friend* had gone travelling. To Thailand or Cambodia or something. One guy fell in love with her. He slipped a letter under her door. And the friend – she liked this guy a lot, he was a real gem of a guy, blah blah blah – only liked this guy as a friend, nothing more. My ears were burning. I made some excuse and left. The next few days were very hard. Then thankfully Motty decided to join me and it was a big relief. Then I saw her in Jaisalmer again. But now she is dating an Australian surfer.'

'Ugh,' Motty and S say in unison.

'Bet she's sorry as hell now,' I say, patting Zvika's hand.

He laughs bravely but it is a hollow laugh and there is pain in his eyes. 'But at least I did *something*. Something stupid, sure. But at least I took some action. Dippy, SJ, you should say something to this Motty. He is too shy. Never says anything to any girl he likes.'

'Is true.' Motty nods in agreement. 'My hands become cold. I can't speak. My tongue feels really heavy. SJ, why don't you give me some tips?'

'Please, if anyone is to be consulted, it's me. *Obviously.*'

'Just wait before you start the consultations, Dippy. I'm feeling hungry,' Zvika announces. He is always hungry. 'I am going to get a slice of cake. Or maybe the apple pie. Anyone want anything?'

He climbs down the plinth and hops to the glass counter, places his request and then walks down to the main doorway. 'Not raining any more,' he calls out from there. 'Nice weather outside.'

The German Bakery is deserted because of the rain, I think. Just one elderly Spaniard sits next to the cakes and reads a book. He doesn't seem to mind us.

'Zvika, get me the newspaper if it's lying around,' S tells him. 'I'll do the Sudoku.'

'Guys, guys, come here a second,' Zvika calls out. 'Now!'

We instantly troop down the plinth and get to the door. I do not even bother with my shoes but pad across the floor in my woollen socks. 'Is it *that girl*? Have you suddenly spotted her?' I ask hopefully, pressing my nose to the glass pane.

Outside, the rain has washed off the dust and grime of Paharganj, leaving a vista that is cleansed, almost newly minted; in fact, Paharganj, where derelict beauty jostles with ugly modernity, is suddenly altered, suffused with a greenish-gold glow as some complex formula of the sun and the grey clouds refracts the light in a peculiarly poetic way. People who were waiting under dripping awnings have begun to crowd the road again. 'Look, it's our rabbi,' Zvika says. And finally I see.

Amid the regulars of Paharganj, the locals, firangs, beggars, hawkers and assorted others, I finally spot a starkly contrasting figure. Like a lone figure from Victorian literature, the rabbi moves through the crowd, pushing a pink pram. In his traditional long beard and black trousers, long black coat, black closed shoes and a Borsalino hat, he would have been an outsider alright, but for the nature of Paharganj, where the margin is the centre. The baby is not visible from where we stand. But the tall thin man walks slowly, reflectively, his eyes lovingly fixed on the pink pram. An old-fashioned umbrella hangs from the back of the pram. Zvika excuses himself and steps out to talk to him. The rest of us go back to our coffee table, but somehow the mood has become serious. S remembers his article. After a few minutes, the three of us decide to clear the tab and go out into the rain-washed streets. Zvika is still deep in conversation with Rabbi Moshe.

49

The next day is surprisingly clement. It's warm and sunny, and there is a spring breeze blowing. We convene for breakfast at around half past ten, early by Paharganj – and our own decadent – standards, and over omelettes, it is suddenly decided that instead of waiting till next week or whenever, *after* the Chabad House party and *after* Saurav finishes his article and what seems to be really *after* the end of time, we should simply consider the blue skies and the mellow breeze and conduct our outing today. I can't remember whose idea it is. But soon we all agree that given how, for once, we've risen above our Paharganj postures to come down for breakfast, not brunch, and given how chirpy each of us is feeling, it is our moral responsibility to act on the plentiful sunshine and *do* something as a group. We are in one of the greatest cities in the world – old, haunting, crazy and new – and all we've done in the last few days is walk up and down the Main Bazaar! It is criminal.

We turn right from Madan Café and begin to walk to the other end of Paharganj – not the railway station side but towards Panchkuiyan Road, a broad avenue famed for its furniture shops. We don't have to go that far down the road though, to where the beds and dressing tables stand by the road. Where Panchkuiyan Road meets Ramakrishna Ashram Marg, on the left, is the huge compound of the Ramakrishna Mission Order of Monks, and next to that stands the eponymous metro station. The station gleams with frosted glass. Smug commuters press forward in endless rolling waves. For S and me, who have in the past conducted a major part of our romance in Calcutta while commuting together on the metro rail, it is a peculiar sensation to take the metro here in Delhi – where we have only ever taken autos and buses and occasional cabs. For a major world city, the metro came to Delhi very late. So whenever we venture underground there is a little thrill, followed by a typical Bengali-style nostalgia for the slightly shabby warmth of the Calcutta stations.

It is rush hour. We, who have nothing to do and sport a distinct backpacker aura, get bitter looks from co-passengers who jostle and hustle, quarrel and shove, balance tiffin boxes with laptop bags and earphones in a compartment that is jam-packed with dead-eyed office-goers. We feel simultaneously grateful and guilty. It's as though our Paharganj posture has suddenly met its nemesis: the purposeful commuter. Three stations later, we emerge, slightly roughed up, onto the leafy avenues of Lutyens's. We relax and find our rhythm again; we stick our eyeballs back in and soothe our bruised egos.

We walk and walk. The sunlight seems more finely spun here, with due regard perhaps to the way square-foot rates have zoomed in the NDMC area. The breeze is delicate as it rustles through the neem trees. We point various landmarks out to the twins: that's the Sahitya Akademi, the government academy of letters, my first-ever job and the place which inspired me to write my novel; that's a restaurant where a friend of ours came with a cockroach in a matchbox to demand a free meal and was caught on CCTV; that's where a Maruti went over Saurav's foot and we fought hard with the driver and went to report him to a police station; there's 'The Imperial' on Janpath, offering classiest service and some of the most expensive rooms in Delhi, as well as lobbies of understated elegance where, people say, foreign agents parlay; that's the round bookshop which has every book you might want – it saved a term paper of mine at the very last minute.

After we get to India Gate on Rajpath, we realize that in addition to the surprise appearance of the sun and blue skies, it is also one of the last few days of winter vacations. There are literally thousands of people teeming in the grounds, mostly harried parents, but also a fair number of lovers who sit tightly entwined, looking towards the water. There is candyfloss and ice cream. A huge number of children, high on sugar, courtesy the said ice cream and candyfloss, shriek and run and demand rides on the bright-red-and-sunflower-yellow paddle boats. They insist on buying whittled wooden flutes, from which the thin men who sell them coax out the most romantic melodies. But when the children place their untrained lips on the flutes, only funny squeaks emerge. Within minutes the flutes transform into rulers that are used to whack each other. Several chips-and-chocolate-wallahs have displayed their wares seductively, and almost on invisible strings Zvika and I are pulled that way. But S grabs me by my long red muffler and I, in turn, pull Zvika by his knapsack.

S takes his role as guide uber-seriously. We realize we are about to be lectured and gather soberly on a green patch next to the Zabta Ganj Masjid, all clean lines and white walls, which floats on a sparkling waterbody. S stands erect against the blue sky and distracting greens and declaims, while Motty is the proverbial first-bencher on a school trip, listening carefully and, later, asking intelligent questions. 'The India Gate was built as a war memorial arch to remember the 70,000 Indian soldiers who died fighting in the First World War on the side of the British. ... It was designed by Edwin Lutyens, the British architect who was the main architect and planner appointed to design the new capital of British India when, during the 1911–12 Durbar, it was announced that the capital would be shifted from Calcutta to Delhi. However, one of the legends of Delhi is that every time a ruler built a new capital, sooner rather than later, his kingdom would fall. Thus the expanse of Delhi is dotted by the several old capitals that the city has witnessed in its time. It was no different for the British. In 1931, when the grand new capital, now named after Edwin Lutyens, was inaugurated, that same week a delegation returned from London after attending the first round-table conference.'

'Papa, we want ice cream. Papa, we want ice cream. Papa we want ice cream,' Zvika begins to chant lustily, and I immediately add my voice in support. Finally, Motty too caves in, and in view of our robust appetite, S relents. Ice creams are handed out. I cannot remember what flavours were selected, only that an inordinate amount of time is spent in decision making. Zvika, like many of the children buying ice cream, drops the wrapper on the grass. S gives him a withering look while Motty fastidiously picks it up and drops it in a bin which the ice-cream seller has solicitously placed next to his cart. 'Pick the other ones up, then,' Zvika tells Motty, 'since you are so goody-goody.' Motty silently begins to, and a few shame faced parents and I join in. Our ice creams begin to melt.

Sucking our poison and dragging our sweaters, we begin to look for an auto that is willing to risk police action by carrying four adults. It is easily found – for a price, of course – and soon we are cruising southward, past the flower shops at the turn of Lodhi Road, past Safdarjung's tomb, past Dilli Haat and AIIMS, to Vasant Vihar, past our old house. S points them out to the boys, they compliment the place, but I only half-hear all this. It is here, outside the gate that we used to rush in and out of several times a day, that I realize, with numbing clarity, this heart-crushing city is no longer ours. Not any more. Not really. We sent our stuff back in a truck. That was it. End of ownership. What a fool I was to have not realized this before!

From the auto, every view of the city is framed by a fluttering tarpaulin that on very cold days is meant to be tied firmly to bar the cold wind from streaming in through the right window. Today it flaps loosely and the sunshine and blue sky fade in and out with regularity.

When we step into Priya Complex, for the twins want to buy us coffee and sandwiches or quiches or croissants or something (since Zvika is hungry again), the sensation solidifies into a bitter freedom. Priya Complex is busy today. We used to come here to the bookstores to browse every other day, to the PVR cinemas for night shows on weekdays, when the prices were low, to the magazine stand to check out their second-hand book collection, to Modern Bazaar to shop and generally amble around the arcade and sit on the benches near the dry fountain where hundreds of pigeons roost. But I resolutely refuse to give in to memory, and am decidedly boisterous over coffee and sandwiches, happy that it has been established, once and for all, that Delhi is not my home. I am a traveller living in Paharganj. In fact, the road is my home.

⌐

Later, at dusk, we will walk around the Qutb Minar Complex, as a fragrant twilight descends on the city. The boys will move ahead, S acquainting them with stories of the sultanate, and a history of the place. I will circle the minar, cross over to the other side, and walk among the pillars. At one end of the compound, I will sit under the arches of what used to be Alauddin's Madrasa, and from outside, the muffled sound of traffic will appear to me as though from another world. A tour group will walk towards me, and a little distance away, a group of Americans will stand in a circle and hear their guide tell them the histories. The Americans wear uniform pastel t-shirts and carry heavy cameras. Several look bored out of their wits. The guide is in his mid-thirties. His voice rises and falls, and from his choice of words it is clear that the episodes he is narrating have passed through the sieve of Bollywood. When a young couple wanders towards the group vaguely and hovers around, looking this way and that, the guide breaks off his narration to address them in cutting Hindi: 'Please don't try to overhear. You want to hear the wonderful stories from history, you have to pay. There are desi guides available. Contact them. Now please go. My stories are not for free.' The couple scoot, and even I get up and walk away.

A quarter of an hour later, after the twins have exhausted themselves with their competitive photography, we stand by the famed iron pillar. Moths circle over our heads.

'We give you five minutes of full attention,' I tell S. 'Shoot.'

'Take ten, take ten,' Motty says, kindly.

'Fine,' S replies. And then he tells us the following. I notice the couple who were shooed off by the guide standing next to us. I smile at them.

'The iron pillar exemplifies the technological prowess of ancient India. It was made by welding together wrought iron, and as you can see, it has not rusted. This technology was perfected in the West as late as the twentieth century, more than 1,500 years later. The process of iron making they had perfected so many years ago in central India produced wrought iron with a relatively high level of phosphorus. Once an initial level of corrosion took place in the pillar, the iron oxides and iron hydroxides formed on the surface would react with the phosphorous to yield iron hydrogen phosphate hydrates that provide excellent resistance to rust and form a passive protective layer that grows over time, reinforcing protection to the metal that lies beneath. It is an ingenious solution which allows some corrosion to take place initially to form a passive protective film that reacts with the environment to grow over time.

'The history of the iron pillar is shrouded in mystery. It is a Gupta era artefact dating from the fourth century AD and its inscriptions state that the pillar was erected in the honour of Vishnu by a certain King Chandra, who is now widely accepted to be Emperor Chandragupta Vikramaditya of the Gupta dynasty and son of Samudragupta.

'In the time of the Delhi Tomars, it was believed that the pillar rested upon the head of Vasuki, the king of serpents, and as long as Vasuki's blessing remained, the kingdom would flourish. One Tomar king decided to investigate this story. He gave orders for the iron pillar to be pulled out. It was, and the king was horrified to see the bottom coated in blood. He tried to put it back immediately, but the pillar would not stay. Soon after, the empire fell.'

Twelve

How (Not) to Go to Heaven Hanging on to a Carrot (or a Book)

Consider, for instance, the national anthem. The Czech anthem begins with a simple question: 'Where is my homeland?' The homeland is understood as a question. As an eternal uncertainty. Or consider the Polish national anthem, which begins with the words 'Poland has not yet'. And now compare this with the national anthem of the Soviet Union: 'The indissoluble union of three republics, has joined for ever by the Great Russia.' Or the British 'Victorious, happy and glorious...' These are the words of a great country's anthem – glory, glorious, victorious, grandeur, pride, immortality – yes, immortality, because great nations think of themselves as immortal. You see, if you're English, you never question the immortality of your nation because you're English. Your Englishness will never be put in doubt. You may question England's politics, but not its existence.

– Milan Kundera to Ian McEwan in an interview published in
The Novel Today.

50

It is 2007. The year rocket leaves have suddenly become popular in Delhi restaurants. Autumn is filled with a strange restlessness, a madness that eggs one towards bad decisions. Among the many *extremely bad decisions* to which I have been drawn, much like a moth to a flame, the acquiring of a timeshare is the crown jewel.

I am twenty-three. I have, for the first time in my life, a job. It pays a measly 15,000 rupees per month but allows me to read through the day and continue with my MPhil. One morning, I read in the newspaper about this resort timeshare, an exclusive club if you will, through which members can stay in the finest getaways tucked away in secret serene hills or dense forests or by the deep blue expanse of the Arabian Sea. All I need to do is call the toll-free number and a representative will come and make a presentation to us.

It is a curious time in my life. I have, for the first time in life, a husband, but somehow we never can manage a honeymoon. Setting up a household from scratch – even with help from the parents – has turned out to be a black hole for cash. There just isn't enough for a proper upper-crust honeymoon that one can tell one's peers about. I pick up the phone. I speak for a long time to the sweet call-centre girl. And I understand the basics. If we take a membership, for a small EMI (and a minor down payment in the beginning), we shall have access to a lifetime of honeymoons. How about that? She is going to send a representative this evening. For a second, I think of S's reaction. But then I remember I am a feminist, and now with some independent means. And a lifetime of weeklong honeymoons? Starched sheets and forests framed on windows? S would be an idiot not to agree. I drool over the website.

In the evening, the guy comes. He is full of jargon and bluster and shows us a short film about the beautiful resorts, one after the other, until my tongue begins to water at the prospect of getting away to Munnar or Binsar or Bangkok – and S is sufficiently numbed into a stupor. After a long day at work, image after image of green forests and sun-dappled backwaters can have that effect on people. I whip out my chequebook. There is that money we got at our wedding that we'd meant to put into a fixed deposit. It will be enough for the down payment. And since S pays for most of the other stuff, I can pay the EMI for four years. I look at him, affecting my best puppy eyes. What? No, really, think it through, but would it be sooo bad?

'What the hell!' he says. 'We only live once!'

He is twenty-four going on twenty-five. We sign. We get a few freebies. The guy zooms off on his motorbike, happily calculating the commission he will receive. We eat dinner and go to bed. In the middle of the night, S gets up from the bed and begins to pace like a bear on heat. 'Worst decision ever,' he fulminates. 'Colossal waste of money if there ever was any *colossal waste of money*! I don't know what came over me.' I sit up, feeling awful. But not *too* awful. Tomorrow morning, I can begin planning the first of my holidays. 'I did the math in my head. It is supremely expensive. Food at the resort will be phenomenally pricey. Then there is a hefty annual maintenance fee. What about that? Damn.'

'But you said we only live once.'

'Exactly. I was *wrong*. We are Hindus. We are born *again* and *again* and *again*. And this bloody mistake – God knows if these resorts flout ecological principles – this mistake will wear *very heavy* on our karma. Mark my words.'

He sighs and returns to bed.

⌐

2009. Unfortunately for me, karma catches up in this life itself when we quit our jobs to write books and travel. The EMI? My brother-in-law offers to buy it from us. But I can hardly bear to give over my dear package of honeymoons-for-life to someone who is already paid hefty sums by a big corporation to go on holidays anywhere in the world, with family, once a year. Instead, I swallow my pride, have several screaming matches with my mother, and after a round of bitter recriminations and slammed doors, she agrees to pay it on my behalf. 'It isn't about the money,' my mother says again and again, like a gramophone record that is stuck. 'How could you – my daughter – be so stupid as to get conned into such a thing?' I have no answer.

⌐

Back to the present. Cold blue room in Paharganj.

Now that the extremely bad decision has already been executed, and the EMI payments are being made on my behalf, one fine day it occurs to me after I hear some travellers gushing about McLeodganj, that we ought to get some paisa wasool out of it. No? Two birds with one stone.

'Let's go to Dharamshala and stay in the timeshare?' I tell S, who is reading an article. 'The rooms will be free. We'll eat outside in cheap places but enjoy the comforts of the room.'

'It sounds like one of your bad ideas.' S says, uncharitably.

'How?' I ask earnestly. 'How is it one of my bad ideas? Purely transparent. Instead of paying 300 rupees a day at a hotel or 400 rupees here in Paharganj, we will stay for three days in Dharamshala, paying *nothing*. Easy way to balance our budget. Isn't it?'

Eventually, he agrees. If only to escape the Paharganj posture for a few days and take in some mountain air.

The call centre gets reservations done in a jiffy. Because it is still frightfully cold in Dharamshala, several rooms are available. Tactfully, I don't say anything about the weather to S and confirm our interest in a room with a view for the morrow. And just like that, in an hour or so, we are ready to roll. It is evening when we text the twins, who are busy with the Chabad House party, and late evening when we finish packing our bags, give up our room and take an auto to the bus depot.

Dharamshala! Here we come!

⌐

At ISBT we get into a bus bound for Kangra Valley. The category of the bus is 'Ordinary' and they have no illusions about themselves. The windows are dirt-encrusted and they don't shut properly since the clasps are broken. From the dirty windows, I gaze at the sea of people billowing around. A madwoman weaves through the masses, a pink dupatta wrapped coyly around her head. She is barefoot and drags a giant plastic bag stuffed with worthless treasures. She behaves with the neat shy movements of a young bride. Once the bus leaves Delhi, it is plunged in darkness. We doze. At some point an icy wind sneaks in through the half-open window, and I shiver for the next few hours. When the bus stops at a dhaba, our co-passengers jump off the bus like flies and pee below my window, their faces turned towards some hedges. I feel thunderous. I doze some more as the bus trundles through darkness.

For the first time, I see daybreak in the hills as it rains and our bus negotiates hairpin bends at high speed. The green is a balm to eyes that have got used to the grey sordidness of Paharganj for a while; the pale blue of early dawn is reminiscent of an ancient joy, a childhood joy of school vacations and books, half-remembered in that cold sleepy state.

The happiness is short-lived. Because of snow, our bus gets stalled on the highway for several hours, after which it breaks down and we have to take another bus. We eventually reach our fancy resort way past noon, bedraggled and drenched. My bladder is fit to burst. It is unbelievably cold. S has finally realized that his bravado in a single jacket is misplaced and he's going to come down with a cold. There is nothing else for us to do but take hot baths in the beautiful bathroom and curl under the duvet in the beautiful bed. The blankets are heavenly. The pillows fluffy and soft.

It is damn comfortable – and nothing like home.

Saurav

'Pretty steep,' D says, as we both look at the snowed-in square that hosts McLeodganj's bus stand right below the wooden cafe where we sit.

'The prices? Absolutely!'

'Uff!' she groans, not wanting that thought to intercede between the cinnamon cappuccino and herself. 'I meant the climb.'

A colonial relic situated 4 kilometres above Dharamshala (about 10 kilometres by a circuitous road), McLeodganj was a backwater until it became the headquarters of the Tibetan government in exile and the chief residence of His Holiness, the fourteenth Dalai Lama. It is now the most popular hangout zone for backpackers in Himachal Pradesh, its idyllic charm as affective as Pushkar's. Outside, the road is white with snow. A yellow-black autorickshaw, a common enough sight across India but a bit of a novelty in McLeodganj, given the terrain, moves across the square. Its wheels add yet another tyre pattern to the other watery vehicle tracks that are visible, brown against the snow. A couple of policemen in black leather jackets throw their heads back in laughter.

A couple of old lamas in maroon walk up the narrow road to Bhagsu with colourful umbrellas and no warm clothes.

Eventually, we begin to walk along the marketplace, slipping on the snow every so often. I acquire a sweater from a small shop where the owner has no memories of Tibet. He came on his mother's shoulder at the age of six in 1959, the same year when the Dalai Lama escaped to India from a Tibet which was invaded by the People's Liberation Army in 1949. Since then, at least 1.2 million people have been killed, and major steps have been taken to wipe out most of the cultural heritage of Tibet. Facing unbelievable levels of persecution, some 250,000 refugees had crossed the mountains on foot.

After this, my next stop is to get a cap. I get one which says 'Free Tibet', and it has a jaunty mix of colours: red, white, yellow, black and blue. Momos from the street, then tomato soup and Tibetan bread. We eat and we walk and we eat and we walk. Then it begins to snow, and we begin to look for cover.

⌐

It is the first time in our lives that we have had to duck into a cafe to save ourselves from snow. Rain often, hail sometimes, even a band of monkeys once (in Bengali Market in Delhi) but not snow. Having spent most of our early lives almost bang on the Tropic of Cancer, that isn't surprising. We've been to the Himalayas before, of course, but we'd never been caught in snowfall somehow. We were snow virgins, in D's language, but now that is over. We grin at each other and peruse the menu.

The cafe is a bit different from the others in McLeodganj. To begin with, it's new. The bright lighting, chairs with steel rods, the plywood gloss all resemble the numerous new-new cafes that are springing up all over India, even in small towns. There is no dim lighting, Tibetan lanterns or heavy wooden furniture here. It is sparse and functional – start-up-ish. On one side, there is a door leading to a balcony that looks down into the valley below. On the other side, to our left, the windows open onto a narrow lane where children pelt snowballs at each other. Their cheeks are pink.

'Please...' A young Tibetan hands us a menu. He has a pen behind his ear.

Instead of asking for her customary cappuccino, D suddenly says, 'Are you from here? I mean, were you born here?'

The Tibetan, however, understands the context of the first question itself and says, probably used to nosy tourists, 'My twelfth year here. Came away from Tibet when I was twenty.'

'Your English is very good,' I remark.

'Yes, thanks, learnt it by speaking to tourists here. Learnt Tibetan also here only. In the Tibetan school here.'

'Why? I thought you came over from Tibet only as an adult?' asks D, mystified.

'In Tibet, less Tibetan. More Chinese. In schools, they teach only Chinese. Like Pema here, he still doesn't speak any Tibetan, only Chinese.'

'So when did he get here?' D asks.

'Just three months ago.'

'Can we talk to him? Would you be kind enough to translate?'

'Sure.'

We order a hot chocolate and a green tea for good measure. In any case, the cafe is deserted, so we are not keeping them from their duties.

It turns out that Permat Pema Tseten, as his full name reads, is mostly a Chinese speaker though he has somehow learnt to scribble his name in the Roman alphabet. He escaped across Tibet's border with Nepal near Lhasa and then made his way here. However, Permat does not come from within the current political boundaries of Tibet within China or the Tibetan Autonomous Region (TAR) as it is called now. He says that he is from Amdo, which, along with U-Stang and Kham, is one of the three traditional ethno-cultural regions of Tibet and today falls mostly within the Chinese province of Qinghai. The present and fourteenth Dalai Lama, Tenzing Gyatso, incidentally, was born there.

To follow this logic, U-Stang is basically China's TAR and Kham is a reference to the Sichuan province. Indeed, this geographic spread of the Tibetan people beyond TAR, in areas that have mostly been under the administrative control of various Chinese dispensations in the last 500 years, was one of the reasons why China moved in to take over what is now called TAR (where the Dalai Lama was the political ruler) not long after the communists consolidated power in the traditional Han heartland of the Yangtze, Hwang-Ho and Xie river basins. Between 1910 and 1949, Amdo was also the stranglehold of three Muslim Chinese warlord families, together known as the 'Ma Clique' who were aligned with the Kuomintang. 'Ma' is the Chinese version of Mohammad and was the first name of each of the three warlords in the clique. It is a common name among Chinese Muslims, who are often called Hui, although there are some Hui who are not Muslims. Moving into TAR was also important in order to deny any retreat to Kuomintang-allied forces. Otherwise, the newly emerging People's Republic of China would have faced its civil war rivals in both the east, i.e., Taiwan, and the west, i.e., Xinjiang and Tibet. In the long-term, Mao also wanted TAR as a buffer against any other 'threat' from China's west, i.e., either India or Russia.

'So how did you make it across? How did you beat the border guards?'

'I hired a guide. I had to pay him 4,000 yuan, 500 as advance. But that wasn't enough. In Mustang, Nepal, he demanded another 3,000 yuan which was paid by the Tibetans there.'

'Where did you get the initial money?'

'I worked as a labourer in Lanzhou for three months along with some other Tibetans. They paid 5,000 yuan lump sum and provided food.'

'But tell me, China has so much economic activity going on. Why did you come here?'

'Not all Tibetans can get jobs in China, especially if they have not gone to government school and learnt Chinese. At times, only some seasonal jobs like the one I did in Lanzhou are available. They also make you join the Communist Party of China if you want to get work.'

'Hmm, I see. But they don't make others, I mean, the Han do that?'

'No, they don't. Nowadays there are many Han in Tibet. They have been settled in the grasslands. Many spies. Many spies in Lhasa.' Permat's reply, of course, is yet another reaffirmation of the well-known Chinese policy of looking to alter the demographics of the western borderlands under their control. In both Tibet and Xinjiang, the Chinese have encouraged Han settlers from the plains by offering them inducements and a favourable share of the 'China Western Development Plan' announced in the year 2000. The plan revolves around building extensive railroad and other infrastructure in China's western territories, including the vast Eurasian borderlands (deemed 'autonomous' regions in China) that lie beyond the traditional Han homeland and continue to defy

Beijing's iron hand to varying degrees. Taken together, China's western provinces and 'autonomous regions' account for three quarters of its territory but only a quarter of its population, and less than 20 per cent of its total GDP.

Now, under the China Western Development Plan, Tibet for the first time has got connected by rail with the Han homeland through the Qinghai Tibet Railway that links Golmud in Qinghai to Lhasa in TAR. While this rail link, the highest existing railway line in the world – considered an engineering feat – has caused great consternation in the minds of Indian strategic thinkers, since it theoretically allows the Chinese to build up military forces much quicker in TAR, ordinary Tibetans are more worried about the droves of Han who might ride this line to migrate to Tibet. According to the Dalai Lama, two-thirds of Lhasa is already Han, and Tibetans often voice fears of being swamped. Although, at the moment, Han Chinese are, at least officially, still less than 10 per cent of Tibet's population.

'But aren't there Buddhists amongst the Han?'

'Yes, there are. But Chinese Buddhism is different from Tibetan Buddhism.'

'But don't they visit Tibetan temples in Lhasa?'

'Some of them do. But they are also building their own temples.'

'What about the monasteries?'

'Young men, whether Tibetan or Chinese, are not allowed to join the monasteries. They actually threw out 2,000 monks from the monastery in Labrang during the 2008 uprising. No TV channels are allowed in Lhasa. In Chinese Internet, if you search Dalai Lama's name you only get a photo of him with Mao from the 1950s.'

'Really? So they do try to control everything?' D exclaims.

'Indeed. While it didn't register much in India, Tibet actually went up in flames in the run-up to the 2008 Beijing Olympics. Some Indians may perhaps remember the Olympic torch controversy, but few would know that Lhasa was burning while Beijing was shining. The 2008 Tibet unrests which spread to all the historically Tibetan regions revealed that China's grip there continues to rely to a great extent on methods that did not really involve any accommodation with the Tibetans. Rapid reaction forces of the Chinese army moved in armoured vehicles to restore order on the streets of Lhasa and to reinforce the confidence of Han settler groups skirmishing with Tibetans.'

When this is loosely translated to Permat, he nods his head. 'Yes, they sent in tanks.'

As a student of geopolitics, I have always felt that China's hold on its periphery continues to be tenuous. Despite consciously altering the demographics of Tibet and building up military infrastructure, China remains extremely worried about the future of its Tibet problem. While Beijing blamed the Dalai Lama for instigating the 2008 unrest and continues to refer to him as a 'splittist', it is probably even more worried about a time when the Dalai Lama is no longer around.

The Dalai Lama in his role as the temporal head of the Tibetan government in exile has kept his people away from armed confrontation with the Chinese and has sought a political settlement whereby the Tibetans retain autonomy in spiritual and cultural matters while the Chinese have the responsibility of foreign affairs and defence. But therein lies the rub. Ever since the rise of Vajrayana Buddhism in Tibet, it has been a country where the Buddhist Sangha and the state have been inextricably linked to each other, with a common temporal and spiritual head. Moreover, Vajrayana Buddhism has not just been the purveyor of common culture but the key defining agency in all political matters. This explains why the Chinese communists have never been comfortable with merely consolidating their administrative hold over Tibet but have first repressed, then sought to control Tibet's religio-cultural ethos.

A key example of this would be the disappearance of the current Panchen Lama as a child and his replacement by someone the Tibetans consider a Chinese-sponsored impostor. The Panchen Lama, since medieval times, has played a key role in locating the reincarnation of an expired Dalai Lama, who is then reared to take over the reins of power in Tibetan state society. The Chinese are known to be worried sick about the possible location of the rebirth of the current Dalai Lama once he gives up his current physical body. Dalai Lamas are typically born in Tibet's ethno-cultural regions and the sixth Dalai Lama was actually born in Tawang, Arunachal Pradesh, India.

Unfortunately for the Chinese, both the Dalai Lama and other high officials of the Tibetan government in exile have repeatedly said that all territories within India that have historically been under Tibetan influence, such as Tawang and Ladakh, are an inalienable part of the Republic of India. Though it's usually not much talked about, the Dalai Lama has given India a huge edge in the Himalayan great game by unabashedly endorsing its control over areas where Tibetan Buddhism is prevalent.

The Chinese are clearly concerned that the next Dalai Lama may again be born in Tawang, thereby putting paid to any easy settlement of the Tibetan issue. What is worse, the Karmapa, who escaped from Tibet in 2000, despite doubts harboured by Indian intelligence agencies regarding his loyalties, is being mentored by the Dalai Lama to be the political beacon of the Tibetan cause, and is likely to serve as a regent till such time as a reincarnated Dalai Lama comes of age.

'But they can't squash things forever now, can they?' D asks.

'There is every chance that Tibet may turn violent after the Dalai Lama's demise and China may not be able to keep a lid on things. What is worse, the Uighur Muslims, to the north of the Tibetans, seem to be on the warpath as well and things are looking quite dicey for the Chinese in these borderlands, the China Western Development Plan notwithstanding.'

D turns to Permat. 'What do you think, Permat, will happen in the future?'

'People are unhappy'. Permat doesn't say more.

I drone on.

'For India, there is an added worry that China may now simply be looking at Tibet as a resource colony and will retain control by force, chiefly to draw upon its water resources. There have been persistent rumours of the Chinese looking to divert the Brahmaputra at the Yarlung Tsangpo Grand Canyon where it "bends" from Tibet into India and even nuclear devices may be considered for this purpose. What lends weight to these fears is that China's civilizational rivers are in very bad shape, with the Hwang-Ho actually not even reaching the sea any more on account of over-diversion for industrial and agricultural purposes. The

Chinese have therefore instituted a sixty-five-billion-dollar north–south water transfer project that aims to divert water from Southern China's rivers to the Hwang-Ho and the Yangtze in the north. It is not difficult to see them try and extend this to the Yarlung Tsangpo, which is what the Brahmaputra is called in Tibet.'

'What about the West? Don't they have a hand to play in this matter?' D interjects.

'Well, the romance of the West with Tibetan Buddhism is not the result of some post-consumerist guilt or even the desire to bring about a synthesis between science and spirituality. For Western strategists like Zbigniew Brezinzki, who has been national security advisor to two US administrations, the entire Himalayan region between India and China represents a so-called 'Eurasian shatter zone'. Tibetan Buddhism, in particular, is attractive since it is the dominant religion of even the Russian regions of Tuva and Buryat in Siberia and of the autonomous republic of Kalmykia on Russia's western Caspian shore. Kalmykia, incidentally, is the only Buddhist-majority region of Europe. Naturally, the West is keen to exploit this particular "Eurasian" fault line.'

'So they will try to exploit this fissure between India and China?'

'I think so.'

Western activities also serve as a source for Chinese suspicions of Indian intentions. Western agents are active in Arunachal Pradesh, and other parts of India's north-east, where the Americans often make requests to search for the remains of USAF pilots who crashed while 'flying the hump' over the Himalayas to bring supplies for the Allied war effort against the Japanese during the Second World War. This 'history-seeking' is dubious, and could be a cover for 'shatter zone' games ultimately detrimental to both Indian and Chinese interests. (Shatter zone is basically a place where people are not integrated with the mainstream. So the American agenda is to target these places and foment trouble.) This is precisely why a sixty-year-old demand by the Americans to set up a consulate in Kalimpong in Darjeeling district of West Bengal has been repeatedly turned down by the Indian side.

'My father and brother are still in Tibet,' Permat tells us. 'They run a small business. But Chinese government takes a lot of money to grant permits for businesses.'

'Officially or under the table?'

Permat laughs after hearing the translation. 'Officially, but if you want to get work done quickly, under the table helps.'

'So don't you miss your family?' D asks.

'I do.' It turns out that Permat's girlfriend is still in China in Ritong. Her father was sick when he left. They are no longer in touch, though he hopes to get her to India at some point.

A group of young tourists comes upstairs now and sits at the next table, followed quickly by a local couple. The men must get back to work. We thank them for their time and venture out into the snow.

The journey to Delhi is long. The first half is redeemed by the views, though. There is a mountain stream warbling down, its water greenish over white rocks. The road curves round it, a grey ribbon climbing up with steep mountains on either side. A man is painting his house lovingly. He's chosen a vivid wisteria. In any case, the houses here favour bright candy colours. There are pine forests, grassy stretches dotted with red flowers and mustard groves. Little white goats nuzzle high up on the slopes. I balance the laptop on my knees, searching for a signal. It connects. 'You might be happy to hear this,' I tell D, 'but we have a party to attend tomorrow night. Shantanu has written to tell me the book is in from the press. Apparently it looks good. He'll bring his copy for us tomorrow. The six author copies would have been sent to Calcutta.'

The book is out.

It feels a bit unreal.

'What are we going to wear?' D pokes me.

'We cannot afford to buy anything if that's what you're saying!'

'I never said that, you always put words in my mouth,' she says, and refuses to talk to me for an hour (except once, to ask about the book). Later, the hairpin bends make her nauseous and she orders me to get her a Coke; that's when we start talking again. We have dinner at a dhaba and reach Delhi in the middle of the night.

51

It is at the dinner to which our editor invites us that we meet Ravi Aneja for the first time. We shall meet Ravi again, at a later date, and he is to tell us about cultural intelligence and other interesting stuff. But I am getting ahead of myself.

This party today, hosted by a renowned publishing house in one of Delhi's finest five-star hotels, is to celebrate the launch of a new imprint – dedicated to only the best of literary fiction – and the guest list is distinguished. 'The nomenklatura of the city as it were,' says S. His eyes glint darkly, and I, nervous in my borrowed sari and heels, clutch his arm and whisper, '*Be nice.*'

But it was a long journey from Kangra, and when we got to Major's Den from Sarai Kale Khan at two in the morning, we had found our Ganesha room assigned to someone else. We are now installed in a tiny room on the first floor, with a bed that is far too small for S and with hardly any floor space to move around. (We had to get dressed at my friend Gee's.) Something of the uncomfortable night and the Dharamshala cold seems to lurk around S, making him unpredictable, even though outwardly he's all crisp shirt and polished shoes and even though inside the hotel, the temperature is perfectly adjusted for bare arms and bare shoulders.

We meet our publisher in the lobby. She's just coming in herself. She hugs us both in turn. Advance copies of S's book have come in from the printer's yesterday morning; they look good. She has just assigned my novel to a copy editor and she's sure I'll love working with her; in fact, the copy editor's supposed to come to the party too. She shepherds us into the elevator and asks about our travels. We both begin to talk at once. S talks about Dharamshala. I chatter about Paharganj and the German Bakery. I tell her that Himachal Pradesh is the most polite state. S tells her about Barmer and the oil question. It is invariably the case that when we meet her, like two attention-seeking kids around a favourite adult, we both start talking to her at the exact same time, as though each of us is aiming for one of her ears. Remarkably, she keeps track of both strings, and responds separately.

The party is in full swing. The ballroom, glossy like the page of a magazine, is full of people. There is that soft swish of expensive clothes and large egos rubbing delicately. The moment we enter, mid-sentence, our publisher is whisked away by a lady with a large bouffant, who I think is a famous socialite. A tray comes floating our way, and by the time our publisher reappears – it *was* the famous socialite, they're bringing out her memoir, and she's a nightmare as far as edits are concerned – we are holding chilled flutes in which champagne bubbles and beads. Somebody else now claims her. It's a nattily dressed young journalist who sees right through us and begins to earnestly talk about a panel discussion on the erosion of liberal values in public discourse. Would our publisher be one of the speakers? It's going to be at India International Centre. We consider this our cue to move on and begin to work the room. Snatches of conversations come our way, along with trays of canapés. A group of foreign correspondents and their spouses stand in a huddle and discuss rents in Golf Links and Jorbagh versus those in Nizamuddin. I know two of them by face. They're both writing books on India, hardbacks that are sure to have a few of the following words in the subtitle: India (well, duh!), Promise, Undone, Market, In spite, (Long) Road Ahead, Fabric, Democracy, Gigantic, Elephant, Exciting. Elephant, though, come to think of it, might actually be in the title and not the subtitle. Ever since Gurcharan Das's *The Elephant Paradigm* was published, the metaphor has caught on.

In a private corner, beside an immaculately curtained French window, two tall women in silk gossip. One of them, the willowy one in blue with shiny waist-length hair, asks a passing waiter to get her a sherry. *Dry*, she wags her finger at him. *Very dry*. We reach the end of the hall where the buffet table is laid out though there's no food on the silver yet, and separate.

I meet a few editors I know, lovely sparkling girls, and we laugh and catch up. One of them, in a dull gold shift dress and a pageboy haircut, introduces me to the best-selling novelist who's the current toast of the town. Behind a giant porcelain vase, I can see a truly famous literary agent, the one behind many Indian successes on the international scene. He is surrounded by a little circle of admirers: three of his authors (who will not stoop to hang out with the published-only-in-India-but-write-in-English authors), one artist he has just taken on, and three or four women of indeterminate age who probably want to grow up and win the Booker. What I *really* want to do is find a powder room, pee, and then sit on the sofa inside, put my feet up, sip my champagne, take in the tinkling music that is playing, and make a list: things to do, money spent and left in the bank accounts, a review of the journey, plans for the future (short term), plans for the future (long term).

But my publisher has appeared at my elbow and I change plans immediately; we march along to do some mingling. She introduces me to a lovely girl, half-Indian, half-Welsh, full American, early thirties, Harvard, Oxford, Harvard, who has come to India for six months to write a book. About women from diverse walks of life. 'Not a book with clichés,' she clarifies immediately. 'I mean, I am literally not going to use the word *exotic*. I'd have axed *colourful* too but that would be plain churlish.' She has just interviewed some midwives in Haryana and, before that, Dalit activists in UP. I'd have liked to keep talking to her – she has that sort of an arresting face and I also want to know which language she conducts her interviews in – but she's leaving for another party.

I weave my way through the beautiful people as they drink and opine, and at some point I find I am walking next to a minister (who's more renowned as an intellectual than as a politician, and has also been, if I recall correctly, a diplomat). Six waiters wheel in a giant cake from the kitchen – shaped, predictably, like the logo of the new imprint that is being launched – and we must stop. So I offer him a slight smile, and am startled to see his hand around my shoulder two-and-a-half seconds later. That was quick. 'Hello, my dear,' he says. 'And you are?' A series of possible answers flits across my brain (human, student, misfit, pagan witch doctor) but instead of mumbling, I decide to suddenly go all Delhi. 'I'm a *novelist*,' I say, for the first time in my life. He seems to like that. *Novelist.* The cake is now a safe distance away, and we are walking again. 'Anything I might have read?' he asks gallantly, his hand now firmly on my back.

'Oh, well, it's only going to be out later this year,' I say. I smile. 'It's called *The Vague Woman's Handbook*. And it'll probably have two women on the cover. A shopping bag or two perhaps. I really *really* doubt it'd be something you'd read. And that...' I stretch my palm outwards and clutch at familiar fabric, 'is my husband.'

S turns, and if he's surprised, he doesn't show it. He greets the minister with an appropriate opener, shakes his hand, and actually talks about recent legislation impacting his ministry for a minute or two. 'Is that the book?' I ask, and S hands me the first copy. The minister coos at it politely as one would greet a new baby. 'Non-fiction, I understand,' he says. 'But it is fiction that I really admire. Something I have never attempted myself.' He looks from one to the other and quips, 'Of course, my detractors have often claimed that my political columns are pure fiction.' We laugh.

After ten-odd minutes, a woman walks up to us. She is about thirty years old, and very chic. 'I'm off, Boo,' she tells him. 'What's your latest number?' He dictates a phone number, and she kisses him on both cheeks and clip-clops away. 'I have no idea who that is,' he tells us, shaking his head. 'She told me her name. I thought it sounded like Moo. I said that. She immediately started calling me Boo. Maybe it's one of A's relatives.' A is our host, the chairman of the publishing house. I have, however, not seen him yet. It's that sort of a party. Apparently, one might not even be introduced to the host.

⌒

At dinner, we find ourselves at a table for eight, and only just. The ballroom is very full now. All the tables are occupied. The people at our table seem to be in a dour mood, though one or two introduce themselves with clever self-deprecation. I think nobody got to sit with anybody who was their first choice and are now all sulking. They keep looking over at other tables, so the conversation is a bit erratic.

To my left are a couple of academics. They are deep in a conversation with each other about the cruelty of the state and the disbursement of grants, alternately, and it would have seemed strange to me that there is so much heartburn involved in being chosen as grantees of the repressive state they so abhor, but I've been in JNU long enough. I smile at them politely when they look towards me.

'I am an anarchist,' says the gentleman who recently retired as the MD of a big evil corporation.

'Me too,' says the young painter sitting next to him, slim and exquisitely featured, in a simple sari that must have cost an arm and a leg. She lives in Lutyens's. (She'd told us so herself, three minutes ago. She's converting the second garage into a studio, installing French windows on the garden side, but the carpenters have disappeared for a whole week! She has an important exhibition coming up.) Her parents are also painters, selling canvases for a few lakh each. Their work is in MOMA, she'd said. 'I *am* an anarchist, and will *die* an anarchist.'

'I am opposed to nuclear power,' the former MD says.

'Perhaps you should read this book then,' Saurav says with a tight smile.

'What do you think about the thorium question?' asks the man sitting next to S, a tall man with a beard and an accent I cannot place. He introduces himself as Ravi Aneja – and they discuss the thorium question for a bit, while the rest of the people at the table ignore us, since they are all avowedly anti-nuclear. Ravi Aneja later tells us that he is a PIO and had served as a diplomat *to* India. One of the things he'd looked at in his tenure was the matter of uranium.

The artist, meanwhile, is talking with the academics about her recent exhibition on mass graves. They purr in appreciation and on the spot issue her an invitation to come and speak at a conference they are organizing on 'Fragments of Nationhood: Notes on a Country That Is Not a Country'.

I can feel the hair standing on S's forearms, though I also feel giggles arising somewhere deep in the pit of my stomach. The former MD excuses himself to get seconds. Ravi Aneja joins the chat and says, 'This is an interesting theme. In fact, one would think from reading several Indian scholars – though I must confess I read only English and not any of the other languages – that the idea of India itself is a creation.'

'Exactly right,' says the younger of the academics, her smug face cracking to reveal a smile.

'Of all the lies,' I hear S saying, 'that the British came up with in their time, this, Ravi, is the very worst.'

The younger academic starts.

'Young man,' she starts to say, but S is looking at Ravi Aneja.

'The idea that only the Westphalian model of nation state is valid is yet another example of Western intellectual arrogance. There are civilizational states too, which have evolved into modern nation states.' He pushes his chair back, and with no regard for the fine sensibilities at hand, the chair screeches rudely. 'The idea of Bharata, Bharatavarsha, is extremely old. And since its spatial contours have been recorded in text after text, it seems strange that strategies which were clearly meant to aid a colonial regime continue to find academic echo. Excuse me,' he says and leaves. The former MD returns, his plate heaped with lavender ice cream and moong dal halwa.

I am left with the awkward task of negotiating this affair. The academics have turned their glassy faces at each other again and have decided to studiously avoid me – who in the world invited us? – but the artist is exhibiting a fluttery sort of energy. I address Ravi. 'I am going to give you one example. There is a text in Sanskrit, called the *Natyashastra*. It is an ancient encyclopaedic work on dramaturgy. Some compare it to Aristotle's *Poetics* but that's plain silly, because the English translation of the *Poetics* is about thirty pages while the *Natyashastra* is immense. About thirty-six chapters averaging eighty to hundred verses each. It's very elaborate. Anyway, what I want to say is that the *Natyashastra* is by no means a religious text. It concerns arts and aesthetics. Chapter 14 of the *Natyashastra* concerns regional variations in performance. There are all the different parts of India mentioned in it – it could be adapted to a Doordarshan programme talking about our unity in diversity in a blink, you know. And this is but one example. Anyway, enjoy your dinner,' I say. 'We must be off.'

I finish my lavender ice cream in two seconds and look for S. I wonder where else he is picking a fight. Then I notice he is talking to his editor, that wonderful man, and I relax. And once I set down my plate, we are ready to leave. Ravi Aneja meets us by the doorway and gives us his card. 'That you are staying in Paharganj has me interested already. Did you know,' he lowers his voice, 'that government files used to be sold in Paharganj once?' We chat for a few moments and then we apologize to Ravi, we really must be off.

'I'll call you guys,' he tells us. Downstairs, in the lobby, as I try to keep pace with S, who always strides extra-fast when he's annoyed, I spy Boo and Moo sitting on one of the sofas.

⌣

'The book?' I ask in sudden panic.

'Right here,' S says, and flips it out from under his arm.

We are in an auto on the way back, and the wind streaming in has dispelled the energy spikes the dinner raised. I take the book from him and run my finger down the spine. It feels solid. The only question is whether it will take our weight.

'What weight?' S asks.

I realize I've spoken loud. 'Oh it's a silly story. You know how we used to have chapel in school every morning, right? So mostly we had stories from the Bible or moral science lessons. But there was one teacher who used to come up with more interesting stories. There was one about an old woman who died and found herself in a room. Apparently, it would be decided there if she would go to heaven or hell. God appeared and asked her, "Have you done anything meaningful in your life?" The old woman thought and thought and thought. Finally she came up with one thing. "I once gave a carrot to a beggar." "Right," God said and went to an anteroom. He returned with a carrot in a plastic bag, like an exhibit in a courtroom drama. "This is that carrot. Now you have to see if this carrot will pull your weight to heaven or not." The old woman is led to an open field and asked to hold the carrot aloft. The carrot does appear to rise in the air, and soon the old woman is dangling from the carrot and rising heavenward. That's the context in which I meant it. We've taken so many decisions in the name of the books – this book, the very first – just wondering if it'll carry our weight heavenward.'

We're in Paharganj now. It's half past ten. Though some of the roadside shops are winding up for the night – the men are packing up their sweaters and bags and watches – the restaurants ought to be buzzing. The cool folks ought to be stepping out into the streets only now, emerging from the alleys in twos and threes.

'So what happened to the old woman?'

'I can't remember the end of the story. Something happened. Bad, I guess. With a moral for schoolchildren. *Bas bhaiya, rok dijiye.*'

We let the auto go outside the German Bakery where the twins are supposed to meet us. My sari is riding up my ankles and the pallu is crumpled.

The twins are sitting in our usual place, though the German Bakery is deserted. Unusually. But before we get to them, Alam, who is standing by the counter, asks us, 'Have you heard the news?'

We cannot read his face. It's an odd mixture of excitement and horror. We wave at the boys. 'Yes,' Alam says in English, 'they have been waiting for you. I am going to shut the place now. We were just waiting for you to come.'

'Why so soon?' I ask, but it is S who asks the moot question. 'What news?'

'There has been a blast in Pune,' Alam says, sitting down on his chair. 'In the German Bakery near Osho ashram. The owner is well known to me. Many people are dead. Indians. Foreigners. The bakery is very close to the Chabad House, so some people are saying that Israelis were the target.'

The boys come and stand by us at the counter, and we talk for a few minutes with Alam. Then we troop out silently. Paharganj is in usual mode, though the owner of the bookstore is unusually bright-eyed; two of the regular layabouts are deep in conversation with the fruit seller. In front of us, three or four policemen arrive with yellow barricades. But they are not sure what they are supposed to do, and they stand in one corner and speak among themselves. The next evening, though, we would see two barricades at either end of Main Bazaar Road; autos would no longer be allowed inside and a couple of policemen would be on duty by the barricades.

'Is that the book?' Motty asks.

'Oh, yes,' S says, and hands it to him.

They pore over it from every angle and unleash a torrent in Hebrew.

'It is big day, SJ,' Zvika finally tells us. 'We would like to take you for a drink. Whatever may have happened, we must celebrate the book. That is what we must always believe. Terrorist attacks are meant to make people afraid – so you have to fight it by not being afraid.'

Together we enter one of the many bars in Paharganj – and truth be told, it is not as seedy as I'd imagined it to be. In the dim light we see it is extremely crowded, and the only table for four that is available is right in front of a TV stuck on the wall.

We order our drinks, and when they arrive, we even manage to raise a toast, but the mood is overshadowed by the Pune tragedy. After they got the news, the boys had rushed to the Chabad House here to enquire if they had more news.

At eleven, Zvika's phone rings. It's their mother. He steps out to take the call. In any case, it's late. We decide to call it a day and Motty clears the tab. By then, Zvika is back. 'They've just got the news. They heard Chabad House, and immediately thought there's been a blast in Delhi. You know how mothers are?'

We step out and walk through the shadowy streets.

'They want us to return home,' Zvika says, finally. 'It's crazy, right?'

We stand outside the ATM, our usual place, but there is a deep emptiness that descends. The boys begin to talk about the book again.

S tells them about the party.

My mind drifts and the edges of the Paharganj streets begin to advance towards me. Perhaps I have drunk too much?

But I don't want to move from that spot.

There is something going on in the air, and I want to understand it.

Even in that state of half-formed drama, suddenly, I realize what is different. The cool but surprisingly sweet breeze that blows in and tangles up my hair says the season has turned.

It is no longer winter.

Thirteen

How to Let Go, How Not to Let Go

Sair kar duniya, ki gaafil zindagaani phir kahaan?
Zindagi gar kuchh rahi, toh naujavaani phir kahaan?

Wander the world, ay drifter, where will you get this life again?
And even if life remained, where would you find this youth again?

– Immortal lines by Ismail Merathi. Quoted by Rahul Sankrityayan
in his famous essay 'Athato Ghumakkad Jigyasa'.

52

I still cannot say how it would have turned out if my mother had not called the next morning and told me that my grandfather was dying. Would we have continued travelling?

But she did call – and in the grey light of the morning after the blast, in our cold blue room – her voice seemed tinny and distant. Was it possible that she – that most practical of practical women – sounded needy? She asked if we had any plans of returning.

I did not know what to say.

Truth was that we had no plans any more.

The Paharganj posture had dug into our soul. We were low on money. We could only mark time in these familiar streets, read second-hand books and wait for S's pitches to be accepted. He could do articles. We could wait for money to come into his account, I could edit a few books, and we could travel again. Until then we might stay here and watch spring take over Delhi.

Or we could return. Enact the same routines by other familiar streets.

There is something frightening about the death of a beloved grandparent for the likes of me, cosseted by generations of ancestors as I was growing up. It puts nothing between death and one's own parents.

S, though, belongs to another land.

And it is only this – the death of an old person who has lived a full life and in the end is surrounded by old children and young grandchildren, perhaps even a great-grandchild or two – it is only this normalcy that has ever stood between us, like a giant distorting mirror mashing up our pasts and presents and making us strangers to each other, scions of an alien species. In his land, there is something odd about this sight. Old people dying surrounded by mourning white-haired children.

And it immediately breeds in him nightmares. He worries about the lone man in the island that is his home – his father.

He tells me that given how low our funds are at the moment, perhaps it is better, more practical, that we return to Calcutta. I can see my grandfather. I can see my mother. He can be with Daddy. We can save up for a couple of months and set out again. This time, the holidays would be on and we could travel unfettered. Not have to worry about the university either.

Consider the parents, he says to me, reasonably. Let's go home.

It is morning in Paharganj. All I can do is lie still.

Saurav

The next day, we are supposed to meet the twins for lunch but we only find Motty in Khosla Café, another thali joint, sitting quietly in a corner. Zvika is having a tough day. He has stayed back in the room to think things over and write his diary. He has not written for days – and is now swirling in a sea of stress. He invariably gets into these stressful situations,

Motty says calmly. It's better if he spends some time on his own until he feels better.

After lunch, none of us want to return to our rooms. It is a pleasant sunny day, and we decide to go to Jantar Mantar. We take the metro and then walk past the protestors, who sit in groups and sip tea. Motty stops to read the placards.

Inside, we walk past the sundial and sit in the shade.

Even I am too exhausted to lecture the others about Sawai Jai Singh's legendary work.

'Our parents are very worried, Dippy,' Motty says, addressing D as everyone does when the matter at hand is complex.

'I can understand,' D replies.

'They are very, how can I say, *sensitive*. Also, they are getting old. But Zvika does not want to listen. He says that blasts happen in Tel Aviv also. He wants to travel to Andaman and help with the Chabad House there. He has apparently promised the rabbi and can't go back on his word. He has got quite involved in this religious thing.'

'Hmm,' D says. 'It has become a spiritual journey for him suddenly.'

'Exactly,' says Motty. 'But he must consider our parents also.'

The sun hides behind the clouds and everything falls into shade. Both D and Motty lose colour from their faces, and from where I sit, they seem strangers.

'What do you want to do?' D asks him.

'I think I will have to return. Zvika can travel on and return when he is ready. But I shall forward my ticket to Bangkok, spend a few days there and go back to Holon. At least one of us will be home. I think, for me, the journey ends here. I would like to travel more – I could do this forever – but I also want to go back to my life. You know?'

Consider the parents: at least one sibling must.

My brother's family is currently in Calcutta with my father – the reason I can travel and be away. But they are supposed to leave for Moscow at the end of summer. And knowing my brother and the path he wants to chart in the corporate world, he is probably never going to return to our hometown. What after that?

D and Motty get up to walk around and take photographs.

I stand near the sundial and watch people come in and children run and lovers kiss. I watch the light dance on the dial.

Epilogue

Summer in Calcutta. White afternoon sky that blurs at the horizon, where buildings stand like toys. In street corners, rickshaw pullers drink sattu dissolved in water, doused with salt and a pinch of sugar. They cover their faces with wet red gamchhas and recline on the seats. When you step out of the house, you feel, first, the sun on your face. It is not the stark sun of Delhi that sucks up moisture from every surface but a hot, dizzy, moist ball that pinches and prickles, that teases and shreds, until beads of sweat begin to gather on the brow and the upper lip. And then, if you are lucky, you will feel on your face a very slight fine breeze that bears the hint of a river. You remember that you are, after all, in a port city and the brown river, the Bhagirathi, named after the king who made unbelievable penances to liberate his ancestors from bondage, sends you this breeze.

It is hot and the streets are deserted. You hug shadows – trees and buildings – as you walk and you realize fleetingly (you will forget this once you've reached your air-conditioned destination) that tree shadows are the most beautiful, most underrated things on earth. Your clothes will be wet with sweat, and unless you are careful, you might catch a cold indoors. Summer in Calcutta is a landmine for the careless, though for the romantic and the eccentric, it is something precious. A season that grows on you by reminding you of the value of truths.

You are late.

Or, at least, you are sure you're late, though your husband looks up from his phone and tells you that the flight from the Andamans has only just landed. It will take your friend at least an hour to get to Park Street. You are, in fact, early.

You walk up and down the pavement beneath the colonnaded mansion, past the bookstore, the Freemasons Hall, the odd little shops, until you pause at the edge of the footpath and watch traffic flowing from every direction. You have been in Calcutta for two months and witnessed the difficult summer unfold: death and longings. You cannot wait to see your friend arriving from the Andamans – you had not thought you would see him again.

After Paharganj, he went off the radar. Then one day you hear there has been an earthquake in the Andamans and you call him. There is no response. You worry. Then, at night, he calls you and says he is coming to Calcutta en route to Bangkok. He would like to see the two of you. You tell him, none of this seeing business, he has to *stay* with you. Period. He begins to laugh. At the back there is a consistent roar. 'Is that the sea?' you ask your friend Zvika Hillel, and he says, 'Yes, yes, it is so beautiful here, Dippy, so blue and white and green that I feel bad Motty could not see it. I will tell you everything when I come.'

You retrace your steps down the pavement, past the magazine stores, back to the bookstore and Trinca's.

'I hope he finds his way,' you sniff.

'He has travelled thousands of kilometres across India. He'll be fine,' your husband tells you, softly.

You enter a glass-fronted cafe and keep your eyes on the road. The afternoon is beginning to dissolve. The tops of the buildings catch the sun and the road is in the shade. Texts are exchanged. At 4:15 a yellow taxi stops outside. Zvika Hillel emerges with two backpacks, a small one in front, a huge one at the back, and his shock of hair and Baghdadi nose and that smile. You catch up excitedly, order coffee and talk nineteen to the dozen. 'When will you guys start travelling again?' he asks.

'In a few days. We will start from Delhi. It's almost as though we had to see you off for the circle to close, so we could start again.'

'But it'll be really hot, no?'

'Oh yes,' Saurav replies. 'It'll be the ultimate heat and dust project.'

A slice of cheesecake arrives for Zvika.

Before he begins to eat, he brings out a little skullcap from his bag and puts it on his head. 'This is a kippa, Dippy.' He smiles. 'I am now grown up and different. I learnt so many things from the rabbis in the Chabad House. I learnt to cook, you know? See' – he shows me a frying pan in his bag and two tomatoes – 'I've been learning the kosher rules. I don't know what will happen after this. But I will study religion.'

You nod, taking this new Zvika seriously.

'And bartending,' he adds, and then you can let go of the little flickers of discomfort and laugh as though all four of you are together again.

At sunset, the three of you stand looking at the river. The breeze is moist. The colours of the sky sparkle in the water, all pink and orange and red and gold. There are boats and barges and ice-cream sellers. There are happy lovers holding hands and sad weird old men, sitting alone. You have made an elaborate plan for this evening: river; Victoria; New Market to eat cookies at the delightful old Baghdadi Jewish institution of Calcutta, Nahoum's; College Street; South City; then home. Even you know this is crazy. You will have to scrap most of it.

'Dippy,' Zvika whispers to you, as the noises of people and boats and sellers coalesce and separate in turns, 'check out these ladies.' You follow his eyes and see two women in their fifties in soft red salwar-kameezes. They sit next to each other, their backs to the river, and placidly share an ice-cream cone as they watch the people coming and going, and the cars streaking on the street. They look as though they could be sisters – they have a certain similarity in manner and dressing – but why would sisters share an ice-cream *cone*? A cup, yes. But a cone? They must be lovers. Old lovers who have grown to look similar. You look at Zvika and nod conspiratorially.

Then you walk ahead and sit by the river and watch people filling little bottles with water, Ganga jal. It will be sprinkled on their heads on special occasions. You watch three women in bright saris sail diyas. 'I am trying to get Motty interested in religion, you know,' Zvika suddenly says, looking at the two of you urgently, and you know immediately what he is saying. He is saying he does not want to break away from the original state – the family. He is saying simultaneously that he will.

You feel the stab, and it is so acute it startles you for a moment.

This is what the land teaches you, after all: you must let go, you must not let go.

You must leave, you must stay.

Lap, lap, lap, the water hits the steps. The tide is coming in.

Acknowledgements

If a book is in gestation for as long as this one was, the burden of its debts are larger than the GDP of some small countries. Many, many thanks are due to:

The parents, Sukumar Jha, Nilanjan Roy, Manidipa Roy, they who have suffered hard and worried long, and learnt to call hand-outs and bailouts 'endowments to the arts'.

Sarajit and Vinu Jha, and Susnato Roy, the second line of defence, who have put up with much moodiness over the years, also called rampant moral high-grounding.

Masood Hussainy, Voruganti Srinivas, Abhishek Mukherjee, Rakesh Ahuja and Ravikant Mishra: five people whose affections made the book – and its authors – stand on a stronger wicket.

The Facebook group 'the heat and dust project – a book in motion'. It had been a flare, sent up from a lonely place, and the response we got – blankets and tinned food and whatnot in virtual terms – kept us warm. (People on the group were awfully patient too. They used the word *finally* only sometimes. *Is the book finally out? Is the subtitle finally decided?*) If you are someone who joined the group, left a comment somewhere, participated in a contest, or forwarded the link to your friends and relatives, know that you kept us going when the going was tough. It was often tough. Thank you.

HarperCollins India: If one keeps one's publishers waiting for this long, they either become friends or, well, the opposite. Fortunately, in our case, they picked a third option: family. Thank you, V.K. Karthika, for never rushing the manuscript, for all the hugs and meals dispensed liberally, and finally, for cutting out the excesses with your fine scalpel. Shantanu Ray Chaudhuri, the best editor one can possibly have, and, to steal a phrase Gulzar used for him (Yes, he is Gulzar's editor too!), the perfect custodian of our ideas. Thank you, Sameer Mahale and Amrita Talwar for captaining the ship, through choppy seas, along with their wonderful teams (hat tip to Prema Govindan, Gokul Kumar, Vinay Anchan, Indranil Roychowdhury). A big hug to Bonita Vaz, who helmed the aesthetics. Finally, S.K. Ray Chaudhuri, whose diligent proofing ensured that the authors did not mix up their streets or their metals.

Arunava Sinha: there are literally a hundred reasons to thank him.

Pinaki De – for that cracking cover. We were lucky you picked us.

Nayantara Chatterjee for her love, generosity, and, of course, her photography skills. Also, to Manasi Subramaniam, who composed the shot and acquired the rickshaw on a mad Paharganj morning, and to Abhishek Chatterjee, cartographer of *The Heat and Dust Project*, and giver of the camera for said author photo.

Gitanjali Chatterjee, who stars as herself – Gee – in the book (well, okay, she just has a cameo in this one but you can always take a look at *The Vague Woman's Handbook*, where she does, indeed, star), and who gifted D the 'yellow notebook'.

Manaspratim Mitra, Neelini Sarkar, Debasri Rakshit, Chitra Viraraghavan, Krishna Shastri Devulapalli ('The French Guide to Bharat' was definitely D's favourite subtitle that, for some reason, did not get picked), Aneela Zeb Babar ('Bhadralok go Backpacking' was a close second), Esha Sil, Karthika Nair, Sarayu Karnoor, Amit Upadhyaya, Asha Ritu, Deepayan Chakravarty, Amrita Singh, Anita Kakar, Deepshika Chakravarty, Shivdev Singh and Yera Tripathi: for various reasons, mostly involving dosti, cake and a history of bad ideas, in some or other combination.

The magnificent Samhita Bianca Chakraborty for giving uncommon good advice and mixing uncommonly good cocktails – vodka with cranberry juice and a secret ingredient distilled from newsprint, for example.

Dipali Taneja and Somak Ghoshal, who, separately, came up with the perfect subtitle. (Of course, it meant we got frazzled phone calls from the parents – refer 1 – who wondered if it might be misunderstood as literal. They were further distressed when we told them that is exactly what we hoped.)

Dipanjan and Arati Rai Chaudhuri, Kapil Kapoor and H.S. Shivapraksh – for teaching us distinct ways of approaching the country and its narratives.

Arhaan Babar Ray, Juhi and Rohini Banerjee, Subit Chakraborty (I want to see those evil dollars support this book, Comrade), Indrayudh Banerjee, Anand Mukherjee, Prateek Chakraborty (who will remember the Jodhpur chapter and the chocolate bombs), Suranjan Mukherjee, the three Boses – Shivangi, Siddharth and Sonia – Pallavi Banerjee Ghosh (who would take over the night shift from the US, in badgering people to pre-order the book), the most generous Tirthajit Maitra and Saumya Srivastav, Sohini Charaborty and Sohini Chakraborty (in the last book, her name had been accidentally missed out): thank you for all the love and support.

Indranath Mukherjee – one and only; best Bengali storyteller this side of the Yamuna.

Mamata Chowdhury and Santosh Bhasin – our beloved grandmothers in Delhi.

Everyone who, in the course of the journey, gave us a discount, put us up or shared their stories, friends old and new, especially Motty and Zvika Hillel (prepare to play yourselves in the movie, dudes!)

The memory of Indira Jha and our grandparents – dramatic people, all; great storytellers too.

Ramkrishna Paramhansa, Aghori Vimalananda, Trailanga Swami and Ramana Maharshi. If we have been able to breathe any life into this book at all, it is owed to their stories and blessings.

Colonel Tod, author of the fascinating *Annals and Antiquities of Rajasthan*, whose three-volume magnum opus was a treasure trove of royal stories.

And finally, you. Thank you for reading the book. Now, go buy a rucksack!

Coming Soon
Book 2 of the Heat and Dust Project

man. woman. road.

Devapriya Roy and Saurav Jha

It is the hottest summer India has seen in decades. Birds are falling from the sky, dead. Most of the gap-year kids and young Israelis have long left for home. The broke couple, D and S, undeterred by family drama or personal finances, have hit the road again. As they travel the land without a compass, from the forests of central India to the seas in the south, an eccentric virtual family comes together on Facebook to root for them. The scorching summer is only matched by the pace at which they travel, from (Sarai) Kale Khan to Kanyakumari, via Khajuraho, Kolhapur, Kozhikode and a hundred other places. At one point, they race the monsoon. At another, they are chased down by a journalist who wants to write a story about the project. Ultimately, forgotten sorrows, lost joys and the cruelties of relationships finally find their way to closure, as the journey offers a rollicking alternative to the grist of life: the road.